W9-CHW-585

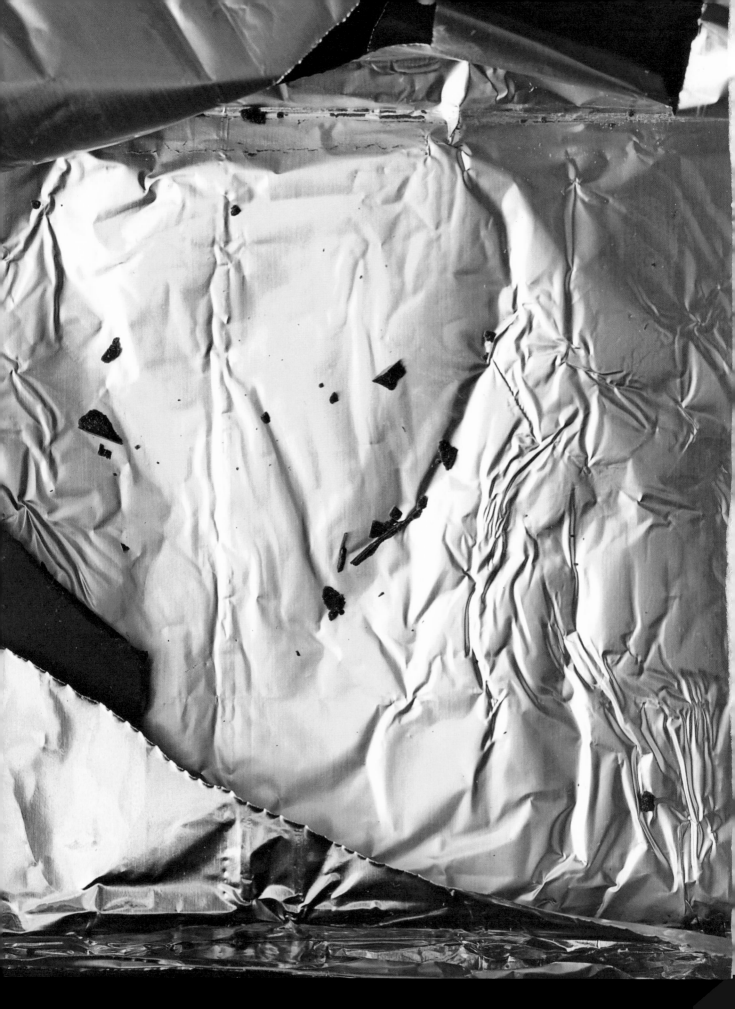

Absolutely

CHOCOLATE

Absolutely CHOCOLATE

irresistible excuses to indulge

FROM THE EDITORS OF FINE COOKING

PHOTOGRAPHS BY ANNA WILLIAMS

The Taunton Press

Text © 2009 by The Taunton Press, Inc.
Photographs © 2009 by Anna Williams-Orchard Represents, except for pp. 40, 48, 49, 60, 63, 65, 68, 113, 116, 117, 124, 139, 149, 160, 184, 197, 202, 207, 239, 252, 253, 255, 266: Scott Phillips © The Taunton Press, Inc.; p. 108: Karl Petzke, courtesy *Fine Cooking* magazine; p. 191: © Ben Fink Photography, Inc.

All rights reserved.

The Taunton Press
Inspiration for hands-on living®

The Taunton Press, Inc.
63 South Main Street
PO Box 5506
Newtown, CT 06470-5506
e-mail: tp@taunton.com

Editor: Martha Holmberg
Copy Editor: Ann E. Compton
Indexer: Heidi Blough
Cover and interior design: Alison Wilkes
Layout: David Giammattei
Photographer: Anna Williams,
  except where noted above
Food stylist: Heidi Johannsen Stewart
Prop stylist: Helen Crowther

Library of Congress Cataloging-in-Publication Data

Absolutely chocolate : irresistible excuses to indulge /
from the editors of Fine cooking.
    p. cm.
  ISBN 978-1-60085-133-9
1. Cookery (Chocolate) 2. Chocolate desserts. 3. Chocolate.
I. Fine cooking.
  TX767.C5A37 2009
  641.3′374--dc22

                    2009016383

Printed in China
10 9 8 7 6 5 4 3 2 1

Fine Cooking® is a trademark of The Taunton Press, Inc., registered in the U.S. Patent and Trademark Office.

The following names/manufacturers appearing in *Absolutely Chocolate* are trademarks: Almond Joy®, Baileys®, Baker's®, Ben & Jerry's®, Bigelow®, Blanton®, Caffé Lolita®, Callebaut®, Chambord®, Coco López®, Cointreau®, Doughmakers®, Droste®, Eagle Rare®, Fleischmann's® RapidRise™, Frangelico®, Ghirardelli®, Godiva®, Grand Marnier®, Guinness®, Heath®, Hershey's®, Hershey's® Special Dark®, Ibarra®, Jif®, Jim Beam®, Kahlúa®, Knob Creek®, Knox®, Lindt®, Michel Cluizel®, Nabisco®, Nestlé®, Nutella®, Old Crow®, Pepperidge Farm®, Post-It®, Pyrex®, Red Star® QuickRise™, Reese's® Peanut Butter Cups®, Rice Krispies®, SAF Perfect Rise®, Scharffen Berger®, Silpat®, Skippy®, Skor®, Valrhona®, El Rey®, Vollrath®, Wild Turkey®, Zeroll®

Contents

for the love of chocolate

CHOCOLATE IS THE SOURCE OF ENDLESS DELIGHT FOR SO MANY OF US, but it can also be the source of some confusion. Within the thousands of options to choose from, there can be as much variation in flavor and quality as there is in, say, wine or cheese, and chocolate is very much the same type of product. While you may buy a bar of beautifully wrapped chocolate from a chic urban boutique, all chocolate starts its life as an agricultural crop, and its quality depends on the care taken by the farmer and those processing the beans at an early stage. The final confection reflects the skill and sensibility of the manufacturer, whether that's an industrial giant such as Hershey's® or a hands-on artisan like one of the many small chocolatiers that have sprung up around the world. Understanding how chocolate is created can help you make the best decisions about which variety to use in cooking and for eating.

Chocolate's delicious journey from bean to bar

All real chocolate comes from the cocoa bean (also called cacao bean), the fruit of a tree, *Theobroma cacao*, that only grows in the tropics. Much of the quality of the chocolate will depend on the origin and quality of the beans. There are three main types of cacao: Forestero (and a subtype called Nacional), which has a robust chocolate flavor but not much finesse; Trinitario, a good middle quality; and Criollo, considered the premium bean. The beans are fermented after being harvested, dried, cleaned, roasted, and finally shelled, to produce the centers, called nibs. These nibs are then pulverized or ground into a smooth liquid that's called chocolate liquor (although it contains no alcohol). When the chocolate liquor cools, it forms solid blocks.

Chocolate liquor is the basis for all things chocolate. Pure chocolate liquor is very dark and bitter and has only two components—cocoa solids and cocoa butter. The solids give chocolate its characteristic dark, strong flavor, and the cocoa butter translates to a smooth mouth-feel.

so many chocolate styles, all good

WHETHER YOU'RE BAKING A CAKE OR MAKING a sauce, chances are you'll have to make a decision about what kind of chocolate to use. Here are the types to look for.

Unsweetened chocolate

Unsweetened chocolate contains no sugar, so is about 99% chocolate liquor. It's extremely bitter and cannot be used interchangeably with semisweet or bittersweet chocolate.

Semisweet and bittersweet chocolate

Generally, these can be used interchangeably, with semisweet giving a slightly sweeter result. Bittersweet usually contains less sugar than semisweet, but the distinction between the two types becomes hazy between brands. For example, a bittersweet chocolate offered by a supermarket brand likely has more sugar than a semisweet chocolate made by a premium chocolate maker.

Milk chocolate

Although popular to eat out of hand, milk chocolate is used less widely in baking than semi- or bittersweet chocolate. In the United States, milk chocolate must contain a minimum of 10% chocolate liquor (though it often contains more) and 12% milk solids. In Europe, milk chocolate must contain 30% chocolate liquor and 18% dry milk solids, as well as 26% total fat.

Gianduia (gianduja)

This silky-smooth, hazelnut-flavored chocolate (pronounced zhahn-DOO-yuh) comes in milk- and dark-chocolate versions. The term is also used to describe the flavor pairing of chocolate and hazelnut.

Couverture

A term for high-quality chocolate that is suitable for candy-making like enrobing truffles.

Chocolate chips

Specially formulated morsels that retain their shape and texture without burning when baked, chips are ideal mix-ins for cookies and quick breads. Since they contain significantly less cocoa butter, they behave differently than bar chocolate when melted, so it's best not to substitute chips when bitter- or semisweet chocolate is called for. But if a recipe calls for chips, you can often substitute coarsely chopped semi- or bittersweet chocolate.

Cocoa nibs

These are simply tiny pieces of roasted cocoa bean that can be used as a crunchy ingredient much as you'd use roasted nuts. They are strongly flavored, sometimes slightly bitter, but appealingly chocolatey.

White chocolate

White chocolate isn't really chocolate at all because it contains no cocoa solids. It's made with cocoa butter (the fat from cocoa beans), sugar, and milk, and usually contains natural vanilla or vanillin, an artificial flavoring. More commonly used in desserts than eaten plain, white chocolate has a quick, even melt and creamy texture that make it ideal for mousses, cheesecakes, truffles, and cookies. It's susceptible to burning, however, so it should be melted over very low heat.

In its natural state, chocolate liquor contains a little more than half (50% to 58%) cocoa butter and the rest is chocolate solids. Early on, producers learned that by increasing the cocoa butter, they could create chocolate with a better sheen and smoother texture. So they developed a high-pressure filter process that breaks down chocolate liquor and separates the solids from the butter. They could then manipulate the chocolate to produce a range of styles.

To create eating chocolate, sugar and flavorings are added to the cocoa butter and solids, and the mixture undergoes hours of a process called conching, using rollers that refine all the particles in sugar and create the luscious mouth-feel we crave in chocolate. While some sugar is needed to make pure chocolate palatable, the best examples contain a high percentage of real chocolate and only small amounts of sugar or other additives.

Deciphering the labels

Fortunately, more and more manufacturers are now listing the percentage of chocolate liquor on the label. A label of 70% chocolate means the bar contains about 70% chocolate liquor (the ingredients actually derived from the cocoa bean) and about 30% sugar. (Vanilla and lecithin generally account for about 1% of the total ingredients.) However, you'll still see the terms bittersweet and semisweet on chocolates and in recipes even though the terms themselves have no real meaning.

In the United States, dark chocolates by law must contain at least 35% chocolate liquor. Most brands of semi- and bittersweet contain 50% or more, but often one maker's semisweet will contain more chocolate liquor and less sugar than another maker's bittersweet. Ultimately, what's most important about the chocolate isn't the exact percentage of cocoa content, but rather whether you like the flavor and whether the chocolate performs well in your recipe. Chocolates between about 55% and 61% are versatile enough for most dishes. As you go higher in cocoa content, however, the chocolate contains less fat and can require slight adjustments. See "A Sweet Math Lesson" on page 7.

Cocoa butter counts, too

Another fact that percentages on labels don't tell you is the proportion of cocoa butter to cocoa solids, since both are part of chocolate liquor. About the only way to figure out whether one chocolate has more cocoa butter than another is to compare the nutritional labels. As long as you're comparing first-quality dark chocolates without any additives, the one with a higher fat content will be the one with more cocoa butter. This will most likely be the more expensive of the two as well, since cocoa butter is more valuable than the solids for its texture and richness. Also, check the ingredient list while you're at it, because if the chocolate contains any dairy products or other types of fat, this will skew the fat percentage.

Choosing chocolates for cooking, baking, or snacking

Even when you've figured out which level of cocoa solids you want, you have a lot of brands of chocolate to choose from. There are mass-market brands (Baker's®, Nestlé®, Hershey's, Ghirardelli®), big European chocolate makers (Valrhona®, Lindt®, Callebaut®, for instance), international brands (like Venezuelan El Rey®), and boutique chocolate makers (such as Scharffen Berger® in California and Michel Cluizel® in France). Which chocolate should you choose?

First, consider taste. The chocolate you bake with should taste good to you when eaten out of hand, so be sure to sample it when you get it home. Better yet, buy a few different kinds and have a chocolate tasting to decide what you like best.

Second, consider value and what you will be baking. The qualities that make high-end chocolates so distinctive right out of the wrapper can become muted in certain baked goods. Since you'll pay more for really good chocolate, save it for when it really counts—when you're making sweets in which the chocolate is most pronounced, such as truffles, a sauce, or a flourless chocolate cake.

Third, consider the form in which the chocolate comes. Chocolate for baking is manufactured in squares, thin bars, and thick blocks. Thin bars are convenient to store and can be easier to chop than blocks, which take a bit of elbow grease to knock apart (but are better for making decorative shavings and curls). Some better-quality chocolates only come in huge blocks, which are great for pros but may be too big a quantity for home cooks. Fortunately, specialty stores often sell smaller chunks of such blocks wrapped in plastic.

Keeping your chocolate delicious

Chocolate will keep for a year at room temperature, if kept below 70°F. Wrap it in a few layers of plastic to keep it as airtight as possible and put it in a dark cupboard, away from strong-smelling foods. (Chocolate, like butter, will absorb strong aromas.) If your cupboard is too hot, you can store chocolate in the refrigerator or freezer, but a moist environment isn't the best. If you do chill your chocolate, bring it to room temperature while still wrapped to prevent condensation from forming, as any water on the chocolate can interfere with its ability to melt smoothly.

If your chocolate has a white film on it (also called bloom), it means it has either been stored too warm, causing the cocoa butter to separate out, or some condensation has occurred, melting its sugar surface. Either way, while it may not feel as good in your mouth when you eat it straight, it will work just fine in baking.

Cocoa's surprisingly deep character

These days, it's easy to get your hands on amazing chocolate from all over the world, but if you're thinking that excellent chocolate is the key to intensely flavored chocolate desserts, think again. When it comes to delivering deep, dark chocolate flavor, plain old cocoa powder is hard to beat.

Cocoa is by no means a lesser product than chocolate. On the contrary, it's a purer form of chocolate. Chocolate has two main components—cocoa solids (where the flavor comes from) and cocoa butter (where the rich texture comes from). Cocoa powder has had most of the cocoa butter pressed out of it; it's mainly cocoa solids. Cocoa powder generally contains around 12% cocoa butter, while pure unsweetened chocolate contains about 55%. So, ounce for ounce, cocoa powder packs a bigger punch of chocolate flavor, because you're getting more cocoa solids and less cocoa butter.

The big question: natural or Dutched?

Cocoa powder comes in two styles: natural (usually simply labeled "unsweetened cocoa powder") and Dutch-processed (or alkalized), which has been treated with alkali to neutralize its natural acidity. Both taste bitter out of the box, but natural cocoa has a fruitier, more acidic chocolate flavor, while Dutched cocoa is mellower, with an almost nutty flavor.

In recipes without a chemical leaven, such as baking soda, taste alone can be your guide, but for most baking recipes, it's best to use the style called for, as Dutched and natural cocoas react differently with baking soda and baking powder. (Baking soda, which is alkaline, is generally paired with natural cocoa to neutralize its acidity; baking powder is paired with Dutched cocoa because both ingredients are essentially neutral already.) A well-stocked baker's pantry includes both types.

a sweet math lesson: using high-percentage chocolates

Many high-quality bittersweet or semisweet chocolates contain significantly higher than average amounts of chocolate liquor, some as high as 80% or more. Despite the fact that these chocolates can be of excellent quality, using them in recipes not specifically designed for them can give you disappointing results: Cakes can turn out dry or overbaked, and ganaches can curdle.

Chocolate guru Alice Medrich has developed a way to convert recipes to work better with high-percentage chocolates: For chocolates labeled 66% or higher, use 25% to 35% less chocolate than called for in the recipe and add up to 1½ teaspoons more granulated sugar for each ounce of chocolate originally called for. For example, if a brownie recipe calls for 8 ounces of chopped semisweet chocolate and 1 cup of sugar, you would use only about 6 ounces of high-percentage chopped chocolate and 1 cup *plus* 4 tablespoons of sugar.

Note that the *Fine Cooking* test kitchen generally tests recipes using chocolate with about a 60% cocoa content.

When to use cocoa and when to use chocolate

In chocolate desserts, flavor isn't the only attribute to consider—texture is also important. The finished texture of a dessert is strongly influenced by the types of fat in the recipe, be it butter, oil, cocoa butter from chocolate, or a combination.

In creamy desserts, chocolate's usually best. Some desserts need the silkiness that only cocoa butter can provide. Cocoa butter is an unusual fat because it melts at a temperature very

getting to know your favorites— try a focused tasting

THE FIRST STEP IN FINDING THE PERFECT CHOCO-late for cooking and baking is finding one that you like to eat out of hand. While many nuances of flavor and texture will get lost in cooking, you want a chocolate whose general flavor profile is pleasing to you. Choose a few chocolates that have something in common—they're all in the same price range at your local grocery store, they're all from the same country, or they're all the same cocoa percentage. It's easier to evaluate differences if there are some unifying qualities, too.

Tasting chocolate is a lot like tasting wine. By walking through several steps, you can focus your senses and understand the character of what you're tasting.

- First, take a look. Is the chocolate shiny or matte. Is the color even?

- Next, break a piece (or pry off a chunk if using a large block). Does it break cleanly or does it seem grainy or soft?

- Now, sniff. Hold a piece in front of your nose and inhale its aromas. Does it remind you of nuts, coffee, tobacco, fruit?

- Start to taste. Put a small piece of chocolate on your tongue and let it melt for several seconds. Consider its flavor notes—do you get smoke, flowers, acid, red fruit, caramel, raisins? What does the texture feel like as you push the chocolate between your tongue and the roof of your mouth? Dry, chalky, creamy, satiny?

- Then actually chew a bit. Do the flavor and texture change?

- At last, swallow the chocolate and evaluate its finish. Does it dissipate quickly or does the flavor linger? A long finish is considered positive.

Finally, did you enjoy the chocolate? That's the most important thing.

close to our body temperature. Chocolate that's hard and solid at room temperature feels rich on the tongue. In puddings, ganache, and mousses, the luxurious mouth-feel of cocoa butter really shines, so for these desserts, chocolate is almost always preferable to cocoa powder. But that doesn't mean cocoa powder is a no-no for such recipes. In fact, adding a tablespoon or two to puddings or mousses along with the chocolate can boost the flavor without altering how the custard sets up.

In cakes, the choice is more complicated. Cakes made with cocoa and cakes made with chocolate can differ remarkably in flavor and texture. And those differences have a lot to do with the other fats used in the recipe.

Cakes made with cocoa powder and oil are tender and intensely flavored. Consider devil's food cake, for example. Its deep flavor, dark color, and moist texture come from pairing cocoa powder with oil. The flavor is intense because there's no milk or butter to dilute the pure chocolate flavor of the cocoa solids. And the texture is moist because vegetable oil is liquid at room temperature (and even when cool), unlike butter and cocoa butter, which are solid. You can serve devil's food cake refrigerator-cold, and it will still be exceptionally tender.

Cake made with chocolate, on the other hand, is temperature-sensitive. If you've ever been served a slice of cold chocolate cake that was dry and crumbly, it may well have been made with chocolate. Remember, cocoa butter is hard even at cool room temperature. The cake's flavor suffers, too, because the cocoa butter is what carries the chocolate flavor, and the colder it is, the longer it takes to melt on your tongue and release the flavor. This is not to say that cakes made with chocolate are unpleasant; you just need to remember to serve them at room temperature. And the fact is, the cocoa butter can make for a pleasantly firm cake, especially if the recipe contains at least 4 ounces of unsweetened chocolate—think of a rich Bundt cake with a dense, springy crumb.

In brownies, cocoa yields chewy results, while chocolate gives a fudgy texture. Chocolate lovers can be snobby about brownies, but the fact is that cocoa powder makes for fabulously rich, chewy brownies. Brownies are chewy when they're high in sugar, fat, and eggs but low in flour. The last variable to their final texture is the nature of the fat used in the recipe—specifically, how hard the fat is at the temperature the brownies are to be served. Butter is soft at room temperature, so brownies made with cocoa plus butter (or oil) have a noticeably soft, chewy texture. And the flavor is intensely chocolatey with a wonderful lingering buttery flavor. By contrast, brownies made with chocolate plus butter are often firmer, almost fudgy, because cocoa butter is harder than butter at room temperature. The more chocolate the recipe contains, the fudgier the brownies will be.

cookies

Chewy chocolate chip cookies

Using butter and eggs right out of the refrigerator keeps the dough cool so the cookies maintain their thickness during baking. To keep the cookies soft and chewy once you've baked them, store them in an airtight container along with a slice of bread.

10¾ ounces (1 ⅓ cups) unsalted butter, cold

1½ cups packed light brown sugar

1 cup granulated sugar

2 large eggs, cold

1 tablespoon pure vanilla extract

17 ounces (3 ¾ cups) unbleached all-purpose flour

1¼ teaspoons table salt

1 teaspoon baking soda

2 cups (12 ounces) semisweet chocolate chips

Arrange the oven racks in the upper and middle positions of the oven. Heat the oven to 375°F.

Using a mixer fitted with a paddle, beat together the butter, brown sugar, and granulated sugar, starting on low speed and gradually working your way up to high speed until the mixture is light and fluffy, about 3 minutes once you reach high speed. Scrape the bowl and beater. Add the eggs and vanilla and beat on low until blended. Beat on high until light and fluffy, about 1 minute. Scrape the bowl and beater.

In a medium bowl, whisk together the flour, salt, and baking soda. Add this to the butter mixture and stir with a wooden spoon until just blended; the dough will be stiff. Stir in the chocolate chips.

Drop rounded measuring teaspoons of dough about 2 inches apart onto two ungreased baking sheets. Refrigerate any unused dough. Bake until the bottoms are golden brown, 8 to 10 minutes, rotating the sheets halfway through for even results. Remove the sheets from the oven, let sit for 3 to 5 minutes, and then transfer the cookies with a spatula to a wire rack to cool completely. Let the baking sheets cool completely before baking the remaining dough.

baking chocolate chip cookies your way

MAKING CHOCOLATE CHIP COOKIES THAT HAVE the texture you like is the subject of many theories, from refrigerating the dough to underbaking the cookies to checking the barometric pressure. But after baking, and eating, many batches of cookies, we think we've broken the cookie code: To get the cookie you like, control the amount and temperature of key ingredients.

Sugar The relative amount of white versus brown sugar has a great effect on chewiness because brown sugar is much wetter than white. Using more brown sugar will produce a softer, chewier cookie, while using more white sugar will turn out cookies that are sandier in texture and crisper overall.

Flour The way you measure flour makes a big difference, because too much flour makes cookies dry and tough while too little causes cookies to spread too much and lose structure. If possible, use a scale to measure the flour in these recipes so your results are as consistent as possible. If you use a measuring cup, follow the tips in "Secrets for Perfect Cookies Every Time" on page 15.

Butter and eggs The temperature of these ingredients helps control how much the dough spreads, so always follow a recipe's instructions. Cool ingredients keep your dough cooler, which means it spreads more slowly in the oven, letting the oven's heat "set" the cookie while the dough is still thick and producing a denser, chewier cookie. Warm dough spreads more quickly in the oven, which makes the cookies thinner and crisper. A high proportion of butter to flour in the dough will also allow it to spread quickly.

Warm eggs quickly by dunking them in warm water for a minute or two. Some people warm butter in the microwave, but just a few seconds too long and it's melted, so it's best just to plan ahead and leave the butter on your counter for an hour or so.

Kitchen temperature The temperature in your kitchen also affects dough temperature, as will dropping cookies onto still-hot baking sheets: For chewy cookies, have cool sheets handy. And humid weather will soften even the crispest cookies in as little as a day, so store them well wrapped.

Crisp chocolate chip cookies

Yields about 72
3-inch cookies

A few tricks make these cookies irresistibly crisp: more white sugar than brown sugar; room-temperature butter and eggs to help the cookies spread thin; and greased baking sheets to encourage the cookies to spread even more.

12 ounces (1½ cups) unsalted butter, softened at room temperature; more for the baking sheets

1 cup granulated sugar

¾ cup packed light brown sugar

2 large eggs, at room temperature

2 teaspoons pure vanilla extract

13½ ounces (3 cups) unbleached all-purpose flour

1 teaspoon table salt

1 teaspoon baking soda

2 cups (12 ounces) semisweet chocolate chips

Position the oven racks in the middle and upper parts of the oven and heat the oven to 375°F. Butter two baking sheets.

Using a mixer fitted with the paddle attachment, beat the butter, granulated sugar, and brown sugar on high speed until light and fluffy, about 1 minute. Scrape the bowl and beater. Add the eggs and vanilla and beat on low until blended. Turn the speed to high and beat until light and fluffy, about 1 minute. Scrape the bowl and beater.

In a medium bowl, whisk the flour, salt, and baking soda. Add this to the butter mixture and beat on medium low until just blended. Stir in the chocolate chips with a wooden spoon.

Drop rounded measuring teaspoons of dough 2 inches apart onto the greased baking sheets. Bake until deep golden brown around the edges and golden in the center, 8 to 10 minutes, rotating the baking sheets halfway through for even results. Remove the sheets from the oven, let sit for 3 to 5 minutes, and then transfer the cookies with a spatula to a rack to cool completely. Repeat until all the dough is baked.

SECRETS FOR PERFECT COOKIES EVERY TIME

The best recipe in the world won't produce a good cookie if you don't pay attention to the first and last steps—measuring and baking. Follow our tips for more precision and control.

Measuring flour

- Always use a true dry measure—not a Pyrex® cup.

- Fluff the flour with a fork to avoid it becoming densely packed.

- Spoon the flour from the bag into the measuring cup and level it with a knife—never scoop right from the bag, which will compact too much flour into the cup.

- Be careful not to shake or tap the cup as you add the flour, as this will pack down the flour as well.

- The *Fine Cooking* test kitchen gets 4½ ounces in weight of all-purpose flour per cup when measured this way.

Baking evenly

- Use baking sheets, not rimmed baking pans. Unrimmed sheets allow better air circulation around the cookies while they're in the oven.

- Be sure to use heavy-duty baking sheets that won't warp. If the sheets warp, your cookies will slide around and bake unevenly.

- Bake cookies one sheet at a time, unless you're using a convection oven. If the dough doesn't fit onto one baking sheet, drop the remaining batter onto a second sheet and bake it after the first batch comes out of the oven. If you're re-using baking sheets, be sure to let them cool down before putting more dough on them.

Mocha cinnamon chocolate chip cookies

Yields 48 cookies

No eggs in this cookie dough means you can take a taste with no worries; the dough's so good that one taste might lead to another—a dangerous thing if you want to actually bake the full amount of cookies.

9 ounces (2 cups) unbleached all-purpose flour

½ teaspoon baking powder

¾ teaspoon ground cinnamon

¼ teaspoon table salt

10 ounces (1½ cups) unsalted butter, softened at room temperature

3 tablespoons instant espresso powder (or 4 tablespoons instant-coffee granules, crushed)

1 cup confectioners' sugar

½ cup packed light brown sugar

1½ cups semisweet chocolate chips

About ¼ cup granulated sugar for dipping

Heat the oven to 350°F. Line a cooling rack with paper towels.

In a medium bowl, combine the flour, baking powder, cinnamon, and salt. In a larger bowl, beat the butter and espresso powder or coffee until well combined. Add the confectioners' sugar and brown sugar and beat until combined. Stir in the flour mixture about ½ cup at a time, mixing well after each addition. Stir in the chocolate chips.

Put the granulated sugar in a small, shallow bowl. Scoop out about 1 tablespoon of dough and flatten it slightly into a disk. Dip one side into the granulated sugar and then set the disk, sugar side up, on an ungreased baking sheet. Repeat with the remaining dough, spacing the disks about 2 inches apart. Bake until the edges start to darken, 12 to 14 minutes. (Begin checking after 12 minutes, but don't be tempted to remove them too soon.)

Let the cookies cool for 1 to 2 minutes on the baking sheets. Transfer them to the paper towel–lined racks to cool completely. Bake the rest of the dough the same way.

Double chocolate cookies

Yields about
36 cookies

These cookies make excellent hostess gifts during the holidays, especially when stacked and tied with a pretty ribbon. To get cookies that look uniform, be sure that the unbaked cookies are all about the same size; that way, they'll all finish baking around the same time. The cookies can be stored in an airtight container for up to three days or frozen for about one month.

5 ounces unsweetened chocolate, chopped

½ pound bittersweet or semisweet chocolate, coarsely chopped

¼ pound (½ cup) unsalted butter, cut into 4 pieces

4 large eggs

1½ cups granulated sugar

¼ teaspoon pure vanilla extract

2½ ounces (½ cup plus 2 tablespoons) unbleached all-purpose flour

½ teaspoon baking powder

¼ teaspoon table salt

3 ounces (¾ cup) walnuts, toasted and chopped

Melt the unsweetened chocolate, half of the bittersweet or semisweet chocolate, and the butter in a small saucepan. Set aside to cool slightly.

Using a stand mixer with the whisk attachment on medium-high speed, whip the eggs and sugar until thick and light, about 10 minutes. With the mixer on low speed, add the melted chocolate mixture and the vanilla, and mix until blended.

With a rubber spatula, fold in the flour, baking powder, and salt, and scrape the bowl. Fold in the remaining chopped chocolate and the walnuts. Refrigerate the dough until it has firmed up enough to scoop, about 1½ hours.

Position a rack in the center of the oven and heat the oven to 350°F. Drop the chilled dough by rounded tablespoonfuls about 3 inches apart on ungreased baking sheets. Bake until the cookies are cracked on top and feel dry on the surface but still soft inside, about 15 minutes. Let the cookies cool on the sheet for 1 minute before transferring them to a rack to cool.

THE BEST WAY TO CHOP CHOCOLATE

Whether you're chopping chocolate to melt it or to create chunks for adding to a recipe, you need to chop it evenly and quickly.

For easy cleanup, first line a rimmed baking sheet with parchment to catch the inevitable flying shards of chocolate; put your cutting board on top of the parchment. Use the paper to gather the shards.

To chop a thick slab of chocolate, use a knife. Set the blade of your biggest knife (preferably a chef's knife) on a corner of the slab and—with your fingers tucked safely away from the blade edge—bear down with both hands to break off a small bit; repeat.

As that corner becomes a flat edge, turn the slab and begin cutting at another corner. Use this same method with flatter bars.

For chopping large amounts of chocolate, use a food processor. Break thin bars into pieces and pulse in the processor with the steel blade until the chocolate is evenly chopped. (Sometimes a few pieces resist chopping; break these into smaller pieces and keep pulsing.) For block chocolate, cut the block into chunks that will fit in the feed tube and use the coarse grating disk (heavy block chocolate might damage the machine if you use the steel blade).

Cocoa cookie dough

The holiday baking marathon just got a little easier. With very little effort, you can transform this one easy dough into three different and dazzling cookies.

Yields 4 cups dough (about 2 pounds, 5 ounces), enough for one batch each of the cookies on pages 22-24.

10 ounces (2¼ cups)
    bleached all-purpose flour

3⅞ ounces (1 cup plus
    2 tablespoons)
    unsweetened natural
    cocoa powder

1⅔ cups granulated sugar

⅜ teaspoon baking soda

⅜ teaspoon table salt

10½ ounces (1 cup plus
    5 tablespoons) unsalted
    butter, slightly softened

4½ tablespoons whole milk

1½ teaspoons pure vanilla
    extract

In a food processor, combine the flour, cocoa, sugar, baking soda, and salt. Pulse several times to mix thoroughly. Cut the butter into about 12 chunks and add them to the bowl. Pulse several times. Combine the milk and vanilla in a small cup. With the processor running, add the milk mixture and continue to process until the dough clumps around the blade or the sides of the bowl. Transfer the dough to a large bowl or cutting board and knead with your hands a few times to make sure the dough is evenly blended. Portion the dough into equal thirds. Each portion should weigh about 12 ounces and each will fill about 1⅓ cups.

The dough must be chilled first for the Bittersweet Mocha Cookies and the Crunchy Cocoa Wafers; follow the chilling directions (including adding any other ingredients before chilling) as described in those recipes.

Bittersweet mocha cookies

Extra chocolatey and laced with freshly ground coffee, these cookies are slightly crunchy on the outside and chewy within.

One-third of a batch (about ¾ pound or 1⅓ cups) freshly made Cocoa Cookie Dough (page 20)

3 ounces bittersweet or semi-sweet chocolate, very finely chopped or pulverized in a food processor to the size of coarse crumbs

¼ teaspoon finely ground coffee beans (regular, not espresso roast), plus 28 whole beans, or as needed

About ¼ cup granulated or coarse decorating sugar

Put the Cocoa Cookie Dough in a mixing bowl. Add the chocolate and ground coffee and mix them in thoroughly with a rubber spatula or your hands. Shape the dough into a log 14 inches long and about 1¼ inches in diameter. Wrap in waxed paper or foil and refrigerate until firm, at least 1 hour or overnight.

Position a rack in the center of the oven and heat the oven to 350°F. Line a baking sheet with parchment.

Put the sugar in a small bowl. Cut the dough into ½-inch slices. Coat both sides with the sugar. Arrange the cookies 1½ inches apart on the lined sheet and press a coffee bean into the center of each cookie. Bake until the cookies puff and show very faint cracks on the surface, 9 to 10 minutes (the cookies will feel soft to the touch). Slide the parchment onto a rack and let the cookies cool completely. Store in an airtight container at room temperature or freeze for longer storage.

Chocolate chunk cookies
with dried cherries & pecans

Tart cherries and toasted nuts not only add flavor but also wonderful and contrasting texture to this chocolate chocolate chip cookie.

One-third of a batch (about ¾ pound or 1⅓ cups) freshly made Cocoa Cookie Dough (page 20)

2½ ounces (⅔ cup) toasted and coarsely chopped pecans

½ cup bittersweet or semisweet chocolate chips or chunks

3 ounces (½ cup) dried tart cherries, very coarsely chopped

Position a rack in the center of the oven and heat the oven to 350°F. Line a baking sheet with parchment.

Put the Cocoa Cookie Dough in a mixing bowl. Mix in the pecans, chocolate, and dried cherries. Drop more or less level tablespoons of the dough 2 inches apart on the lined sheet. Bake, rotating the sheet about halfway through, until the surface looks dry and the cookies are soft but not too squishy when pressed lightly with your finger, about 12 minutes. Slide the parchment onto a rack and let the cookies cool completely. Store in an airtight container at room temperature or freeze for longer storage.

Crunchy cocoa wafers

The most basic of all the cookies using the Cocoa Cookie Dough, a couple of
these crisp cookies hit the spot at the end of a big meal; while they offer a good
hit of chocolate, they're not too rich and filling. Offer them with espresso.

One-third of a batch
(about ¾ pound or
1⅓ cups) freshly made
Cocoa Cookie Dough
(page 20)

Shape the dough into a log about 7 inches long and 1¾ inches in diameter. Wrap the log in waxed paper or foil. Refrigerate until firm, at least 1 hour or overnight.

Position a rack in the center of the oven and heat the oven to 350°F. Line a baking sheet with parchment.

Cut the log into slices a scant ¼ inch thick and arrange them 1 inch apart on the lined sheet. Bake for 12 to 15 minutes, rotating the sheet about halfway through. As they bake, the cookies will puff a little and then deflate; they're done about 1 minute after they deflate. The tops of the cookies will look slightly pitted, and they'll feel dry but soft when touched (the cookie will hold an impression). Slide the parchment onto a rack and let the cookies cool completely, at which point they should be perfectly dry and crunchy. Store in an airtight container at room temperature or freeze for longer storage.

Dark chocolate crackles

These cookies are fragile when hot, so be sure to let them cool
on the baking sheet for 5 minutes.

11¼ ounces (2½ cups)
    unbleached all-purpose
    flour

1 teaspoon baking soda

¼ teaspoon table salt

8 ounces (1 cup) unsalted
    butter, at room
    temperature

2 cups firmly packed
    light brown sugar

2 ounces (⅔ cup)
    unsweetened natural
    cocoa powder (not
    Dutch-processed), sifted
    if lumpy

2 teaspoons finely grated
    orange zest

1 teaspoon pure vanilla
    extract

3 large eggs

8 ounces bittersweet
    chocolate, melted and
    cooled until barely warm

4 ounces chopped
    chocolate (white,
    bittersweet, or
    semisweet)

⅓ cup granulated sugar;
    more as needed

Position a rack in the center of the oven and heat the oven to
350°F. Line three large baking sheets with parchment or nonstick
baking liners.

In a medium mixing bowl, whisk together the flour, baking soda,
and salt. In the bowl of a stand mixer fitted with the paddle attachment (or in a large mixing bowl with a hand mixer), beat the butter, brown sugar, cocoa, orange zest, and vanilla on medium speed
until well combined, about 4 minutes. Add the eggs one at a time,
beating briefly between additions. Add the cooled chocolate and
mix until blended, about 1 minute. Add the dry ingredients and mix
on low speed until almost completely blended, about 1 minute. Add
the chopped chocolate and mix until blended, about 15 seconds.

Shape the dough into 1¼-inch balls with a small ice-cream scoop
or two tablespoons.

Pour the granulated sugar into a shallow dish. Dip the top of each
ball in the sugar and set the balls sugar side up about 1½ inches
apart on the prepared baking sheets. Bake one sheet at a time
until the cookies are puffed and cracked on top, 11 to 12 minutes.
Let the cookies cool on the baking sheets for 5 minutes before
transferring them to a rack to cool completely.

Chocolate soufflé cookies

Chocolatey and moist with a light, crisp exterior, these flourless cookies are an excellent showcase for high-quality chocolate. If you want a chocolate-only experience, you may omit the walnuts.

2 large egg whites, at room temperature

⅛ teaspoon cream of tartar

½ teaspoon pure vanilla extract

¼ cup granulated sugar

¾ cup finely chopped walnuts

6 ounces bittersweet or semisweet chocolate, melted and cooled slightly

Position oven racks in the upper and lower third of the oven and heat the oven to 350°F. Lightly grease two baking sheets or line them with parchment.

Using a hand or stand mixer, beat the egg whites with the cream of tartar until soft peaks form. With the beaters running, gradually add the vanilla and sugar until the egg whites hold stiff peaks but don't look dry.

Pour the nuts and melted chocolate over the whipped whites. Gently fold the mixture with a large rubber spatula, trying not to deflate the egg whites, until the color is just uniform. Immediately drop level measuring teaspoons of the batter onto the baking sheets, leaving at least 1 inch between the cookies. Bake until the cookies are shiny and cracked, 10 to 12 minutes; they should be firm on the outside but still gooey inside when you press them. Slide the parchment liners onto racks or use a metal spatula to transfer the cookies to racks and let cool completely. The cookies are best eaten on the day they're baked but will last two to three days if stored in an airtight container.

MAKE AHEAD & FREEZE The balls of dough may be frozen for one month before baking. Thaw them overnight in the refrigerator before proceeding with the recipe.

Chocolate brownie cookies

Yields about
54 cookies

These cookies share the moist chewiness of a brownie but are much lighter.
You can make a mint version by substituting 1½ teaspoons mint extract for
the vanilla and the nuts.

¾ pound bittersweet
chocolate, chopped

2 ounces (¼ cup) unsalted
butter; more for the pan

3 large eggs, at room
temperature

¾ cup granulated sugar

2 teaspoons pure vanilla
extract

1½ ounces (⅓ cup) unbleached
all-purpose flour

¼ teaspoon baking powder

¼ teaspoon table salt

¼ pound (1 cup) chopped
toasted pecans

Position a rack in the center of the oven and heat the oven to
350°F. Line two baking sheets with parchment (or butter and
flour the sheets). Melt the chocolate and butter together in a
metal bowl set over a pan of simmering water (don't let the bowl
touch the water). Let cool.

With a stand mixer fitted with the whisk attachment, beat the eggs
and sugar on medium-high speed to a ribbon consistency (when
the stilled beater is lifted, the batter falls back onto the surface,
forming a ribbon-like pattern that takes a few seconds to sink back
into the batter), about 4 minutes. Take the bowl off the mixer.
Add the cooled chocolate mixture and the vanilla; stir to combine.

Sift together the flour, baking powder, and salt. Stir the flour mixture and the nuts into the batter; let rest for 5 minutes. Spoon the
batter into a pastry bag fitted with a #4 tip (or into a heavy-duty
zip-top bag; snip one bottom corner to create a ²/₃-inch diagonal
opening). For each cookie, pipe 1 tablespoon batter onto the lined
baking sheet. While you pipe the second tray, bake the first until
the cookies are puffed and
cracked and the tops barely
spring back when pressed, 8 to
10 minutes. The cracks should
be moist but not wet. Let the
cookies cool on a rack.

**Shape your cookies quickly and neatly
using a pastry bag instead of a spoon;
use a #4 tip. It's fine to pipe the cookies
close together; they won't spread much
during baking.**

Peanut butter-chocolate chip sandwich cookies

Yields 18
2½-inch sandwiches

This recipe can be mixed by hand or in an electric mixer. Even if you prefer natural peanut butter for sandwiches, use a smooth "processed" peanut butter such as Skippy® to get the right texture for these cookies.

For the cookies

6 ounces (1⅓ cups) unbleached all-purpose flour

2 ounces (⅔ cup) cake flour

½ teaspoon baking soda

¼ teaspoon table salt

6 ounces (¾ cup) unsalted butter, completely softened at room temperature

¾ cup smooth peanut butter

½ cup sugar

½ cup firmly packed light brown sugar

1 teaspoon pure vanilla extract

1 large egg

continued

Make the cookies: Heat the oven to 350°F. Line two baking sheets with parchment. In a medium bowl, sift together the two flours, baking soda, and salt. In the bowl of an electric mixer, cream the butter, peanut butter, and sugars with the paddle attachment until light and fluffy. Add the vanilla and egg; continue creaming until smooth and fluffy, about 3 minutes with an electric mixer (longer by hand). Stir in the flour mixture by hand just until it's incorporated; don't overmix or the cookies will be tough. Drop heaping tablespoonfuls of batter, spaced about 2 inches apart, onto the lined baking sheets. With floured fingers, flatten each dab of batter into a 2-inch round. Bake until the cookies are puffed and golden, 12 to 14 minutes, rotating the baking sheets if needed for even baking. Transfer the cookies to a rack to cool.

Make the filling: In a small bowl, cream the confectioners' sugar, butter, and peanut butter until smooth. Add the heavy cream; continue creaming until smooth and fluffy. Stir in the chopped peanuts and chocolate.

continued

An offset spatula is handy for spreading the cookie filling easily and evenly. A blunt table knife works, too.

For the filling

1½ cups confectioners' sugar

3 ounces (6 tablespoons)
   unsalted butter, softened at
   room temperature

¾ cup smooth peanut butter

3 tablespoons heavy cream

¼ cup coarsely chopped
   roasted unsalted peanuts

¼ cup coarsely chopped
   semisweet chocolate,
   or mini semisweet
   chocolate chips

Assemble the sandwiches: Transfer the cooled cookies to a work surface, flipping half of them over. With an offset spatula or a butter knife, spread a scant teaspoon of filling onto each turned-over cookie. Set another wafer on top of each filled cookie, pressing gently to spread the filling. Store sealed at room temperature or in the refrigerator.

MAKE AHEAD You can assemble these cookies ahead because they won't get soggy—even when filled—and they'll keep in the refrigerator or at room temperature for a couple of days . . . if they don't get eaten up before that!

A NEAT TRICK FOR SHAPING DROP COOKIES

A handsome sandwich starts with perfectly matched pairs of cookies. The easiest way to get drop cookies that are uniform in size and shape—and that will bake evenly, too—is to use a small ice cream scoop, the "disher" style with the sweep arm that scrapes the dough (or ice cream) from the bowl of the scoop. Not only do you get the perfect amount of dough in every cookie but using a scoop also makes the task go fast.

Look for the Zeroll® brand, which makes both a tablespoon and teaspoon size. The tablespoon size will give you a dough ball that's just over a true tablespoon, about the same amount you'd get if you scraped out your dough using two kitchen tablespoons.

Milk chocolate pecan lace cookie sandwiches

Yields 15 sandwiches

Delicate and elegant, lace cookies seem challenging to make, so it may surprise you to learn that the batter is mixed in one pot with just a spoon and that these buttery crisp cookies are actually simple drop cookies. The only catch is that you must line your baking sheets with a nonstick liner. For the sandwiches, choose cookies of the same size to pair together, and let the milk chocolate for the filling cool and thicken slightly before spreading it on so it doesn't drip through the lacy holes of the cookies.

2 ounces pecans (to yield ½ cup ground pecans)

2 ounces (4 tablespoons) unsalted butter

⅓ cup granulated sugar

2 tablespoons light corn syrup

1½ ounces (⅓ cup) unbleached all-purpose flour

Pinch table salt

1 teaspoon pure vanilla extract

½ cup coarsely chopped pecans

4 ounces milk chocolate, chopped

Position racks in the middle and upper third of the oven. Heat the oven to 350°F. Line two baking sheets with nonstick liners, like Silpat® brand, or with parchment.

In a food processor, grind the 2 ounces of pecans finely and measure out ½ cup. Heat the butter, sugar, and corn syrup in a medium saucepan over low heat, stirring often, until the butter melts and the sugar dissolves. Increase the heat to medium high and, stirring constantly, bring the mixture just to a boil. Remove the pot from the heat and stir in the flour and salt until incorporated. Stir in the vanilla, the ground pecans, and chopped pecans.

Drop the batter by the teaspoon 3 inches apart on the baking sheets, about 6 cookies per baking sheet. Bake the cookies until evenly light brown, 11 to 12 minutes total. About 5 minutes into baking, switch the sheets from top to bottom and back to front to promote even baking. The cookies won't begin to spread until about 6 minutes into baking.

Line a cooling rack with paper towels. Remove the cookies from the oven and, as soon as they're firm (which will take just a few minutes), use a wide spatula to transfer them to the rack to cool completely.

continued

Melt the milk chocolate in a bowl in a microwave or in a metal bowl set over a pan of simmering water (don't let the bowl touch the water). Let it cool enough to thicken slightly.

Arrange the cookies in pairs of similar size. Turn half of the cookies bottom up. Leaving a ½-inch border around the edge, spread a thin layer of milk chocolate over the cookies that are bottom up. Gently place the remaining cookies, bottom down, onto the milk chocolate. Let the cookies sit until the filling firms, about 30 minutes.

FOLLOW THESE TIPS FOR PERFECT LACE COOKIES

- Grind the nuts finely to give the batter the correct body. A food processor makes quick work of grinding. Almonds and walnuts are also delicious in these cookies.

- When boiling the batter, take the pan off the heat soon after you see bubbles. A boiled batter is unusual in a cookie dough, but crucial to these lace cookies.

- Incorporate the dry ingredients with a few quick strokes. The batter's texture will remain quite soft.

- Allow ample room between cookies to prevent "kissing." The silicone baking liner encourages the right amount of spreading.

- Spread the chocolate with a small off-set spatula or the back of a teaspoon, leaving a ½-inch margin to allow the chocolate to squeeze out a bit when you add the top cookie.

Chocolate-nut wafers

Yields about
144 cookies

A very sharp knife makes it easy to slice this nutty dough into neat squares. The pistachios add lovely color to these cookies, but feel free to use whatever combination of nuts you like.

9 ounces (2 cups) unbleached all-purpose flour

2 ounces (½ cup) natural (nonalkalized) unsweetened cocoa powder

½ teaspoon ground cinnamon

8 ounces (1 cup) unsalted butter, softened at room temperature

¾ teaspoon salt

10 ounces (2⅔ cups) confectioners' sugar

1 large egg, at room temperature

8 ounces (scant 2 cups) chopped walnuts

4 ounces (scant 1 cup) chopped pistachios

Blend the flour, cocoa, and cinnamon; set aside. With the paddle of an electric mixer (or regular beaters), cream the butter on medium speed until soft and creamy but not melted. Add the salt and confectioners' sugar; mix on medium-low speed until thoroughly combined, about 5 minutes, scraping the bowl as needed. Reduce the speed to low and add the egg; mix until blended. Add the walnuts, pistachios, and the flour mixture; as soon as the dough comes together, stop the mixer. Scrape the dough onto a large sheet of plastic wrap. Using the wrap to help shape and protect the dough, gently press it into a 6-inch square that's 1½ inches thick. Wrap in plastic and refrigerate until the dough is firm enough to slice, at least 4 hours.

Heat the oven to 400°F. Line a baking sheet with parchment. Unwrap the dough, trim the edges, and slice the square into four 1½-inch-square logs. Slice each log into square cookies between ¼ and ⅛ inch thick. Lay the squares ½ inch apart on the baking sheet. Bake until the tops look dry and the nuts look slightly brown-tinged, 8 to 10 minutes, rotating the sheet halfway through. Cool the cookies on the baking sheet until cool enough to handle (about 10 minutes) and then transfer the cookies to a rack.

MAKE AHEAD & FREEZE This recipe makes a lot of cookies, which is helpful during holiday time, but if you don't feel like baking them all at once, freeze the shaped logs; defrost them in the refrigerator the night before you plan to bake, and then bake as much as you need.

Pistachio-chocolate shortbread wedges

Yields 12 or 16 wedges

This outrageous shortbread is conveniently made with what are essentially pantry ingredients, perfect for spontaneous holiday entertaining or gift giving.

For the shortbread

¼ pound (½ cup) unsalted butter, at room temperature; more for the pan

½ cup granulated sugar

¾ ounce (¼ cup) unsweetened cocoa powder, preferably Dutch-processed

¼ teaspoon table salt

1 large egg yolk

½ teaspoon pure vanilla extract

4½ ounces (1 cup) unbleached all-purpose flour

For the glaze

3 ounces bittersweet or semisweet chocolate, coarsely chopped (a generous ½ cup)

1 ounce (2 tablespoons) unsalted butter, cut into 2 pieces

2 ounces (½ cup) coarsely chopped pistachios

Position a rack in the middle of the oven and heat the oven to 350°F. Lightly butter the bottom and sides of a 9½-inch fluted tart pan with a removable bottom.

Make the shortbread: In a medium bowl, combine the butter, sugar, cocoa, and salt. Beat with an electric mixer on medium speed until well blended. Scrape the bowl. Add the egg yolk and vanilla and continue beating on medium speed until just combined. Add the flour and mix on low speed, scraping the bowl as needed, until the flour mixes in and the dough begins to clump together, about 1 minute. Scrape the dough into the pan, scattering the pieces of dough evenly. Using your fingertips (lightly floured, if necessary), pat the dough onto the bottom (not up the sides) of the prepared pan to create an even layer. Bake until the top no longer looks wet and the dough just barely begins to pull away slightly from the sides of the pan, about 25 minutes.

Shortly before the shortbread is done, make the glaze: Melt the chocolate and butter together. Stir until smooth.

When the shortbread is done, transfer the pan to a rack. Pour the warm glaze over the shortbread and, using an offset spatula, spread the glaze evenly to within ½ inch of the edge. Scatter the pistachios evenly over the glaze and gently press them into the glaze. Let cool completely until the glaze is set. Remove the shortbread from the tart pan and cut it into 12 or 16 wedges. Serve at room temperature.

Chocolate-dipped espresso shortbread cookies

Yields about 84
1½-inch heart-shaped cookies

Melting chocolate with shortening helps the chocolate set without the need to temper it. You can omit the shortening and the dipping and instead drizzle the cookies with plain melted chocolate.

For the cookies

½ pound (1 cup) cold unsalted butter, cut into ½-inch pieces

½ cup granulated sugar

½ teaspoon table salt

10 ounces (2¼ cups) unbleached all-purpose flour

2 tablespoons finely ground espresso coffee beans

For the dipping chocolate

9 ounces semisweet chocolate, chopped

1 tablespoon vegetable shortening

Make the shortbread: Line two baking sheets with parchment. With a stand mixer bowl fitted with the paddle attachment or in a large mixing bowl, combine the butter, sugar, and salt. Mix on low speed until the butter combines with the sugar but isn't perfectly smooth, 1 to 2 minutes. Add the flour and ground espresso and mix on low speed, scraping the bowl frequently, until the dough has just about pulled together, about 3 minutes; don't overmix.

On a lightly floured surface, roll the dough to about ¼ inch thick; aim for uniform thickness to ensure even baking. Using a 1½-inch heart-shaped (or similar-size) cookie cutter, cut out shapes as close to one another as possible. Press the scraps together, roll them out, and cut out more cookies. Arrange the cookies on the prepared baking sheets and refrigerate until well chilled, at least 20 minutes.

Heat the oven to 300°F. Bake the cookies until the tops look dry and the color has darkened slightly, 30 to 60 minutes, depending on how golden you like them. For the most even baking, swap the position of the baking sheets and rotate them. Let the cookies cool on a rack before dipping them.

Dip the cooled cookies: Set a sheet of parchment or waxed paper on a work surface. Put the chocolate and shortening in a small heatproof bowl and set the bowl over a pan of simmering water. Melt the chocolate, stirring, until smooth and warm; don't let it get hot. Dip half of each cookie into the chocolate, set on the parchment, and let cool at room temperature, about 2 hours.

Chocolate-glazed chocolate hazelnut cookies

These cookies are bittersweet and complex, not only from dark chocolate and cocoa powder but also from espresso powder, which deepens and enriches the other flavors. Store these cookies in the fridge for up to five days to keep the chocolate glaze shiny. Remove them about 10 minutes before serving to keep that sheen. If the cookies stand unrefrigerated for longer than an hour, the chocolate surface will still taste great but may begin to dull.

5 ounces (1 cup) whole hazelnuts, toasted

1½ teaspoons instant espresso powder

5⅓ ounces (⅔ cup) unsalted butter, slightly softened; more for the baking sheets

¾ cup granulated sugar

1⅛ ounces (⅓ cup) unsweetened Dutch-processed cocoa powder

1 large egg

1½ teaspoons pure vanilla extract

¼ teaspoon table salt

8¼ ounces (1¾ cups) unbleached all-purpose flour

3 ounces bittersweet or semisweet chocolate, melted

Chocolate Glaze (page 40)

In a food processor, process the hazelnuts and espresso powder until they're ground to a paste, 2 to 3 minutes.

In a large bowl, beat the butter, sugar, cocoa, and hazelnut mixture with a stand mixer (use the paddle attachment) or a hand-held mixer on medium speed until very well blended and fluffy, 1½ to 2 minutes; scrape the bowl as needed. Add the egg, vanilla, and salt; beat until completely blended and smooth, about 1½ minutes. Add half of the flour and mix on low speed, and then add the melted chocolate and mix just until evenly incorporated. Mix or stir in by hand the remaining flour until evenly incorporated. Set aside for 10 minutes; the dough will firm up slightly.

Cut the dough into thirds. Set each third between sheets of parchment or waxed paper. Roll out each portion to ⅛ inch thick; check the underside and smooth any wrinkles. Stack the rolled pieces (paper still attached) on a tray. Refrigerate until firm, about 45 minutes or several hours.

Position a rack in the center of the oven and heat the oven to 350°F. Butter several large baking sheets or coat with nonstick spray. Working with one piece of dough at a time and keeping the remainder chilled, gently peel away and then replace the top sheet of paper. Flip the dough over. Peel off and discard the second sheet of paper. Cut out cookies using a 2½- to 2¾-inch fluted round, oval, or other cutter. (If the dough softens too much to handle easily, transfer the paper and cookies to a tray and refrigerate until firm again.) Using a spatula, carefully transfer the cookies to the baking sheets, arranging them about 1½ inches apart. Reroll the dough scraps. Continue cutting out the cookies until all dough is used.

Bake the cookies one sheet at a time (keep the rest refrigerated) until they feel dry and almost firm when pressed in the center, 7 to 10 minutes. Let cool on the sheets for 3 or 4 minutes before transferring to racks to cool completely. Prepare the cookies for glazing by freezing them for at least 20 minutes or up to several hours. (You can also freeze the cookies at this point, tightly wrapped, for up to two months.) To glaze the cookies, follow the directions on page 40.

chocolate glaze

Yields enough to coat at least one batch of Chocolate-Glazed Chocolate Hazelnut Cookies

Holding the glaze over warm water keeps it fluid and easy to handle during dipping.

1 pound bittersweet or semi-sweet chocolate (not unsweetened), broken up or coarsely chopped

1 tablespoon corn oil or other flavorless vegetable oil

Combine the chocolate and oil in a medium metal bowl. Set the bowl over a saucepan containing about an inch of barely simmering water and stir with a spatula until melted. Turn off the burner under the saucepan but leave the bowl over the hot water to keep the chocolate warm; stir the chocolate occasionally. (Replace the water in the pan with hot water as it cools off during the dipping process, but be careful not to splash water into the chocolate.)

DIPPING FOR A SHINY GLAZE

Make the glaze as directed in the Chocolate Glaze recipe above and line several baking sheets with aluminum foil. Working with only about five or six cookies at a time (keep the remainder frozen), dip the cookies in the chocolate glaze. For best results, tip the bowl so the chocolate pools on one side.

Hold a cookie vertically and dip until half is submerged in the chocolate. Lift out the cookie and shake off any excess chocolate. Gently scrape the bottom of the cookie against the side of the bowl to remove excess chocolate from the bottom surface.

Arrange the dipped cookies on the foil-lined sheets, spacing them slightly apart. When a pan is full, refrigerate it for 30 minutes so the chocolate can firm up. Then peel the cookies from the foil, pack them in airtight containers, and return them to the refrigerator.

Chocolate cherry coconut macaroons

Yields about 20 macaroons

These rich macaroons are moist and fudgy inside—they're something like a cross between a cookie and a chocolate truffle.

1¾ cups sweetened shredded coconut

⅔ cup cream of coconut, such as Coco López® (not coconut milk)

⅓ cup unsweetened cocoa powder, preferably Dutch-processed

2 large egg whites

1 teaspoon pure vanilla extract

Pinch table salt

3 ounces (½ cup) dried cherries (preferably tart ones), coarsely chopped

Heat the oven to 325°F. Spread 1½ cups of the shredded coconut on a rimmed baking sheet. Bake, stirring frequently, until some of the shreds begin to turn a light golden brown, 8 to 10 minutes (you're not so much toasting the coconut as you are drying it). Let cool. Turn off the oven.

In a medium bowl, whisk the cream of coconut, cocoa, egg whites, vanilla, and salt until well combined. Stir in the dried cherries and the "toasted" coconut. Cover and refrigerate until thoroughly chilled and firm, at least 2 hours and up to 24 hours.

About 20 minutes before you plan to bake the macaroons, heat the oven to 325°F. Line a heavy baking sheet with parchment. With damp hands, shape slightly heaping tablespoons of the batter into balls. Arrange them on the baking sheet about 2 inches apart (they should all fit on one sheet). Top each macaroon with a pinch of the remaining untoasted coconut. Bake in the center of the oven until the outsides are no longer sticky but the insides still feel somewhat soft when poked with a finger and the coconut topping is golden brown, about 20 minutes. Let the macaroons cool for 3 minutes on the baking sheet before transferring them to a rack to let cool completely.

Chocolate-orange biscotti

These fragrant and chocolatey cookies are an inventive departure from more Christmasy-looking cookies while still being sparkly, festive, and full of delicious nuggets like hazelnuts, candied ginger, and chocolate chunks. Another bonus for holiday giving: The biscotti are sturdy enough to travel well, arriving at their destination unbroken and as delicious as the day you baked them.

For the dough

2½ cups whole skin-on hazelnuts

12 ounces high-quality bittersweet or semisweet chocolate

8 ounces (1 cup) unsalted butter, completely softened at room temperature

4 large eggs

1 cup packed light brown sugar

1 cup granulated sugar

2 teaspoons pure vanilla extract

½ teaspoon almond extract

2 tablespoons instant espresso powder or finely ground coffee

¾ cup high-quality unsweetened Dutch-processed cocoa powder, sifted

1 cup candied orange peel

continued

Position the oven racks in the middle and top of the oven and heat the oven to 350°F. Toast the hazelnuts on a baking sheet until they're well browned, about 10 minutes. Let cool. You won't need to skin them—the skins taste great—but if the nuts are bigger than ½ inch, chop them roughly. Chop the chocolate into slivers that are a scant 1 inch long and ⅛ inch wide.

With an electric mixer fitted with the paddle attachment, beat the butter on medium-high speed until light and creamy. Add the eggs one at a time. Add the brown and white sugars, vanilla extract, almond extract, espresso powder, and cocoa powder, scraping down the sides of the bowl as needed. Add the candied orange peel, flour, baking powder, and salt. Add the hazelnuts and chocolate slivers, mixing just to combine. The dough will be stiff and a bit sticky. Let the dough rest in the refrigerator for 15 to 30 minutes before shaping.

Line two large baking sheets with parchment. Divide the dough into six equal pieces. Using as little flour as possible on the work surface, roll each piece into logs that are 12 to 14 inches long and 1¼ inches wide, working out the air pockets as you go. (If you're working ahead, wrap the logs in plastic wrap and refrigerate them overnight.) Transfer the logs to the lined baking sheets, setting the dough about 3 inches apart, patting the sides to smooth and

continued

18 ounces (4 cups)
   unbleached all-purpose flour

1 teaspoon baking powder

1 teaspoon kosher salt

For finishing

4 egg whites

1 teaspoon best-quality
   orange extract

¾ cup granulated sugar

straighten. In a small bowl, beat the egg whites with the orange extract until foamy. Brush the tops and sides of the logs with some of the whites. Sprinkle with ¼ cup of the sugar. Bake until firm in the center, about 35 minutes, rotating the sheets to ensure even baking. Set the sheets on racks until the logs are cool enough to handle and so the dough won't compress when you cut it, about 30 minutes.

Reduce the oven to 300°F and line the baking sheets with fresh parchment, if needed. With a serrated knife, saw the strips into ½-inch-thick slices, cutting crosswise. Lay the slices flat on the baking sheets. Brush the tops with the beaten egg white and sprinkle with another ¼ cup of the sugar. Bake for about 15 minutes, rotating the baking sheets as needed. Turn the biscotti over. Brush again with the egg white and sprinkle with the remaining ¼ cup sugar. Bake for another 10 to 15 minutes, watching carefully to make sure the chocolate doesn't burn. The centers will feel soft even when fully baked; they'll harden as the cookies cool. Set the baking sheets on racks, letting the cookies cool and crisp completely on the sheets. If stored airtight, the biscotti will keep for about two weeks.

creaming butter and sugar

WHAT DOES CREAMING BUTTER AND SUGAR MEAN, and why does it matter? For cookie-baking, perfectly creamed butter is key to smooth and workable dough, which will ensure that the remaining ingredients blend easily into the butter. Thorough creaming is also critical for cookies to hold their neat shape because uncreamed flecks of butter in the dough will melt during baking and cause the cookies to lose their shape, spread into blobs, and bake unevenly.

Cream the butter thoroughly until it has softened and whitened, using the paddle attachment of your mixer or, if you've got the energy, a wooden spoon. This can take up to 5 minutes, depending on the amount of butter. Scrape the bowl thoroughly during mixing to avoid lumps.

Chocolate-mint cut-outs

Yields about 48
2½-inch cookies

Use natural (nonalkalized) cocoa, such as Hershey's or Nestlé, rather than Dutch-processed for more straight-ahead chocolate flavor. Simple shapes such as circles or squares suit this dough, but you could use a more whimsical cookie cutter, provided there are no super-thin parts, which might burn.

10 ounces (2¼ cups) unbleached all-purpose flour

1½ ounces (½ cup) unsweetened natural cocoa powder (not Dutch-processed)

Pinch table salt

8 ounces (1 cup) unsalted butter, at room temperature

¾ cup granulated sugar

½ teaspoon pure vanilla extract

½ teaspoon peppermint extract

Combine the flour, cocoa, and salt. In a large bowl, beat the butter, sugar, vanilla, and mint extract until well blended. Add the flour mixture; beat until well blended (if you're using an electric mixer, set it on low speed). Divide the dough and shape it into two flat disks; wrap one in plastic while you work with the other.

Heat the oven to 350°F. On a lightly floured surface, roll one disk ⅜ inch thick. Cut out shapes of your choice using cookie cutters and set them 1 inch apart on parchment-lined baking sheets. Repeat with the other disk. Combine the scraps, chill them if they feel warm, and reroll.

Bake the cookies until the tops look dry and you see flaky layers when you break a cookie in half. This will take about 15 minutes. Transfer to a rack to cool completely. Decorate the cooled cookies with royal icing or gold leaf, if you like.

Chocolate-vanilla pinwheel cookies

Yields about 120
2-inch cookies

These pretty pinwheels look professionally made, but they're easily baked at home following the dough-layering technique outlined here. Once the layers of chocolate and vanilla dough get rolled together, these essentially become slice-and-bake cookies. You can freeze the logs for up to three months before baking them.

13½ ounces (3 cups) unbleached all-purpose flour

½ teaspoon table salt

¼ teaspoon baking soda

10 ounces (1¼ cups) unsalted butter, slightly softened

1¼ cups granulated sugar

1 large egg

1½ teaspoons pure vanilla extract

1 teaspoon instant espresso powder

3 tablespoons unsweetened Dutch-processed cocoa powder

3 ounces bittersweet chocolate, melted and still warm

Sift together the flour, salt, and baking soda. In the bowl of a stand mixer fitted with the paddle attachment, cream the butter on medium-low speed until smooth, about 2 minutes. Add the sugar in a steady stream and mix for another 2 minutes. Add the egg and vanilla and mix until well combined, scraping the bowl as needed. Reduce the speed to low and add the dry ingredients in two additions, mixing just until combined. Remove 2 cups less 2 tablespoons of the dough and set aside.

Dissolve the espresso powder in 2 tablespoons boiling water and set aside briefly to cool. Then mix the espresso and cocoa powder into the remaining dough. Reduce the mixer speed to low, add the warm melted chocolate, and mix just until thoroughly combined. Divide and shape the dough and roll it into pinwheel logs, following the photos and directions on pages 48-49.

Position racks in the upper and lower thirds of the oven. Heat the oven to 350°F. Line two rimmed baking sheets with parchment. Working with one log at a time, use a sharp, thin-bladed knife to slice the dough into 3/16-inch rounds. Lay the rounds about 1 inch apart on the prepared pans and bake until the tops of the cookies feel set, 12 to 14 minutes (don't let the edges become too brown). To ensure even browning, rotate the sheets as needed during baking. Let the baked cookies stand for 1 minute on the pan. While they're still warm, use a thin metal spatula to transfer them to racks. When cool, store between sheets of waxed paper in an airtight container for up to two weeks, or freeze for up to three months.

STACK AND ROLL FOR IMPRESSIVE PINWHEEL COOKIES

For perfectly round cookies, chill the dough logs on a level surface and turn them every 15 minutes for the first hour to keep the bottoms from flattening. If the bottoms do flatten, give each log a quick roll before returning it to the refrigerator.

1. Portion each flavor of dough into three equal pieces. (For accuracy, use a scale.) Shape each piece into a 5x5-inch square on a piece of plastic wrap and wrap well. The chocolate will be thicker than the vanilla. Refrigerate the dough for 30 minutes. (If the dough becomes too hard, let it stand at room temperature for a few minutes before rolling.)

2. While the dough is chilling, tear off twelve 12-inch squares of waxed paper. Roll each piece of dough into a 7x7-inch square between two sheets of the waxed paper. Without removing the waxed paper, layer the squares of dough on a baking sheet and refrigerate for 10 to 15 minutes. Have ready three 15-inch sheets of plastic wrap.

3. To shape the cookies, remove one square of the vanilla dough and one square of the chocolate dough from the refrigerator and peel off the top sheet of waxed paper from each. Invert the chocolate square over the vanilla square (or vanilla can go on top of chocolate; try some of each for variety), taking care to align the two doughs as evenly as possible. Using your rolling pin, gently roll over the dough to seal the layers together. Peel off the top layer of waxed paper.

Use a sharp knife and a ruler for even slices. To cut even slices of your pinwheel dough, lay a ruler alongside the log of dough. Use your sharpest thin-bladed knife and a continuous slicing motion to cut each cookie.

4. Starting with the edge of the dough closest to you, carefully curl the dough up and over with your fingertips, so no space is visible in the center of the pinwheel.

5. Using the waxed paper as an aid, continue rolling the dough into a tight cylinder. After the cylinder is formed, roll it back and forth on the counter to slightly elongate and compact it. Transfer the log to the plastic wrap, centering it on the long edge closest to you. Roll tightly, twisting the ends of the plastic firmly to seal. With your hands on either end of the log, push firmly toward the center to compact the dough. The log should be about 9 inches long and 1½ inches thick. Repeat with the remaining dough. Refrigerate the logs until firm enough to slice, about 3 hours, or freeze for up to three months.

Clever solutions for keeping your logs round

To keep your perfectly shaped round log from flattening out on the bottom while it chills, try these ideas:

Turn frequently. Put the logs on a level shelf or flat baking sheet in the refrigerator or freezer and turn each log every 15 minutes for the first hour. As the logs chill, the bottoms will flatten from the weight of the dough. To correct this, remold the logs by rolling them back and forth a few times on the countertop.

Use a cradle. If you happen to have a baguette pan, it makes a perfect cradle for chilling logs of dough. If you don't, save a few empty paper towel rolls, cut each in half lengthwise to make two cardboard troughs with rounded bottoms, and then place a log in each half for chilling. For both of these methods, after the logs have chilled for 15 to 20 minutes, turn them over once and chill until firm.

brownies & bars

Chewy brownies

Added flour helps to give these brownies their pleasant chewiness.
Be super careful not to overbake these or they'll dry out.

Yields 16
2-inch squares

¼ pound (½ cup) unsalted
butter; more for the pan

¼ pound unsweetened
chocolate

1½ cups granulated sugar

Scant ¼ teaspoon table salt

2 teaspoons pure vanilla
extract

2 large eggs, at room
temperature

4½ ounces (1 cup)
all-purpose flour

2 tablespoons unsweetened
natural cocoa powder
(not Dutch-processed)

Position a rack in the middle of the oven; heat the oven to 350°F. Butter an 8-inch-square pan, line the pan bottom with parchment (or waxed paper), and then butter the parchment.

Melt the butter and chocolate together in a medium metal bowl set over a pan of simmering water (don't let the bowl touch the water). Let the chocolate cool slightly before stirring in the sugar, salt, and vanilla.

Add the eggs one at a time, stirring each time until blended. Add the flour and cocoa and beat until the mixture is smooth, 30 to 60 seconds. Scrape the batter into the prepared pan and bake until the top is uniformly colored with no indentation and a

toothpick inserted in the middle comes out almost clean, with a few moist crumbs clinging to it, 35 to 45 minutes. Set the pan on a rack until cool enough to handle. Run a paring knife around the inside edge of the pan, and then invert the pan onto a flat surface and peel off the parchment. Flip the baked brownie back onto the rack to cool completely. Cut into squares.

Fudgy brownies

Using both bittersweet and unsweetened chocolate gives these brownies a deep, sophisticated chocolate flavor. The consistency is fudgy but not gooey or underdone.

5 ounces (10 tablespoons) unsalted butter, softened at room temperature; more for the pan

5 ounces bittersweet chocolate

2 ounces unsweetened chocolate

1 cup granulated sugar

2 teaspoons pure vanilla extract

Pinch table salt

2 large eggs, at room temperature

1 large egg yolk, at room temperature

3 ounces (⅔ cup) unbleached all-purpose flour

Position a rack in the middle of the oven and heat the oven to 350°F. Butter an 8-inch-square pan, line the pan bottom with parchment (or waxed paper), and then butter the parchment.

In a medium bowl, melt the butter and both chocolates together in a medium metal bowl set over a pan of simmering water (don't let the bowl touch the water) and let cool slightly. Whisk in the sugar and then the vanilla and salt. The mixture will be somewhat grainy. Whisk in the eggs and egg yolk, one at a time, stirring each time until blended. Add the flour, beating until thickened and smooth, 30 to 60 seconds.

Pour into the prepared pan and bake until a toothpick inserted in the middle comes out with moist crumbs (not wet batter) clinging to it, 35 to 45 minutes. Set the pan on a rack until cool enough to handle. Run a paring knife around the inside edge of the pan, then invert the pan onto a flat surface and peel off the parchment. Flip the baked brownie back onto the rack to cool completely. Cut into squares with a sharp knife.

Cakey brownies

These are rich and luscious, with a cakey lightness. This brownie improves
on sitting at least one and even two days after you bake it.

2 ounces (¼ cup) unsalted
butter, softened at room
temperature; more for
the pan

¼ pound unsweetened
chocolate

¾ cup granulated sugar

1 tablespoon plus 1 teaspoon
light corn syrup

2 large eggs, at room
temperature

2 teaspoons pure vanilla
extract

¼ cup whole milk, lukewarm

2¼ ounces (½ cup) unbleached
all-purpose flour

½ teaspoon baking powder

Pinch table salt

Position a rack in the middle of the oven and heat the oven to
350°F. Butter an 8-inch-square pan, line the pan bottom with
parchment (or waxed paper), and then butter the parchment.

Melt the chocolate in a medium metal bowl set over a pan of
simmering water (don't let the bowl touch the water); let cool
slightly. In a medium bowl, cream the butter with a fork. Beat
in the sugar and corn syrup; be sure there are no lumps in the
mixture. Add the eggs, one at a time, whisking thoroughly. Add
the vanilla and milk. Whisk until incorporated, about 30 seconds.
The batter may appear broken; this is fine. Whisk in the melted
chocolate, beating until the batter is smooth and has thickened
slightly, 30 to 60 seconds. Stir the flour, baking powder, and salt
so they're well blended; stir the dry ingredients into the chocolate
mixture until incorporated. Scrape into the prepared pan and
bake until a toothpick inserted in the middle comes out clean
with a few moist crumbs clinging to it, 20 to 30 minutes. Set the
pan on a rack until cool enough to handle.

Run a paring knife around the inside edge of the pan, then
invert the pan onto a flat surface and peel off the parchment.
Flip the baked brownie back onto the rack to cool completely.
Cut into squares.

what gives a brownie its texture?

ALL OF THESE BROWNIE RECIPES HAVE ENOUGH chocolate flavor to satisfy a chocolate yearning, but because of the varying amounts of chocolate, butter, sugar, and flour, the texture of each brownie is quite different.

A fudgy brownie is dense, with a moist, intensely chocolatey interior, somewhere between a rich truffle torte and a piece of fudge. The recipe on page 54 uses both bittersweet and unsweetened chocolate to give the brownies a deep, intense chocolate flavor. An egg yolk contributes fudgy richness without greasiness. Because the batter is quite dense, beat it vigorously with a wooden spoon to ensure a smooth, even texture.

A chewy brownie is moist but not quite as gooey as a fudgy one. The chewiness seems to come from a couple different factors: more all-purpose flour, whose proteins provide "bite" (cake flour, which is lower in protein, results in a light, crumbly texture that can be too delicate for brownies); and whole eggs, whose whites give structure and "set."

A cakey brownie has a moist crumb and a slightly fluffy interior. The batter contains less butter than the other recipes and includes milk and a little corn syrup for moistness (the milk and corn syrup are also great ways to extend a brownie's shelf life). The recipe doesn't include much flour (even less than for most cakes), and while brownies typically don't use chemical leavens, this cakey version has some baking powder in it for lightness.

The cakey brownie method also uses a bit of cake-baking technique: creaming the butter and sugar first (rather than melting the butter) and then whisking the batter to aerate the mixture and get a light crumb.

Rich cocoa brownies

These brownies are made with only cocoa powder—no chocolate—yet they're surprisingly rich and deeply flavored. Use cake flour for a brownie with an ultra-smooth texture or all-purpose flour for one with just a hint of crumb.

6 ounces (12 tablespoons) unsalted butter

⅔ cup unsweetened cocoa powder

1¼ cups granulated sugar

¼ teaspoon salt

1 teaspoon pure vanilla extract

3 eggs

2⅔ ounces (⅔ cup) cake flour or 2½ ounces (½ cup) unbleached all-purpose flour

½ cup chopped pecans or walnuts (optional)

Heat the oven to 350°F and grease a 9x9-inch pan. In a 2-quart saucepan, melt the butter, allowing it to get quite hot. Take the pan from the heat and whisk in the cocoa. Let the mixture cool completely. Whisk the sugar, salt, and vanilla into the cooled cocoa mixture. Add the eggs all at once and whisk again to combine. With a rubber spatula, fold in the flour just until incorporated. Fold in the nuts, if using.

Spread the batter in the pan and bake until a toothpick comes out moist and gooey but not wet, 18 to 20 minutes. Be careful not to overbake the brownies, as they'll toughen. Allow them to cool completely before cutting.

Brownie cream-cheese bites

The tang of cream cheese plays beautifully against the earthiness of dark chocolate in these mini cupcakes, which add a delicious burst of fudgy flavor and a playful element to the usual cookie assortment.

For the brownies

¼ pound unsweetened chocolate, coarsely chopped

¼ pound (½ cup) unsalted butter, cut into 3 pieces

4 large eggs, at room temperature

¼ teaspoon table salt

2 cups granulated sugar

1 teaspoon pure vanilla extract

5¾ ounces (1¼ cups) unbleached all-purpose flour

For the cream cheese topping

6 ounces cream cheese, softened at room temperature

3 tablespoons granulated sugar

1 large egg yolk, at room temperature

½ cup mini semisweet chocolate chips

Heat the oven to 350°F. Line mini muffin tins with foil or paper liners. (If you don't have enough tins to make 5 dozen cupcakes at one time, you'll need to bake the cupcakes in batches.)

Make the brownie batter: Melt the chocolate and butter together in a small bowl. Set aside.

With a stand mixer (use the whisk attachment) or a hand mixer, beat the eggs and salt in a large bowl on medium speed until very foamy, about 2 minutes. Continue beating while gradually adding the sugar. Beat until thick and pale, about 3 minutes. With a large rubber spatula, scrape the chocolate mixture into the eggs, add the vanilla, and fold until the two mixtures are just barely incorporated. Add the flour and continue folding until just incorporated. Scrape the batter into a 1-gallon heavy-duty zip-top bag. Squeeze out as much air as possible and seal.

Make the cream cheese topping: In a medium bowl, beat the cream cheese and sugar with a wooden spoon until smooth and creamy. Add the egg yolk and mix until blended. Pour in the chips and mix until blended. Scrape into a 1-quart zip-top bag. Squeeze out as much air as possible and seal.

Assemble and bake: Snip off ½ inch from one corner of each bag. Fill each lined muffin cup about two-thirds full with the brownie batter and then top with about 1 teaspoon of the cream cheese mixture. Bake the tins in the center of the oven until the

continued

brownies are puffed and a toothpick inserted in a brownie comes out just barely clean, about 20 minutes. Let the brownies cool in the tins on racks for 5 minutes before carefully lifting the liners out of the tins and transferring them to racks to cool completely. Let the tins cool completely before lining and filling them with the remaining batter.

Store the brownie bites at room temperature for up to two days or freeze in an airtight container, separating the layers with waxed paper, for up to two months.

SIMPLE TOOLS GIVE BROWNIES AND BARS A PROFESSIONAL LOOK

One of the advantages of making bar cookies is that you don't need any fancy equipment. Though not essential, a couple of simple tools will make your bar cookies look more professional.

- **Straight-sided 9x13-inch metal pans,** such as those made by Parrish and Doughmakers®, are great for baking bars and brownies. Regular Pyrex pans, with their rounded corners, are fine, but your yield will be smaller because you'll need to trim to get sharp edges.

- **Small offset spatulas,** especially the short, square 2-inch-wide size, are best for lifting

out squares neatly. For evenly spreading batters and glazes, a 3-inch- or 4-inch-long offset icing spatula is perfect.

- **Parchment** to line the bottom and edges of the pan makes it much easier to lift out bar cookies.

- **A bench scraper** is the perfect tool for cutting bar cookies. Its squared-off shape allows you to see just what you're doing and lets you aim straight down for the cleanest cut.

- **A ruler** helps you measure, so you get an even and consistent yield if you're making multiple batches.

- **Toothpicks** are helpful for marking off where you'll need to cut.

Double chocolate-glazed peppermint brownies

Yields about 30 brownies

Chocolate and mint are a perfect duo, but we improve upon perfection in these brownies by topping them with a gorgeous dark chocolate glaze marbleized with a white chocolate drizzle. These brownies only get better after a couple of days, as their texture gets fudgier and their flavor richer.

10 ounces (1¼ sticks) unsalted butter; more for greasing the pan

10 ounces unsweetened chocolate, chopped

2 teaspoons peppermint tea leaves (from about 2 tea bags)

2 cups granulated sugar

4 large eggs

2 teaspoons peppermint extract

¼ teaspoon kosher salt

4½ ounces (1 cup) unbleached all-purpose flour

2 ounces semisweet chocolate, chopped

2 tablespoons light corn syrup

2 ounces white chocolate, chopped

Center a rack in the oven and heat the oven to 350°F. Butter the bottom and sides of a 9x13-inch baking pan, line it with parchment (the paper should extend at least an inch above the long sides to act as handles for getting the brownies out), and butter the paper.

Put about 2 inches of water in a small pot and heat to a gentle simmer. In a heatproof bowl set over the water, melt 8 ounces of the butter and 8 ounces of the unsweetened chocolate. Be sure that the water is hot but not boiling and that it doesn't touch the bottom of the bowl. Stir occasionally with a heatproof spatula until the mixture is completely melted and uniform, 6 to 7 minutes. Turn off the heat, but leave the bowl over the water.

In a food processor, finely grind the peppermint leaves with the sugar. In a medium bowl, whisk together the eggs, peppermint extract, salt, and peppermint sugar until just combined. Whisk in the melted chocolate mixture (reserve the pot of water for later). Slowly add the flour, gently folding it in with a spatula, until incorporated. Spread the batter into the prepared pan and bake until a pick inserted into the center comes out almost clean (a few bits of batter should cling to the pick), 35 to 40 minutes. Put the pan on a rack to cool to room temperature, about 2 hours. Lift the paper lining to pull the brownies out of the pan. Peel the paper off the brownies and put them on a cutting board.

continued

To make the glaze, bring the pot of water back to a gentle simmer. Set a heatproof bowl over the pot and add the semisweet chocolate, corn syrup, and the remaining 2 ounces of both the butter and unsweetened chocolate. Stir frequently with a heatproof spatula until the mixture is melted and smooth; set aside. Put the white chocolate in a separate heatproof bowl and set it over the water. Stir frequently until it's melted and smooth; remove it from the heat.

Spread the chocolate glaze over the cooled brownies in an even layer using a spatula. Drizzle the white chocolate over the glaze in evenly distributed lines. Use a toothpick or a wooden skewer to drag the white chocolate into the glaze and make a marbleized pattern. Lift the cutting board and firmly tap it on the counter to settle the glaze.

Refrigerate until the glaze is set, at least 20 minutes and up to 12 hours. Cut into 30 bars, about 2 inches square (a knife rinsed in hot water and then dried will cut more cleanly than a cold knife). Keep well covered and serve at room temperature.

CREATE A GLOSSY MARBLEIZED GLAZE

1. A long offset spatula is ideal for spreading and smoothing the glaze, but if you don't have one, use a straight metal spatula or a long table knife. Spread the glaze in as even a layer as possible, all the way to the edges, letting the excess drip over.

2. White chocolate can be gloppy, so do a practice drizzle before you drizzle onto the brownies. For even more control, you can put the melted white chocolate into a clean, totally dry squeeze bottle, but work fast so it doesn't cool down too much. The closer your lines, the more marbling you'll get.

3. Use a toothpick or the back of a small knife to make vertical lines. Dragging the point slowly through the chocolate in one direction for the first line and the opposite direction for the next one creates the prettiest look.

Double chocolate chunk fudge brownies

Yields 12 brownies

If you use a metal pan, the edges of these brownies will be flat and the texture will be even. If you use a Pyrex baking dish, your brownies will have puffier, drier edges. Lining either type of pan with parchment will make it easier to get the brownies out (see how on the facing page).

6 ounces (¾ cup) unsalted butter, cut into 6 pieces; more for the pan

2 ounces (⅔ cup) unsweetened cocoa powder (natural/nonalkalized or Dutch-processed)

1⅔ cups granulated sugar

¼ teaspoon table salt

2 large eggs

1 teaspoon pure vanilla extract

4½ ounces (1 cup) unbleached all-purpose flour

¼ pound very coarsely chopped semisweet or bittersweet chocolate (¾ cup)

2 ounces (½ cup) coarsely chopped walnuts or pecans (optional)

Position a rack in the middle of the oven and heat the oven to 350°F. Generously butter the bottom and sides of an 8-inch-square Pyrex dish or metal baking pan.

Melt the butter in a medium saucepan over medium heat, stirring occasionally. Turn off the heat and add the cocoa. Whisk until smooth. Add the sugar and salt, and whisk until blended. Add 1 egg and whisk until just blended. Whisk in the vanilla and the second egg until just blended. Sprinkle the flour over the mixture and stir with a rubber spatula until just blended. Add the chopped chocolate and stir until combined.

Scrape the batter into the prepared baking pan and spread evenly. Scatter the nuts evenly over the batter, if using. Bake until a toothpick inserted in the center comes out with small, gooey clumps of brownie sticking to it, 33 to 38 minutes. Don't overbake or the brownies won't be fudgy. Transfer the baking dish to a rack and let cool completely.

Run a knife around the edges of the brownie and then pry it from the pan in one piece. Using a sharp knife, cut the cooled brownie into three equal strips and cut each strip into four equal pieces. Or, use a bench scraper to cut the brownie in the baking pan and then use a spatula to lift out the cut brownies. The cooler the brownie is, the cleaner the cutting will be, but these fudgy brownies will always leave some sticky crumbs on the knife.

CUTTING BROWNIES INTO NEAT SQUARES

The solution to neat brownies without any wasted edges left in the pan starts with parchment.

1. Run a sharp paring knife around the edge of the pan. This helps to ease the whole baked brownie out of the pan.

2. When the pan is cool enough to handle, flip out the whole brownie and then peel off the parchment.

3. Invert the whole brownie onto a rack and let cool completely before cutting.

Brownies will cook more quickly in metal pans than in glass, which is what accounts for the wide time windows in many recipes. If you're using metal, cooking times will be on the short side; with Pyrex, they'll be longer. For any brownie recipe—regardless of the pan you're using—start testing for doneness after 20 minutes of baking.

Port ganache-glazed brownies with dried cherries

A port-ganache topping and port-soaked dried cherries transform the classic fudgy brownie into an elegant, grown-up dessert, but you can also omit them for an indulgent afternoon snack.

For the port-soaked dried cherries

½ cup dried cherries, very coarsely chopped (or whole dried cranberries)

⅓ cup tawny port

For the brownies

8 ounces (1 cup) unsalted butter; more softened butter for the pan

3 ounces (⅔ cup) unbleached all-purpose flour; more for the pan

2 cups granulated sugar

4 large eggs, at room temperature

½ teaspoon pure vanilla extract

2½ ounces (¾ cup) unsweetened natural (non-alkalized) cocoa powder (not Dutch-processed)

½ teaspoon baking powder

½ teaspoon table salt

continued

Soak the cherries: In a small saucepan, bring the cherries and port to a boil over medium heat. Reduce the heat to low and cook for 2 minutes. Take the pan off the heat and let cool to room temperature.

Make the brownies: Position a rack in the center of the oven and heat the oven to 350°F. Butter and flour a 9-inch-square metal baking pan, tapping out the excess flour.

Melt the butter in a medium saucepan over medium heat. Remove the pan from the heat. Whisk or stir in the sugar, followed by all four of the eggs and the vanilla. Stir in the flour, cocoa, baking powder, and salt, starting slowly to keep the ingredients from flying out of the pan and stirring more vigorously as you go. Stir until the batter is smooth and uniform, about 1 minute. If you're using the port-soaked cherries, stir them in at this time, along with any remaining liquid from the saucepan.

Spread the batter into the prepared baking pan, smoothing it so it fills the pan evenly. Bake until a toothpick or a skewer inserted ¾ inch into the center of the brownies comes out with just a few moist clumps clinging to it, about 40 minutes. Let the brownies cool completely in the pan on a rack.

Make the topping: In a small saucepan over medium heat, bring the port to a boil. Boil until the port is reduced to 2 tablespoons, 3 to 6 minutes. Pour it into a small cup or bowl. Thoroughly rinse

continued

For the port-ganache topping

½ cup tawny port

½ cup heavy cream

6 ounces semisweet
chocolate, finely chopped
(about 1 cup)

the pan. Bring the heavy cream to a boil in the pan over medium-high heat, stirring occasionally. Take the pan off the heat. Stir in the chopped chocolate and reduced port until the mixture is smooth and the chocolate is melted.

Pour the ganache into a bowl and cover the surface with plastic wrap to prevent a skin from forming. Put the bowl in a cool part of the kitchen and let the ganache cool to room temperature, stirring occasionally. When it's cool, spread it evenly over the cooled brownies and give the ganache about an hour to set (it will still be quite soft and gooey). Cut into 16 squares. Keep the brownies at room temperature, well wrapped, for several days. You can freeze them, too, for up to two months.

LOOK FOR SUBTLE CLUES THAT INDICATE WHEN A BROWNIE IS DONE

To cook a brownie perfectly, you need to pay close attention toward the end of cooking, and you should always start testing for doneness before the recipe says to. Press gently in the center of the pan—the brownie should feel like it has just set. Then insert a toothpick to be sure. When in doubt, lean toward underdone rather than overdone.

Brownies are underdone when smudges of wet batter cling to the toothpick

Brownies are just right when traces of moistness and fudgy crumbs cling to the toothpick. Brownies are overdone when the toothpick comes out perfectly clean.

Macadamia double-decker brownie bars

These gorgeous two-layer bars have a brownie base topped with a gooey
nut-and-coconut-studded topping. Dipping the knife in warm water and wiping
it dry between cuts will keep the gooey topping from sticking to the knife.

For the brownie layer

Cooking spray

6 ounces (¾ cup) unsalted
butter, cut into large chunks

1½ cups granulated sugar

2¼ ounces (¾ cup)
unsweetened cocoa powder

¼ teaspoon table salt

2 large eggs

1 teaspoon pure vanilla extract

3½ ounces (¾ cup) unbleached
all-purpose flour

continued

Position a rack in the center of the oven and heat the oven to 325°F.
Line the bottom and sides of a 9x13-inch baking pan with foil, leaving some overhang on the sides, and spray with cooking spray.

Make the brownie layer: In a medium saucepan over medium
heat, whisk the butter until it is melted. Remove the pan from the
heat and add the sugar, cocoa powder, and salt. Whisk until well
blended, about 1 minute. Add the eggs and vanilla and whisk until
smooth. Add the flour and stir with a rubber spatula until blended. Scrape into the prepared pan and spread evenly. Bake until the
top is shiny and dry-looking and the brownie springs back very
slightly when pressed with a fingertip, about 20 minutes. (The
brownie should not be completely baked.) Remove from the oven
and put on a rack.

While the brownie layer is baking, make the macadamia topping:
In a large mixing bowl, combine the brown sugar and flour.
Whisk until well blended, breaking up any large clumps. Add
the corn syrup, melted butter, and vanilla. Whisk until blended,
about 1 minute. Add the eggs and whisk just until combined,
about 30 seconds. (Don't overmix or the batter will be foamy.)
Add the nuts and coconut and stir with a rubber spatula until
evenly blended.

continued

For the macadamia layer

½ cup firmly packed light
   brown sugar

1½ ounces (⅓ cup)
   unbleached all-purpose flour

⅔ cup light corn syrup

1½ ounces (3 tablespoons)
   unsalted butter, melted

1½ teaspoons pure vanilla
   extract

2 large eggs

1½ cups roughly chopped
   salted macadamia nuts

⅓ cup sweetened coconut
   flakes

Pour the topping over the partially baked brownie layer: Using a spatula, carefully spread the mixture into an even layer. Return the pan to the oven and bake until the top is golden brown, 37 to 40 minutes. Transfer the pan to a rack to cool completely.

Using the foil as handles, lift the rectangle from the pan and invert onto a work surface. Carefully peel away the foil. Flip right side up. Using a sharp knife, cut into 2x2-inch squares and then cut each square into triangles.

MAKE AHEAD & FREEZE After the brownie and macadamia layers have been baked and cooled, the entire pan can be wrapped in plastic wrap, then foil, and frozen for up to one month.

Nutty butterscotch & chocolate bars

Yields 24

2¼- x 2-inch bars

This cookie goes by many aliases: blondie, golden brownie, congo bar. No matter what you call them, they're butterscotch-flavored, chewy, and loaded with texture.

11¼ ounces (2½ cups) unbleached all-purpose flour

¾ teaspoon baking soda

½ teaspoon table salt

½ pound (1 cup) unsalted butter, softened at room temperature; more for the pan

1¾ cups very firmly packed light brown sugar

2 large eggs

1½ teaspoons pure vanilla extract

7½ ounces (1¼ cups) semi-sweet chocolate chips

1¼ ounces (½ cup) sweet-ened coconut flakes

4½ ounces (1 cup) medium-finely chopped pecans or walnuts

Position a rack in the middle of the oven and heat the oven to 325°F. Lightly grease the bottom and sides of a 9x13-inch baking pan.

In a medium bowl, whisk the flour, baking soda, and salt to blend. In a large bowl, combine the butter and brown sugar. With a hand-held mixer or a stand mixer fitted with the paddle attachment, beat the butter and brown sugar on medium speed until very well blended and fluffy, about 2 minutes. Add the eggs and vanilla and continue to beat on medium speed until well blended, about another 1 minute. Add the flour mixture and mix on low until just blended, about 1 minute. Pour in the chocolate chips and coconut; mix on low until combined.

Scrape the dough into the prepared pan and spread evenly. Scatter the nuts evenly over the top. Bake until a toothpick inserted in the center comes out almost clean with a few moist crumbs clinging to it, about 40 minutes. Transfer the pan to a rack and let cool completely. Cut into bars, squares, or triangles. Cover with plastic and store at room temperature for up to two days or freeze for up to one month.

Mexican-style pecan-chocolate squares

Using bittersweet chocolate for the layer between the cookie base and the gooey pecan topping helps keep the balance of flavors from tipping toward the too-sweet side. These pecan bars keep well for a few days.

For the cookie base

6 ounces (¾ cup) cold unsalted butter, cut into ½-inch pieces

9 ounces (2 cups) unbleached all-purpose flour

½ cup packed light brown sugar

2 teaspoons ground cinnamon

½ teaspoon table salt

2 ounces finely grated bittersweet chocolate (a scant ½ cup)

For the pecan topping

10 ounces (3 cups) pecans, toasted

¼ pound (½ cup) unsalted butter

1 cup packed dark brown sugar

⅓ cup honey

2 tablespoons heavy cream

½ teaspoon table salt

Position a rack in the middle of the oven and heat the oven to 350°F.

Make the cookie base: Put the 6 ounces of butter in a food processor, along with the flour, light brown sugar, cinnamon, and salt. Pulse until the mixture is well combined (about 20 pulses). Scatter the dough into a 9-inch-square baking pan and press it evenly over the bottom. (Wipe out the processor bowl but don't bother washing it.) Bake the base until firm and lightly browned, about 25 minutes. When the cookie base comes out of the oven, sprinkle the grated chocolate evenly over the top. (Don't turn off the oven.) Set the pan aside.

Make the pecan topping: As the cookie base bakes, pulse the pecans in the food processor until coarsely chopped. In a medium-size heavy saucepan, melt the ¼ pound of butter. Stir in the dark brown sugar, honey, cream, and salt. Simmer for 1 minute, stirring occasionally. Stir in the pecans. Pour the pecan mixture over the chocolate-sprinkled cookie base, spreading evenly. Bake until much of the filling is bubbling (not just the edges), 16 to 18 minutes. Let cool completely in the pan.

When ready to serve, cut into 16 squares; a bench scraper is the best tool for cutting these chewy bars. Tightly covered, these bars will keep for about five days (though they never last that long).

Kahlúa fudge bites

Yields about 96
1-inch squares

These are oh-so-chocolatey and rich, which is why they're best cut into smaller, bite-size squares.

For the fudge

9 ounces (2 cups) unbleached all-purpose flour

½ teaspoon baking powder

½ teaspoon table salt

¾ pound (1 ½ cups) unsalted butter; more for the pan

3 ounces (1 cup) unsweetened natural cocoa powder (not Dutch-processed)

3 cups very firmly packed light brown sugar

4 large eggs

2 tablespoons coffee-flavored liqueur (such as Kahlúa®) or 1½ teaspoons pure vanilla extract

For the chocolate glaze

6 ounces bittersweet chocolate, finely chopped

3 ounces (6 tablespoons) unsalted butter, cut into 6 pieces

1 tablespoon light corn syrup

Position a rack in the middle of the oven and heat the oven to 325°F. Lightly grease the bottom and sides of a 9x13-inch baking pan.

Make the fudge: In a medium bowl, whisk the flour, baking powder, and salt to blend. Melt the butter in a large saucepan over medium heat, stirring occasionally. Remove the pan from the heat and whisk in the cocoa until smooth. Whisk in the brown sugar until blended. Add the eggs, one at a time, whisking until just blended. Whisk in the coffee liqueur along with the last egg. Sprinkle the flour over the mixture and stir with a rubber spatula until just blended. Scrape the batter into the prepared pan and spread it evenly. Bake until a toothpick inserted in the center comes out with a few small, moist clumps sticking to it, about 30 minutes. (Don't overbake or the squares won't be fudgy.) Transfer the pan to a rack to let cool completely.

Make the glaze: In a medium metal bowl set over a pan of simmering water, melt the chocolate, butter, and corn syrup together (don't let the bowl touch the water). Whisk the mixture to smooth it if necessary. Pour the glaze onto the center of the cooled, uncut fudge bars. Using an offset spatula, spread the glaze evenly to cover completely. Refrigerate until the glaze is set, about 30 minutes. Cut into 1-inch squares.

Hazelnut toffee squares

Yields about

72 squares

You can make a lot of these nutty, buttery treats in one batch, making them great for entertaining or giving. Be sure to let the chocolate set before you cut the cookies.

8 ounces (1 cup) unsalted
butter, at room temperature

8 ounces (1 cup firmly packed)
dark brown sugar

1 large egg yolk

1 teaspoon pure vanilla extract

¼ teaspoon table salt

9 ounces (2 cups) unbleached
all-purpose flour

10 ounces bittersweet
chocolate, chopped

¼ cup whole milk

3½ ounces (1 cup) chopped
hazelnuts, toasted

Heat the oven to 350°F. Lightly grease a 9x13-inch baking pan. With a wooden spoon or a mixer, cream the butter and brown sugar until smooth and no lumps remain. Add the egg yolk, vanilla, and salt; beat until well blended. Add the flour; mix until the dough begins to come together (if you're using an electric mixer, set it on low speed). Pat the dough into the pan. Bake until the dough begins to pull away from the sides of the pan and keeps a slight indentation when pressed lightly, 26 to 28 minutes.

Meanwhile, melt the chocolate and the milk in a double boiler, stirring as little as possible to prevent separating. Pour the warm ganache over the warm baked cookie crust and spread it evenly. Sprinkle with the nuts and let cool completely until the chocolate has set, about 4 hours. Cut into 1½-inch squares.

Caramel turtle bars

Yields about 48
1½-inch-square bars

The secret to these spectacular treats? A crust that's as buttery and tender as shortbread but that's crisp and strong enough to be the foundation of these bar cookies.

For the crust

Nonstick cooking spray, vegetable oil, or melted butter for the pan

7 ounces (14 tablespoons) unsalted butter, melted and cooled to just warm

½ cup packed light brown sugar

½ teaspoon table salt

9 ounces (2 cups) unbleached all-purpose flour

For the caramel topping

2 cups pecan halves, toasted and coarsely chopped

1 cup packed light brown sugar

¾ cup heavy cream

4 ounces (½ cup) unsalted butter, cut into chunks

½ cup light corn syrup

¼ teaspoon table salt

continued

Line a straight-sided 9x13-inch metal baking pan with foil, letting the ends create an overhanging edge for easy removal. Lightly coat the sides of the foil (not the bottom) with nonstick cooking spray, oil, or melted butter to prevent the caramel from sticking.

Make the shortbread crust: In a medium bowl, stir together the butter, brown sugar, and salt. Stir in the flour to make a stiff dough. Press the mixture evenly into the bottom of the prepared pan. Prick the dough all over with a fork. Refrigerate the pan for 30 minutes (or freeze for 5 to 7 minutes), until the dough is firm.

Meanwhile, position a rack near the center of the oven and heat the oven to 325°F.

Bake the dough for 20 minutes, and then decrease the oven temperature to 300°F and bake until the crust is golden all over and completely set, about 15 more minutes.

Make the topping: Sprinkle the pecans evenly over the crust.

In a heavy medium saucepan, bring the brown sugar, cream, butter, corn syrup, and salt to a boil over medium-high heat, stirring until all the ingredients are melted and smooth. Let the mixture continue to boil, without stirring, until a candy thermometer registers 240°F, about 6 more minutes. Turn off the heat and immediately (but carefully) pour the caramel evenly over the prepared crust. Let the bars cool completely, about 2 hours, before garnishing with the ganache.

For the ganache

2 ounces good-quality
 bittersweet chocolate, finely
 chopped (about ½ cup)

6 tablespoons heavy cream

Make the ganache: Put the chocolate in a small heatproof bowl. In a small saucepan, bring the heavy cream to a boil. Remove from the heat and pour over the chocolate. Let it sit for 3 minutes. Stir gently with a rubber spatula until combined and smooth.

Fill a plastic zip-top baggie with the ganache, snip the tip off a corner, and drizzle the ganache decoratively over the caramel bars (you don't have to use all the ganache; keep the extra in the fridge for up to five days). Let the ganache set for 30 to 60 minutes. Carefully lift the bars from the pan using the foil sides and transfer them to a cutting board. Separate the foil from the bars by sliding a spatula between them. Cut the bars into 1½-inch squares. They will keep at room temperature for a week.

A BAR-COOKIE BASE THAT'S RICH BUT STURDY

The Caramel Turtle Bars have a buttery shortbread base that's a notch more luxurious than most bar cookie bases. But in order to make the shortbread strong enough to support the toppings and allow for easy cutting, we've changed the classic shortbread method.

Most shortbread recipes begin with soft butter and use a classic creaming method, which yields a tender, slightly sandy shortbread. In this recipe, melted, not creamed, butter is the key. Simply stirring melted butter into the dry ingredients delivers a crisp yet tender crust.

Another important key is to refrigerate the dough before baking. Cold dough doesn't puff up and shrink as much during baking as room temperature dough, so the crust is perfectly crispy-crunchy.

Kahlúa truffle triangles

Yields about 72
1½- to 2-inch triangles

These luscious cookies are perfect for a party. Because they're a bar cookie,
they're not fussy to make and they yield a big batch of pretty and delicious treats.

For the crust

6¾ ounces (1½ cups) unbleached
   all-purpose flour

3 ounces (¾ cup)
   confectioners' sugar

¼ teaspoon table salt

6 ounces (¾ cup) cold,
   unsalted butter, cut into
   10 pieces, more for the pan

½ teaspoon pure vanilla
   extract

For the filling

1 pound semisweet or
   bittersweet chocolate,
   broken into squares or very
   coarsely chopped

¾ cup whole or 2% milk

4 ounces (½ cup) unsalted
   butter, cut into 6 pieces

4 large eggs

⅔ cup granulated sugar

2 tablespoons Kahlúa

Make the crust: Position an oven rack in the center of the oven and heat the oven to 350°F. Line the bottom and sides of a 9x13-inch baking pan with foil, allowing foil to overhang the long sides of the pan to act as handles for removing the cookie later. Lightly butter the foil.

In a food processor, combine the flour, confectioners' sugar, and salt. Process the ingredients briefly to combine, about 15 seconds. Scatter the cold butter pieces and the vanilla over the flour mixture and process, using short pulses, until the dough begins to form small clumps, 1 to 1½ minutes. Turn the dough into the prepared pan. Using lightly floured fingertips, press the dough into the pan in a smooth, even layer. Bake until pale golden, especially around the edges, 22 to 25 minutes. Do not overbake or the crust will be hard and crispy. Transfer the pan to a cooling rack and lower the oven temperature to 325°F.

Make the filling: In a medium bowl, melt the chocolate, milk, and butter together over a pot of barely simmering water or in the microwave. Whisk until smooth and set aside to cool slightly.

In a stand mixer fitted with a paddle attachment or in a large mixing bowl using a hand-held electric mixer, beat the eggs, sugar, and Kahlúa on medium-high speed until foamy and lighter in color, 2 minutes. Reduce the speed to low and gradually add the chocolate mixture. Stop the mixer and scrape down the bowl and beater. Beat on medium speed until well blended, about 30 seconds.

continued

Pour the chocolate batter over the baked crust and spread evenly. Bake until the sides are slightly puffed and a toothpick inserted near the center comes out wet and gooey but not liquid, 30 to 35 minutes. Transfer the pan to a rack. As it cools, the center may sink a bit, leaving the edges slightly (about $\frac{1}{2}$ inch) elevated. While the filling is still warm, use your fingertips to gently press the edges down to the level of the center, if necessary.

When completely cool, cover with plastic and refrigerate until very cold, at least 12 hours or up to 2 days. Using the foil as handles, lift the rectangle from the pan and set it on a cutting board. Tipping the rectangle, carefully peel away the foil. Using a hot knife, cut the rectangle lengthwise into $1\frac{1}{2}$-inch strips, wiping the blade clean before each cut. Cut each strip on alternating diagonals to make small triangles. Let sit at room temperature for about 5 minutes before serving. The baked truffles can be refrigerated, wrapped in plastic, for up to two days.

MAKE AHEAD & FREEZE You can bake these up to one month ahead: Wrap the cooled baking pan in heavy-duty plastic wrap and freeze (no need to cut them into triangles first).

Apricot, pistachio & chocolate chip bars

Yields 18
3- x 2-inch bars

With oatmeal, dried fruit, and nuts, these bars are a healthful indulgence. To ensure thoroughly crisp results, the bottom layer gets partially baked before the filling and crumb topping go on.

9 ounces (2 cups) unbleached all-purpose flour

1¼ cups old-fashioned oats

1 cup packed dark brown sugar

½ teaspoon ground cinnamon

½ teaspoon table salt

½ pound (1 cup) chilled, unsalted butter, cut into ½-inch cubes

4 ounces (about 1 cup) chopped, shelled natural pistachios

½ cup diced dried apricots

½ cup white chocolate or semisweet chocolate chips

15¼-ounce jar apricot preserves

Heat the oven to 325°F. With an electric mixer, combine the flour, oats, brown sugar, cinnamon, and salt; mix on low speed until well combined. Add the butter and mix on medium speed until the butter is mostly blended and the mixture appears moist and begins to pull together, about 3 minutes. Stir in the pistachios. Reserve 1½ cups of this crumb mixture, stir the dried apricots and chocolate chips into it, and refrigerate. Firmly press the remaining mixture into the bottom of an ungreased 9x13-inch baking pan. Bake in the middle of the oven for 25 minutes. Let cool for about 20 minutes.

Spread the apricot preserves evenly on top, leaving a ⅛-inch border around the edge of the crust. Crumble the reserved crumb mixture over the top. Continue baking until lightly browned and the fruit filling is bubbling all over, including in the center of the pan, 35 to 40 minutes. Let cool completely before slicing into 18 bars (or into smaller pieces, if you like).

cakes

Chocolate-espresso mousse torte

This torte is delicious alone or with lightly sweetened whipped cream. Be sure to wrap your springform pan with heavy-duty aluminum foil (or two layers of regular foil); even the best pans can let water in.

1 tablespoon softened unsalted butter for the pan

12 ounces semisweet chocolate (55% to 60% cacao), coarsely chopped or broken into pieces (2 slightly heaping cups)

1 cup heavy cream

1 tablespoon instant espresso granules

6 large eggs, at room temperature

½ cup granulated sugar

1⅛ ounces (¼ cup) unbleached all-purpose flour

1 tablespoon confectioners' sugar

¼ teaspoon ground cinnamon

Position a rack in the center of the oven and heat the oven to 400°F. Generously butter a 10-inch springform pan and wrap the bottom and sides in heavy-duty aluminum foil. Have ready a roasting or baking pan just big enough to accommodate the springform, and put a kettle of water on to boil.

Grind the chocolate in a food processor until it reaches the consistency of coarse meal, about 30 seconds. Bring the cream to a boil in a small saucepan over medium heat. Add the cream to the food processor and process until smooth, about 10 seconds.

Dissolve the espresso powder in 1 tablespoon hot water and add it to the warm chocolate mixture still in the food processor. Process until fully incorporated, about 10 seconds. Transfer to a large bowl.

In the bowl of a stand mixer fitted with the whisk attachment, whip the eggs, sugar, and flour at just under high speed until pale, light, and fluffy and at least doubled in volume (if not tripled), about 6 minutes. Add about one-third of the egg mixture to the chocolate mixture and mix with a rubber spatula until combined. Add the remaining egg mixture and gently fold together until just combined and no obvious streaks of egg remain.

Pour the batter into the prepared springform pan. Set the pan inside the roasting pan and fill the roasting pan with 1 to 1½ inches of boiling water. Bake until a dry crust forms on the top of the torte and the edges seem set but the center is still a bit wobbly when you jiggle it, 15 to 20 minutes. Remove the torte from the water bath and its foil wrap. Cool the torte on a wire rack to room temperature and then refrigerate until cold and completely set, at least 3 hours or overnight.

To unmold, carefully remove the springform ring. Put a piece of plastic wrap over the top of the torte. Invert the torte onto a baking sheet and remove the pan bottom; use a thin-bladed knife to help separate the torte and pan bottom if necessary. Invert the torte again onto a serving plate and remove the plastic wrap. Just before serving, put the confectioners' sugar and cinnamon in a small fine strainer and sift over the top of the torte.

To cut the torte as cleanly as possible, dip your knife in hot water to heat the blade and wipe dry before each cut. Or for a cleaner cut, use unwaxed dental floss.

Flourless chocolate & vanilla marble cake

Serves 16

This dense, luscious cake has a texture a little like fudge and a little like cheesecake. A small slice goes a long way. To slice this moist cake neatly, use a hot knife (run it under hot running water and dry it), and wipe the blade clean between slices.

For the vanilla batter

8 ounces cream cheese, softened to room temperature

⅔ cup granulated sugar

1 large egg

1 teaspoon pure vanilla extract

For the chocolate batter

10 ounces bittersweet chocolate, finely chopped

5 ounces (10 tablespoons) unsalted butter, cut into 6 pieces

3 large eggs

⅓ cup granulated sugar

1 tablespoon dark rum or espresso

1 teaspoon pure vanilla extract

Pinch table salt

Unsweetened cocoa powder, for dusting

Position an oven rack in the middle of the oven and heat the oven to 300°F. Lightly grease a 9x2-inch round cake pan and line the bottom with parchment.

Make the vanilla batter: In a medium bowl, beat the softened cream cheese with an electric mixer until smooth. Add the sugar and continue beating until well blended and no lumps remain. Add the egg and vanilla and beat just until blended. Set aside.

Make the chocolate batter: In a medium bowl, melt the chocolate and butter in a large metal bowl over a pan of simmering water or in the microwave. Whisk until smooth and set aside to cool slightly. Using a stand mixer fitted with the whip attachment (or with a hand mixer), beat the eggs, sugar, rum or espresso, vanilla, and salt on medium high until the mixture is pale and thick, 3 to 4 minutes. With the mixer on low, gradually pour in the chocolate mixture and continue beating until well blended.

Combine and bake: Spread about half of the chocolate batter in the bottom of the pan. Alternately add large scoopfuls of each of the remaining batters to the cake pan. Using a knife or the tip of a rubber spatula, gently swirl the two batters together so they're mixed but not completely blended. Rap the pan against the countertop several times to settle the batters.

continued

Bake until a pick inserted about 2 inches from the edge comes out gooey but not liquid, 40 to 42 minutes; don't overbake. The top will be puffed and slightly cracked, especially around the edges. It will sink down as it cools. Let the cake cool on a rack until just slightly warm, about 1½ hours. Loosen it from the pan by holding the pan almost perpendicular to the counter; tap the pan on the counter while rotating it clockwise. Invert onto a large flat plate or board, then remove the pan and carefully peel off the parchment. Sift some cocoa powder over the cake (this will make it easier to remove the slices when serving). Invert the cake again onto a similar plate so that the top side is up and let cool completely. Cover and refrigerate until very cold, at least 4 hours or overnight, or freeze.

MAKE AHEAD & FREEZE Wrap the cooled cake (unmolded as directed in the recipe) in plastic and refrigerate until firm and well chilled. Slide the cake from the plate and wrap it again in plastic. Freeze for up to a month. To serve, unwrap the cake and set it on a flat serving plate that's been sprinkled with a little more cocoa powder. Cover with plastic wrap and thaw in the refrigerator overnight or at room temperature for an hour or two.

Flourless chocolate-almond cake with almond-cherry-caramel glaze

Dried cherries and toasted almonds are folded into a caramel topping and then drizzled over this cake, giving it a crisp (think peanut brittle) topping. The cake is made with margarine, which ensures that it keeps with kosher rules, making it a wonderful conclusion for a Passover meal. Most large supermarkets carry matzo cake meal around the holidays.

For the cake

8 ounces (1 cup) unsalted stick margarine, softened; more for the pan

8 ounces bittersweet or semisweet chocolate, coarsely chopped

¾ cup slivered almonds, toasted

1 cup granulated sugar

⅛ teaspoon table salt

6 large eggs, separated

1 teaspoon pure vanilla extract

½ cup matzo cake meal

For the glaze

⅓ cup dried cherries

¼ cup Kirschwasser or other cherry liqueur

1 cup granulated sugar

½ cup slivered almonds, toasted and coarsely chopped

Position a rack in the center of the oven and heat the oven to 350°F. Line the bottom of a 9-inch springform pan with parchment paper, then grease the paper and sides of the pan.

Make the cake: Melt the chocolate in a medium metal bowl set in a small skillet of hot, barely simmering water. Remove the chocolate from the heat and let cool for a couple of minutes.

Meanwhile, process the almonds in a food processor until finely ground and set aside. In a stand mixer fitted with the paddle attachment (or with an electric hand mixer), beat the margarine with ¾ cup of the sugar and the salt on medium speed until soft and fluffy, 2 to 3 minutes. Add the egg yolks and vanilla and mix on medium-low speed until smooth. Gently fold in the chocolate, ground almonds, and matzo cake meal.

In another large bowl, using the whisk attachment or clean beaters, beat the egg whites on high speed until they form soft peaks, about 3 minutes. Add the remaining ¼ cup sugar and beat until the egg whites form stiff peaks, about 1 minute more.

In three batches, use a rubber spatula to gently fold the egg whites into the chocolate mixture. Scrape the batter into the prepared pan, spread evenly, and bake until the top starts to brown and a

continued

toothpick inserted into the center comes out with just some moist crumbs attached, 35 to 40 minutes. Let the cake cool in the pan on a rack for 15 minutes.

While the cake is baking, soak the cherries in the liqueur in a small bowl.

Meanwhile, make the glaze: In a heavy-based medium saucepan, stir the sugar and $\frac{1}{2}$ cup water together over medium heat until the sugar dissolves. Raise the heat to medium high and cook, swirling occasionally and brushing down the sides of a pan with a wet pastry brush to wash down any sugar crystals, until the caramel turns a deep, amber brown, about 6 minutes. Carefully add $\frac{1}{4}$ cup water (it will bubble up) and whisk together until the mixture acquires an even, syrupy consistency. Drain the cherries and then stir them into the caramel, along with the chopped almonds.

Remove the sides of the springform pan and set the cake on a large rimmed baking sheet. Pour the caramel mixture evenly over the cake (it's fine if it spills over the sides). Let the cake cool completely to room temperature before transferring to a cake stand and serving.

Flourless chocolate cake with chocolate glaze

Everyone needs a good flourless chocolate cake in their dinner-party repertoire. This one is drop-dead delicious—a pure chocolate indulgence.

For the cake

¾ ounce (¼ cup) unsweetened natural cocoa powder, sifted if lumpy; more for the pan

12 ounces bittersweet chocolate, coarsely chopped (2 ¼ cups)

6 ounces (¾ cup) unsalted butter, cut into 6 pieces; more for the pan

5 large eggs

1 cup granulated sugar

1½ teaspoons pure vanilla extract

¼ teaspoon table salt

For the glaze

¼ pound bittersweet chocolate, coarsely chopped (¾ cup)

1½ ounces (3 tablespoons) unsalted butter

Make the cake: Position a rack in the middle of the oven and heat the oven to 300°F. Lightly butter the bottom of a 9x2-inch round cake pan and line the bottom with a round of parchment. Lightly butter the parchment and the sides of the pan and dust with cocoa. Tap out any excess cocoa.

Melt the chocolate and butter together in a medium bowl and let cool slightly. With a stand mixer fitted with the whisk attachment, combine the eggs, sugar, vanilla, salt, and 2 tablespoons water. Beat on medium-high speed until the mixture is very foamy, pale in color, and doubled in volume, 2 minutes. Reduce the mixer speed to low and gradually pour in the chocolate mixture. Increase the speed to medium high and continue beating until well blended, about 30 seconds. Add the cocoa and mix on medium low just until blended, about 30 seconds.

Pour the batter into the prepared pan. Bake until a pick inserted in the center comes out looking wet with small gooey clumps, 40 to 45 minutes. Don't overbake. Let cool in the pan on a rack for 30 minutes. If necessary, gently push the edges down with your fingertips until the layer is even. Run a small knife around the edge of the pan to loosen the cake. Cover the cake pan with a

continued

wire rack and invert. Remove the pan and parchment and let the cake cool completely. The cake may look cinched in around its sides, which is fine. Transfer to a cake plate. Cover and refrigerate the cake until it's very cold, at least 6 hours or overnight.

Glaze the cake: Melt the chocolate and butter in the microwave or in a medium metal bowl set in a skillet of barely simmering water, stirring with a rubber spatula until smooth. Pour the warm glaze over the chilled cake and, using an offset spatula, spread the glaze evenly to within ¼ inch of the edge. Refrigerate the cake until the glaze is set, 20 to 40 minutes. Before serving, remove the cake from the refrigerator and let it come to room temperature, 20 to 30 minutes. To serve, cut the cake into small, if not tiny, slices using a hot knife.

**Flourless chocolate cake
with chocolate glaze**

Chocolate strawberry shortcakes

How can you make the quintessential summer dessert even better?
By making the biscuits chocolate. Tender and rich, they're the perfect
partner for seasonal berries; try a mix of strawberries, raspberries,
and blackberries for a variation.

For the chocolate biscuits

10 ounces (about 2¼ cups)
unbleached all-purpose flour

1½ ounces (about ¼ cup
plus 3 tablespoons)
unsweetened Dutch-
processed cocoa powder,
such as Droste®

¼ cup granulated sugar; plus
about 3 tablespoons for
sprinkling

1½ tablespoons baking powder

¾ teaspoon table salt

4½ ounces (9 tablespoons)
cold unsalted butter, cut into
small pieces

6½ ounces semisweet
chocolate, grated or finely
chopped (the food proces-
sor works well); more for
garnish

1¼ cups heavy cream; plus
about 3 tablespoons for
brushing

1½ teaspoons pure vanilla
extract

continued

Make the biscuits: Line a heavy baking sheet with parchment. Sift the flour, cocoa powder, sugar, baking powder, and salt into a large bowl. Toss with a fork to combine. Cut the butter into the dry ingredients with a pastry cutter or a fork until the largest pieces of butter are the size of peas. Add the grated chocolate and toss to combine. Combine the cream and vanilla in a liquid measure. Make a well in the center of the flour mixture and pour the cream into the well. Mix with a fork until the dough is evenly moistened and just combined; it should look shaggy and still feel a little dry. Gently knead by hand five or six times to pick up any dry ingredients remaining in the bottom of the bowl and to create a loose ball.

Turn the dough out onto a lightly floured work surface and pat it into an 8-inch square, ³/₄ to 1 inch thick. Transfer the dough to the parchment-lined baking sheet, cover with plastic wrap, and chill for 20 minutes. Meanwhile, heat the oven to 425°F. Remove the dough from the refrigerator and trim about ¼ inch from each side to create a neat, sharp edge (a bench knife or a pastry scraper works well, or use a large chef's knife, being sure to cut straight down). Cut the dough into 9 even squares (about 2½ inches square) and spread them about 2 inches apart on the baking sheet. With a pastry brush or the back of a spoon, brush each biscuit with a thin layer of cream and sprinkle generously with sugar. Bake until the biscuits look a little dry and are mostly firm to the touch (they should spring back slightly when gently pressed), 18 to 20 minutes.

continued

For the strawberries

5 cups ⅛-inch-thick strawberry
    slices (from about 3 pints);
    9 to 18 whole strawberries,
    for garnish

1 to 3 tablespoons granulated
    sugar, depending on the
    sweetness of the berries

For the whipped cream

1 ½ cups heavy cream

2 tablespoons granulated sugar

¾ teaspoon pure vanilla extract

Grated chocolate, for garnish

Meanwhile, prepare the berries: Toss the berries with 1 tablespoon sugar and taste. If they're still tart, sprinkle with another 1 to 2 tablespoons sugar. Let sit at room temperature until the sugar dissolves and the berries begin to release their juices, at least 30 minutes but no more than 2 hours.

Whip the cream: Pour the cream into a cold mixing bowl and beat with a hand mixer until it begins to thicken. Add the sugar and vanilla extract and, using a whisk, continue to beat by hand until the cream is softly whipped or until the whisk leaves distinct marks in the cream; it should be soft and billowy but still hold its shape.

Assemble the shortcakes: While the biscuits are still warm, split them in half horizontally with a serrated knife. For each serving, set the bottom half of a biscuit on a plate. Scoop about ½ cup of the berries and their juices over the biscuit. Add a generous dollop of whipped cream and cover with the top half of the biscuit. Top with a small dollop of cream, a sprinkling of grated chocolate, and one or two whole, hulled strawberries.

three ways to streamline your shortcakes

For the biscuits: Although the biscuits are best warm—not hot—from the oven, you can make them several hours in advance. (You can even bake the biscuits a day ahead or freeze them for up to three months, but keep in mind that their texture will suffer slightly.) Just before serving, reheat the prepared biscuits in a 200°F oven until warmed through.

For the berries: You can slice the berries hours ahead of time and refrigerate them. Half an hour before assembling the shortcakes, toss the berries with the sugar and let them sit at room temperature.

For the whipped cream: Underwhip your cream and refrigerate it, covered, until ready to serve. Then use a whisk to finish whipping.

Almond crunch & chocolate confetti chiffon cake

This cake is light, lovely, and impressive with its height and crunchy topping. The sweet coating on the baked almonds keeps crisp for several days.

For the almond crunch topping

1 large egg white

1¼ cups sliced almonds

2 tablespoons granulated sugar

For the cake

1½ cups miniature semisweet chocolate chips

9 ounces (2¼ cups) cake flour

1½ cups granulated sugar

1 teaspoon baking powder

½ teaspoon table salt

½ cup canola or corn oil

7 large eggs, separated

1 teaspoon pure vanilla extract

½ to 1 teaspoon pure almond extract

2 tablespoons almond-flavored liqueur, such as Amaretto (optional)

¼ teaspoon cream of tartar

continued

Make the almond crunch topping: Heat the oven to 325°F. Have ready an ungreased nonstick baking sheet. In a medium bowl, whisk the egg white with a fork until foamy, about 30 seconds. Stir in the nuts until they're evenly coated. Sprinkle the sugar over the nuts and stir the mixture. Spread the nuts in a single layer onto the baking sheet. Bake for 5 minutes. Stir the nuts with a wooden spoon to loosen them from the baking sheet. Bake until golden, another 5 to 8 minutes. Remove the nuts from the oven and immediately stir them to loosen them from the baking sheet. The nuts will become crisp as they cool. Set aside.

Make the cake: Heat the oven to 325°F. Have ready a 9½- or 10-inch tube pan with sides at least 3¾ inches high.

In a food processor, pulse the chocolate chips until some of them are finely grated and the rest have formed small crumbs.

In a large bowl, sift together the cake flour, 1 cup of the sugar, the baking powder, and the salt. Make a well in the center and put in the oil, egg yolks, vanilla, almond extract, almond liqueur, and ⅔ cup water. Beat the mixture on medium speed until smooth and thick, at least 3 minutes. With a rubber spatula, fold in the chocolate chips. Set aside.

In a large, clean bowl with clean beaters or whisk attachment, whisk the egg whites and the cream of tartar on medium speed until the cream of tartar is dissolved and the whites are foamy.

continued

Increase the speed to high and beat the whites until the movement of the beaters forms lines in the mixture. Slowly pour in the remaining ½ cup sugar, about 2 tablespoons at a time, and beat the mixture until soft peaks form.

With a large rubber spatula, stir about one-third of the egg whites into the yolk mixture. Gently fold in the remaining egg whites until no white streaks remain. Pour the batter into the tube pan, spreading it evenly. Bake until you can gently press your fingers on top of the cake and it feels firm, about 75 minutes. Any cracks that form on the top should look dry.

Invert the pan onto a bottle with a narrow neck and let cool thoroughly, about 90 minutes. Use a small, sharp knife to loosen the cake from the sides of the pan and the center of the tube, if necessary. Remove the cake from the pan and slide it onto a serving plate.

Make the glaze: In a small bowl, stir together the confectioners' sugar, milk, and almond extract, adding enough milk to make a smooth glaze with a thick, syrupy consistency. Set aside 2 tablespoons of the glaze. Spread the remaining glaze over the top of the cake, letting it drip down the sides of the cake and into the center hole; you may not need to use all of it. Cover the top of the cake with the prepared almonds. Drizzle the reserved glaze over the almonds.

Frangipane-ripple chocolate pound cake

Serves 6
plus leftovers

Frangipane is a sweetly fragrant almond filling for cakes and pastries. For the best flavor and easiest slicing, serve this cake a day after you bake it.

For the frangipane

⅓ cup sliced blanched almonds

½ cup almond paste

¼ cup granulated sugar

1 large egg

4 tablespoons unsalted butter, softened at room temperature

For the cake

2 ⅓ cups cake flour; more for the pan

2 teaspoons baking powder

¼ teaspoon table salt

¾ cup unsweetened Dutch-processed cocoa powder

1¼ cups (2 ½ sticks) unsalted butter, softened at room temperature; more for the pan

2 cups granulated sugar

3 large eggs

1 teaspoon pure vanilla extract

1 cup whole milk

Make the frangipane: In a food processor, blend the almonds, almond paste, and sugar until the nuts are finely ground. Add the egg and butter; process until smoothly blended. Cover and refrigerate.

Make the cake: Have all ingredients, including the frangipane, at room temperature. Position a rack in the lower third of the oven and heat the oven to 350°F (325°F for pans with a dark finish). Grease and flour a 12-cup bundt pan. Sift together the cake flour, baking powder, salt, and cocoa; set aside. Using the beater attachment on an electric mixer (or the paddle attachment, if you have one), beat the butter at medium speed until creamy, 30 to 45 seconds. Add the sugar. Beat until fluffy and light in color, 4 to 5 minutes, scraping the bowl as needed. Add the eggs one at a time, beating well after each. Add the vanilla. At very low speed, add the dry ingredients alternately with the milk in three additions, starting and ending with the dry ingredients, blending just until smooth. Scrape the sides of the bowl as needed. Spoon 2 cups of batter into the pan, spreading evenly.

Spoon half of the frangipane filling in dollops over the center of the batter. Spread the filling evenly over the batter, avoiding the center tube and sides of the pan. Spoon about 1½ cups of batter evenly over the filling. Spoon the remaining frangipane over the batter, spreading evenly. Spoon the remaining batter over evenly.

Bake just until the cake springs back when touched in the center and just starts to come away from the sides of the pan, 60 to 65 minutes (65 to 70 minutes with a dark pan at 325°F). Cool the cake upright in the pan on a cooling rack for 15 to 20 minutes, invert, and cool completely.

Brown-butter banana cake
with chocolate chips

This comforting cake—just one delicious layer—is terrific plain, but it can be dressed up, too, with a dusting of confectioners' sugar if you want to take it to a party. And it's so simple—all you need is a bowl and a whisk.

8 ounces (1 cup) unsalted butter; more for the pan

1⅓ cups granulated sugar

3 large eggs

1 cup finely mashed ripe bananas (2 medium bananas)

1 teaspoon pure vanilla extract

½ teaspoon table salt

7½ ounces (1⅔ cups) unbleached all-purpose flour; more for the pan

1¼ teaspoons baking soda

⅔ cup mini semisweet chocolate chips

Position a rack in the center of the oven and heat the oven to 350°F. Butter and flour a 10-cup decorative tube or bundt pan. Tap out any excess flour.

Melt the butter in a medium saucepan over medium-low heat. Once the butter is melted, cook it slowly, letting it bubble, until it smells nutty or like butterscotch and turns a deep golden hue, 5 to 10 minutes. If the butter splatters, reduce the heat to low. Remove the pan from the heat and pour the browned butter through a fine sieve into a medium bowl and discard the bits in the sieve. Let the butter cool until it's very warm rather than boiling hot, 5 to 10 minutes.

Using a whisk, stir the sugar and eggs into the butter. (Since the butter is quite warm, you can use cold eggs for this.) Whisk until the mixture is smooth (the sugar may still be somewhat grainy), 30 to 60 seconds. Whisk in the mashed bananas, vanilla, and salt. Sift the flour and baking soda directly onto the batter. Pour the chocolate chips over the flour. Using a rubber spatula, stir just until the batter is uniformly combined. Don't overmix.

Spoon the batter into the prepared pan, spreading it evenly with the rubber spatula. Bake until a skewer inserted in the center comes out with only moist crumbs clinging to it, 42 to 45 minutes. Set the pan on a rack to cool for 15 minutes. Invert the cake onto the rack and remove the pan. Let cool until just warm and then serve immediately or wrap well in plastic and store at room temperature for up to five days.

Chocolate chip butter pound cake

This updated version of the traditional "pound of butter, pound of sugar, pound of eggs, pound of flour" recipe produces a pound cake that's soft and moist, yet still has the classic's buttery flavor and springy texture.

10 ounces (1 ¼ cups) unsalted butter, softened at room temperature; more for the pan

10¼ ounces (2 ½ cups) cake flour or 11 ounces (2 ⅓ cups) unbleached all-purpose flour; more for the pan

1½ teaspoons baking powder

½ teaspoon table salt

1 ¾ cups granulated sugar

2 large egg yolks, at room temperature

3 large eggs, at room temperature

⅔ cup whole milk, at room temperature

1 ½ teaspoons pure vanilla extract

4 ounces very finely chopped semisweet chocolate or ⅔ cup mini semisweet chocolate chips

Confectioners' sugar, for sprinkling (optional)

Position a rack in the center of the oven and heat the oven to 350°F. Butter a 12-cup bundt pan, dust the pan with flour, and tap out the excess. In a small bowl, whisk together the flour, baking powder, and salt until evenly combined.

In the bowl of a stand mixer fitted with the paddle attachment, beat the butter and sugar at medium speed until light and fluffy, about 2 minutes.

On low speed, beat in the yolks until smooth. Stop the mixer and scrape the bowl and the paddle. With the mixer running on medium-low speed, add the whole eggs, one at a time, mixing for at least 20 seconds after each addition. Stop the mixer and scrape the bowl and paddle again.

With the mixer running on the lowest speed, add half of the flour mixture and mix just to combine. Add the milk and mix until combined, and then add the remaining flour mixture and mix just until combined.

Scrape the bowl one last time, add the vanilla extract, and mix at medium speed until the batter is smooth and fluffy, 20 to 30 seconds. Carefully fold in the chopped chocolate.

Scrape the batter into the prepared pan and spread it evenly. Run a knife through the batter and tap the pan against the counter to dislodge trapped air. Bake until golden brown and a toothpick inserted in the center comes out with only moist crumbs clinging to it, 45 to 55 minutes.

Cool in the pan for 10 to 15 minutes and then invert onto a wire rack to cool completely. If you like, sprinkle the cake with confectioners' sugar before serving. The cake will keep at room temperature for three days.

BAKING A CAKE THAT GLIDES OUT OF THE PAN

For cakes that slide flawlessly out of their pans every time, follow these steps.

1. Grease the pan liberally with a visible coating of vegetable shortening, soft butter, or vegetable oil spray. The best way to get into all the corners of a pan, especially the fluting of a bundt pan, is to use a pastry brush.

2. To flour the pan, spoon a generous amount of flour into the pan and tilt it so the flour slides over all the inside surfaces. Dump out any extra and then give the pan a few hard knocks over a trash can to get rid of any excess.

3. If your recipe calls for using parchment, be sure the paper lies flat and fits inside the edges of the pan. Grease the pan first, insert the parchment, then grease (and flour, if directed by your recipe) again.

Chocolate nut upside-down cake

Using a mixture of toasted nuts brings complexity to this fabulous cake;
try a blend of whole hazelnuts (roughly chopped after toasting and skinning),
slivered almonds, and large walnut pieces. This cake is easiest to cut with a
serrated knife when the cake is at room temperature.

For the caramel-nut mix

¾ cup packed dark brown sugar

2½ ounces (5 tablespoons) unsalted butter

1¼ cups toasted assorted unsalted nuts (see note above)

For the cake

6 ounces (1⅓ cups) unbleached all-purpose flour

1½ ounces (½ cup) unsweetened natural cocoa powder (not Dutch-processed)

¾ teaspoon baking powder

¼ teaspoon baking soda

¼ teaspoon table salt

5 ounces (10 tablespoons) unsalted butter, at room temperature

1 cup granulated sugar

1 teaspoon pure vanilla extract

3 large eggs

½ cup buttermilk

Heat the oven to 350°F and lightly butter the sides of a 9x2-inch round cake pan.

Make the caramel: In a small saucepan, combine the brown sugar, butter, and 3 tablespoons water. Cook over medium heat, stirring often, until the butter is melted and the mixture is smooth. Bring to a boil and pour into the prepared pan, swirling to coat the bottom evenly. Scatter in the nuts evenly and gently press them in.

Make the cake: Sift together the flour, cocoa powder, baking powder, baking soda, and salt. In a medium bowl, beat the butter with an electric mixer until smooth. Gradually add the sugar and continue beating until fluffy. Beat in the vanilla. Add the eggs one at a time, beating briefly after each addition. Sprinkle half of the flour mixture over the butter and mix on low speed just until the flour disappears. Add the buttermilk and mix until just blended. Gently mix in the remaining flour. Scoop spoonfuls of batter onto the nuts and gently spread the batter evenly in the pan. Lightly tap the pan on the counter to settle the ingredients.

Bake until a pick inserted in the center comes out clean, about 45 minutes. Immediately run a paring knife around the inside edge of the pan. Set a flat serving plate on top of the pan and invert the cake. Let the inverted pan rest for about 3 minutes to let the topping settle. Gently remove the pan and serve slightly warm or at room temperature.

Old-fashioned chocolate layer cake with mocha milk chocolate frosting

For homey charm, few desserts beat a chocolate layer cake. (If you're not a mocha fan, simply leave the espresso out of the frosting.) If you like to prepare ahead of time—a good idea during holiday season—know that the baked, cooled cake layers will stay fresh, well wrapped, for two days at room temperature or in the freezer for up to three months.

For the cake

10½ ounces (3 cups) sifted cake flour

1½ teaspoons baking soda

½ teaspoon table salt

2½ ounces (¾ cup plus 2 tablespoons) unsifted unsweetened natural cocoa powder

½ cup cold plain yogurt (regular or low-fat)

1 tablespoon pure vanilla extract

6 ounces (¾ cup) unsalted butter, softened at room temperature

2⅔ cups granulated sugar

3 large eggs, at room temperature

continued

Bake the cake: Position a rack in the lower third of the oven and heat the oven to 350°F. Line the bottoms of three 9-inch round cake pans with parchment and lightly grease the sides. Combine the flour, baking soda, and salt. Sift together three times and set aside.

In a mixing bowl, pour 1 cup boiling water over the cocoa and stir to blend. Refrigerate to cool to lukewarm, stirring occasionally to speed cooling. Stir in ³/₄ cup cold water, yogurt, and vanilla. If necessary, refrigerate again to cool to room temperature before continuing.

With an electric hand-held mixer, beat the butter and sugar at high speed until light in color and texture, 6 to 7 minutes. If you're using a stand mixer, use the paddle attachment at medium speed (the whisk attachment will aerate the batter too much). The butter and sugar mixture will remain somewhat granular; this is fine. Whisk the eggs briefly and dribble them slowly into the butter mixture, 2 to 3 minutes, stopping as needed to scrape the bowl and beaters.

Stop the mixer and spoon one-third of the flour mixture into the bowl. Beat on low speed, scraping the bowl at least once, just until all traces of flour are incorporated. Stop the mixer and pour in half of the cocoa mixture. Beat on low to medium speed, scraping the bowl at least once, just until the mixture is blended. Stop mixing and spoon half of the remaining flour into the bowl.

For the frosting

1½ pounds milk chocolate, chopped into matchstick-size pieces

3 ounces (6 tablespoons) unsalted butter, cut into small pieces

4½ teaspoons instant espresso powder

Scant ⅛ teaspoon table salt

1 cup plus 2 tablespoons heavy cream

1½ teaspoons pure vanilla extract

Beat as before. Stop mixing to add the remaining cocoa mixture and beat as before. Add the last of the flour mixture and beat it in.

Divide the batter evenly among the prepared cake pans, spreading the batter to level it.

Bake, rotating the pans halfway through, until the cake just begins to shrink from the sides of the pan and a toothpick inserted in the center comes out clean, 30 to 35 minutes. Let the cakes cool on racks for about 5 minutes. Invert the pans to unmold. Peel off the parchment liners and turn the layers right side up to cool on the rack. Let cool completely before filling and frosting.

Make the frosting: Put the chocolate, butter, espresso powder, and salt in a large bowl. Bring the cream to a boil and pour it over the chocolate mixture. Stir until the chocolate is completely melted and smooth. Stir in the vanilla. Refrigerate until the mixture is cold and feels quite firm when you touch it, at least 2 hours. When you're ready to frost the cake, beat the frosting with a hand-held electric mixer (it will seem a bit firm to beat at first) until the frosting lightens in color, has a spreadable but not-too-stiff consistency, and holds a nice shape. Frost the cake immediately, using about ⅔ cup between each layer and the rest for the top and sides.

EVEN A BEGINNER CAN FROST LIKE A PRO

A layer cake may be homey, but it shouldn't be messy. Follow these tips for a frosted cake that stands tall and beautiful.

- Let the cake layers cool completely before frosting them so the frosting doesn't melt and make the cake slip and slide.

- Brush stray crumbs from all cake layers.

- Set the first layer, flat side down, on a serving plate or a piece of cardboard; cover the top evenly with ⅔ cup of the frosting.

- Set the second cake layer on top, flat side up; cover the top evenly with another ⅔ cup of frosting.

- Set the third layer on top, flat side down.

- If the frosting is very soft and the cake layers start to slide, refrigerate the cake for about 20 minutes.

- Before frosting the sides, slide four wide strips of waxed paper under the cake to keep the serving platter clean.

- When ready to frost, spread a very thin layer of frosting all over the top and sides of the cake just to cover and smooth the cracks and secure loose cake crumbs (this is called a "crumb coat"). As you work, be sure to keep cake crumbs from getting into the frosting bowl.

- To spread the rest of the frosting lavishly over the cake, smooth it with a spatula and then create texture with a cake comb, a serrated knife, or the back of a spoon.

Vanilla layer cake with whipped rum-ganache icing

Serves 12

You're all set for the next birthday bash with this festive cake. To get the texture of both the cake and the icing perfect, serve the cake at room temperature. Store it in the refrigerator, but take it out about 30 minutes before serving.

For the cake

6 ounces (¾ cup) unsalted butter, at room temperature; more for the cake pans

10¼ ounces (2¼ cups) unbleached all-purpose flour; more for the cake pans

2 teaspoons baking powder

¾ teaspoon table salt

3 large eggs, at room temperature

4 large egg yolks, at room temperature

3 tablespoons vegetable oil

2 teaspoons pure vanilla extract

2 cups granulated sugar

¾ cup buttermilk, at room temperature

continued

Position a rack in the center of the oven and heat the oven to 350°F. Butter and flour two 9x2-inch round cake pans and line the bottoms with parchment.

Make the cake: In a medium bowl, whisk the flour, baking powder, and salt. In another medium bowl, whisk the eggs, yolks, oil, and vanilla.

In the bowl of a stand mixer fitted with the paddle attachment, mix the butter on medium-high speed until smooth and light in color, about 2 minutes. Scrape the sides of the bowl with a rubber spatula. Add the sugar and mix on medium-high speed until very well blended, about 2 minutes longer. Scrape the bowl again.

With the mixer running on medium-high speed, add the egg mixture to the butter mixture in a steady stream. Beat until light and fluffy, about 2 minutes.

Reduce the mixer speed to low. Add half the dry ingredients to the butter mixture and mix until combined. Add half the buttermilk and mix until combined. Repeat with the remaining flour and buttermilk.

Scrape the sides of the bowl and divide the batter evenly between the prepared pans. The batter will be thick; spread it in the pans as smoothly as possible.

continued

For the whipped ganache

12 ounces semisweet
  chocolate (55% to 60%),
  coarsely chopped or
  broken into pieces

2 cups heavy cream

2 to 3 tablespoons dark
  rum or brandy

Bake the cakes until they're golden-brown on top and a toothpick inserted into the middle of each comes out clean, 30 to 35 minutes. Cool them in the pan on a cooling rack for 15 to 20 minutes and then turn them out onto a rack and cool completely.

Make the whipped ganache: While the cake cools, prepare the ganache. Clean and dry the stand mixer bowl. Grind the chocolate in a food processor until it reaches the consistency of coarse meal, about 30 seconds. Bring the cream to a boil in a small saucepan over medium heat. Add the cream and rum to the food processor and process until smooth, 10 to 20 seconds. Transfer to the cleaned and dried mixer bowl and refrigerate, stirring occasionally, until the ganache reaches 55°F to 65°F, about 1½ hours.

In the stand mixer fitted with the whisk attachment, whip the chilled ganache on medium-high speed until lightened in color and fluffy, about 1 minute. Don't overwhip or the ganache may seize. Scrape the sides of the bowl with a rubber spatula and mix gently.

Assemble the cake: Put one cake layer on a cake plate and tuck strips of waxed paper under the cake to keep the plate clean. Using an offset spatula, spread about 2 cups of the whipped ganache over the top in an even layer right to the edges of the cake. Top with the second cake layer.

Brush any large, loose crumbs off the cake and quickly ice the top and sides with a thin layer of the whipped ganache to seal the cake. Spread most or all of the remaining ganache over the sides and top of the cake, using the spatula to decoratively dimple and swirl the icing. Carefully pull the waxed paper from under the cake and discard. Store the cake in the refrigerator, but let it sit at room temperature for 20 to 30 minutes before serving.

Sour cream chocolate cake with coconut buttercream frosting

Serves 12 to 16

Cocoa and coconut? Of course! Baking the layers at 300°F keeps this cake exceptionally moist. Serve it at room temperature because the coconut softens when refrigerated.

For the cake

¾ cup unsweetened cocoa powder

6 ounces (¾ cup) unsalted butter, cut into six pieces

¾ cup sour cream

3 large eggs

1 teaspoon pure vanilla extract

12 ounces (3 cups) cake flour

3 cups granulated sugar

2¼ teaspoons baking soda

1½ teaspoons table salt

For the buttercream frosting

6 large egg yolks

1 cup granulated sugar

½ cup coconut milk

1 to 2 teaspoons coconut extract (or to taste)

1 pound (2 cups) unsalted butter, cut into tablespoons, softened (but not melted)

4 cups large-shaved coconut (fresh or desiccated), toasted

Heat the oven to 300°F. Line the bottoms of two 9-inch cake pans with parchment (there's no need to grease the pans).

Make the cake: Put the cocoa powder in the bowl of an electric mixer fitted with the whisk attachment. Pour 1½ cups boiling water over the cocoa and whisk until smooth. Add the butter and sour cream and blend on low speed until the butter melts. Let the mixture cool for a minute if still very hot, and then add the eggs and vanilla and whisk until smooth. Let cool for 10 minutes.

Meanwhile, sift together the cake flour, sugar, baking soda, and salt. With the mixer on low speed, add the dry ingredients a little at a time to the butter mixture, scraping down the sides once or twice. Increase the speed to medium and blend for another 3 minutes.

Pour the batter into the prepared pans and bake until the center of each cake feels firm and the cake just barely begins to pull away from the sides of the pan, 50 to 60 minutes (begin checking after 45 minutes). Remove the cakes from the oven and let cool completely before frosting.

Make the frosting: Put the yolks in the bowl of an electric mixer fitted with a whisk attachment.

In a small saucepan, combine the sugar and coconut milk. Stir to combine and then bring to a boil. As the mixture heats,

continued

begin whipping the eggs on high speed. Boil the coconut milk and sugar until the mixture reaches the soft-ball stage (238°F on a candy thermometer). Remove the mixture from the heat. Stop the mixer and pour a small amount of the syrup into the egg yolks. Quickly beat on high again. Repeat twice more until all of the syrup is incorporated. (You can also add the sugar syrup in a steady stream with the mixer on, but be careful not to let it hit the beater or the syrup will be flung to the sides of the bowl, where it will harden.) Continue beating until the mixture is cool.

Add the coconut extract. With the mixer on medium speed, begin beating in the butter 1 or 2 tablespoons at a time. When the butter is completely incorporated, scrape down the sides of the bowl and beat for another minute.

Use the frosting right away to fill and frost the cooled cake, or cover tightly and refrigerate until ready to use. Once frosted, pat on a generous coating of the shaved toasted coconut over the sides and top and, if you like, between the layers.

MAKE AHEAD The buttercream can be made in advance and refrigerated until ready to use. Bring chilled buttercream to room temperature before using, beating briefly to smooth it, if necessary.

CREATING DRAMA WITH CHOCOLATE SHAVINGS AND CURLS

Curls and shavings add whimsy to your favorite desserts, whether they're fancy or simple. To make shavings or curls, you'll need a thick block of bittersweet, semisweet, milk, or white chocolate (10 to 12 ounces is a good size). Then follow the directions below.

To make shavings Set out a large sheet (11x17 inches) of parchment or waxed paper. Rub the chocolate with your palm to warm it slightly. Wrap a paper towel or sheet of plastic wrap around half of the chocolate block so it's easier to grip. Drag a vegetable peeler across the side of the chocolate block, letting the shavings fall on the paper. As your hand warms the chocolate, turn the block around. You'll get larger shavings from the warmer side.

To make curls Curls are made like shavings, only the chocolate must be a bit warmer. To warm it, microwave the block very briefly, using 5-second bursts on high, until it feels just slightly warm. One or two 5-second bursts should be sufficient; white chocolate needs even less time. Use the peeler as for shavings, but apply a bit more pressure. If the chocolate still makes shavings or won't give big curls, it isn't warm enough, so heat it again for 5 seconds. If it melts against the peeler, it's too warm, so let it cool. Let the curls fall in an even, single layer on the sheet of parchment.

Luscious chocolate mousse layer cake

This dessert is on every chocolate-lover's list of favorites, but it's a dish you'd order in a restaurant rather than make at home, because it's the embodiment of "fancy." But even a novice baker can create this spectacular cake if you take it step by step. Divide the work of making this show-stopper by baking the chocolate cake well ahead of making the mousse.

For the chocolate cake

Vegetable oil or nonstick cooking spray for the pan

6 ounces (1½ cups) cake flour; more for the pans

1 ounce (6 tablespoons) unsweetened natural cocoa powder

2 teaspoons baking powder

¼ teaspoon baking soda

¼ teaspoon table salt

1 cup granulated sugar

¼ cup vegetable oil

1 large egg

2 teaspoons pure vanilla extract

For assembling the cake

8 cups Classic Chocolate Mousse (page 159)

For decorating the cake

See choices on page 117

Position a rack in the center of the oven and heat the oven to 325°F. Lightly grease a 9x2-inch round cake pan, line the bottom with parchment, and flour the sides (but not the bottom).

Make the cake: Sift the cake flour, cocoa, baking powder, baking soda, and salt into a large bowl. Add the sugar and whisk until well blended. Measure the oil into a 1-cup liquid measure, add the egg and vanilla, and mix with a fork. Add the egg-oil mixture to the dry ingredients and then add 1 cup water. Whisk until the dry ingredients are just moist, about 1 minute, scraping down the sides of the bowl. Pour the batter into the prepared pan.

Bake until a pick inserted into the center of the cake comes out clean, 32 to 34 minutes. Let cool on a rack for 20 minutes. Lightly grease a wire rack, invert the cake onto it, lift off the pan, peel off the parchment, and let the cake cool completely. The cake can be wrapped in plastic and kept at room temperature for a day.

Cut the layers: Chill the cake briefly in the refrigerator to help cut neater layers. Set the cake, bottom side up, on a parchment-lined work surface. Cut the cake into three equal layers (see "A Beautiful Layer Cake Needs Even Layers" on page 116). Set aside without separating the layers.

continued

a beautiful layer cake needs even layers

To help you turn one cake into three delicate and even layers, use two toothpicks to divide the cake into three equal layers. Do this at four points around the cake. Cut the cake using the picks as guides.

Using your longest serrated knife, place the section of the blade near the handle one-third of the way down the side of the cake. With a firm, slow sawing motion, cut around the cake at this level, focusing on where the blade enters the cake. When you have cut through the layer, place the knife two-thirds of the way down the cake, using the toothpick guides, and repeat, creating three layers.

Make the chocolate mousse following the recipe on page 159 only after the layers are cut. Before chilling the mousse, scoop out about 1 cup into a bowl, cover, and refrigerate for finishing touch-ups. Use the rest of the mousse to assemble the cake.

Assemble the layers: Set the ring of a 9-inch springform pan on a large, flat cake plate that you'll use to serve the cake. Gently flip the top cake layer (really the bottom) upside down and center it in the springform ring so the mousse can flow over the edge to frost the sides (don't worry if a little mousse leaks out of the bottom). Handle the cake carefully (if it breaks, just piece it together). Scoop about one-third of the mousse onto the cake layer in the ring and gently spread to cover.

Flip the next cake layer (the center) on top of the mousse and press gently to level it. Scoop half of the remaining mousse over the layer and spread gently. Flip the remaining cake layer upside down and set it on top of the mousse. Press gently to level it. Spread on the remaining mousse and smooth the top or add texture by scoring it with a cake comb or a serrated knife, if you like. Refrigerate the cake for at least 6 hours and up to 24 hours before decorating so it will hydrate from the mousse and the layers will set.

To finish, run a long, thin knife under hot water and dry it well. Slide the warm knife between the chilled cake and the springform ring, pressing the knife against the ring. Carefully release the springform clasp; gently pry it all the way open. Lift off the ring and clean the plate edge. Mold strips of foil around the cake plate to keep it clean as you decorate. If the cake's sides have bare patches, use a small metal spatula to touch them up with some of the reserved mousse. Chill.

Decorate according to your choice of finish (see below). Once decorated, keep the cake refrigerated and serve it within 8 hours. Remove it from the refrigerator 10 to 15 minutes before serving.

MAKE AHEAD & FREEZE The cake can be baked and cut into layers ahead; wrap each layer in plastic and freeze for up to a month.

TWO WAYS TO DECORATE, FROM SIMPLE TO SPECTACULAR

Simple—chopped toasted nuts You'll need 1½ cups toasted whole walnuts, chopped medium fine. Scoop up a handful and pat them onto the side of the cake; many will fall off, but that's fine; just keep adding more while turning the cake until all sides are covered. Brush extra nuts from the plate before removing the foil strips.

Spectacular—curls and shavings You'll need 1½ to 2 cups chocolate shavings and enough chocolate curls to fill an 11x17-inch piece of parchment or waxed paper in a single layer. Make the curls and shavings following the techniques on page 113. Using a soupspoon, scoop up some shavings. Starting at the bottom of the cake and using light pressure, gently drag the spoon up the side so the shavings stick; continue until the sides of the cake are covered. Arrange the curls on the top.

Bourbon chocolate cake

This mousse-like cake really does melt in your mouth. It can be baked up to a day before serving and stored lightly wrapped at room temperature. If you don't have a 9x3-inch cake pan, use a standard 9x2-inch pan and construct a parchment collar so the cake has room to rise. For this cake, it's worth splurging on the best chocolate you can buy.

For the cake

11 ounces semisweet chocolate, chopped

6 ounces (12 tablespoons) unsalted butter

6 large eggs, separated, at room temperature

¾ cup packed light brown sugar

1 ounce (¼ cup) unbleached all-purpose flour

¼ cup bourbon

1 teaspoon pure vanilla extract

½ teaspoon kosher salt

For serving

1 cup heavy cream

1 to 2 tablespoons granulated sugar

Confectioners' sugar, for dusting

Position a rack in the middle of the oven and heat the oven to 350°F. Butter a 9x3-inch cake pan. Line the bottom of the pan with a round of parchment and butter the parchment. Set the cake pan in a roasting pan large enough to accommodate it.

Melt the chocolate and butter together. Remove from the heat and let cool slightly.

With an electric mixer (a stand mixer with the whip attachment or a hand mixer), beat the egg yolks with the brown sugar on medium speed until very pale, thick, and fluffy, about 3 minutes. Reduce the speed, add the chocolate mixture, and mix just to combine. Add the flour, mixing just to combine and scraping the bowl as needed. Blend in the bourbon and vanilla. Transfer to a large bowl and set aside.

In a clean, dry mixing bowl with clean, dry beaters, beat the egg whites with the salt on high speed until they hold soft peaks, 1 to 2 minutes. With a rubber spatula, fold one-third of the egg whites into the chocolate mixture to lighten it, and then gently fold in the remaining whites. Scrape the batter into the prepared cake pan.

Set the roasting pan on the oven rack and add enough warm tap water to come halfway up the sides of the cake pan. Bake until the top feels set, 40 to 45 minutes. Remove the cake pan from the water bath and run a paring knife around the inside of the pan (or the inside of the parchment collar) to loosen the cake, and then let the cake cool completely in the cake pan on a rack. When the cake is completely cool, loosen the sides once more with a paring knife. Cover the cake with a serving plate and invert the cake onto the plate. The bottom of the cake is now the top. Peel off the parchment. (Don't worry if the surface looks a little ragged; you'll be dusting with confectioners' sugar.)

To serve: In a chilled bowl with chilled beaters, beat the cream and sugar to medium-soft peaks. Dust the top of the cake generously with confectioners' sugar, slice, and serve each slice with the whipped cream.

When making desserts with bourbon, save expensive bourbons like Blanton's®, Eagle Rare®, or Knob Creek® for sipping. For cooking, a regular bourbon such as Jim Beam®, Wild Turkey®, or Old Crow® is fine.

Deep, dark chocolate stout cake

Yields 1 large bundt cake or
12 miniature bundt cakes

Rich, dark, and toasty stout beer plus deeply flavored molasses give the
chocolate flavor of this cake some wonderful nuance. With this recipe,
you can bake one big beautiful cake, perfect for entertaining, or a dozen
irresistible miniature bundt cakes, perfect for gift giving.

For the cake

1¼ cups stout, such as
   Guinness® (don't include
   the foam when measuring)

⅓ cup dark molasses
   (not blackstrap)

7½ ounces (1⅔ cups)
   unbleached all-purpose flour

2¼ ounces (¾ cup) unsweetened natural cocoa powder
   (not Dutch-processed);
   more for the pan

1½ teaspoons baking powder

½ teaspoon baking soda

½ teaspoon table salt

10 ounces (1¼ cups)
   unsalted butter, softened
   at room temperature;
   more for the pan

1½ cups packed light
   brown sugar

3 large eggs, at room
   temperature

6 ounces semisweet chocolate,
   very finely chopped

continued

Position a rack in the middle of the oven and heat the oven to
350°F. Butter a 10- or 12-cup bundt pan (or twelve 1-cup mini
bundt pans) and then lightly coat with sifted cocoa; tap out any
excess cocoa.

Make the cake: In a small saucepan over high heat, bring the
stout and molasses to a simmer. Remove the pan from the heat
and let stand while preparing the cake batter.

Sift together the flour, cocoa, baking powder, baking soda, and
salt. With a stand mixer (use the paddle attachment) or a hand
mixer, cream the butter in a large bowl on medium speed until
smooth, about 1 minute. Add the brown sugar and beat on medium speed until light and fluffy, about 3 minutes. Stop to scrape
the sides of the bowl as needed. Beat in the eggs one at a time,
stopping to scrape the bowl after each addition. With the mixer
on low speed, alternate adding the flour and stout mixtures, beginning and ending with the flour. Stop the mixer at least one last
time to scrape the bowl and then beat at medium speed until the
batter is smooth, about 20 seconds. Stir in the chopped chocolate.

Spoon the batter into the prepared pan (or pans), spreading it
evenly with a rubber spatula. Run a knife through the batter to
eliminate any air pockets. Bake until a wooden skewer inserted in
the center comes out with only a few moist crumbs clinging to it,
45 to 50 minutes (or about 35 minutes for mini cakes).

continued

For the chocolate glaze (optional)

¾ cup heavy cream

6 ounces semisweet chocolate, chopped

Set the pan on a rack to cool for 20 minutes. (If you let it sit longer, it may break apart when you try to take it out.) Invert the cake onto the rack and remove the pan. Let cool until just barely warm. If you're making the cake ahead, wrap it in plastic wrap while still barely warm and without the glaze; it will keep for about a week at room temperature. You can also freeze well-wrapped cakes for up to a month.

Make the glaze: If you plan to freeze the cake, don't glaze it until you're ready to serve it or give it away. Bring the cream to a boil in a small saucepan over high heat. Remove the pan from the heat and add the chocolate. Let stand for 1 minute and then whisk until the chocolate is melted and smooth. Let cool for 5 minutes before drizzling over the barely warm cake. Let the glaze cool to room temperature before serving.

Rich chocolate olive-oil cake

Full of deeply chocolate flavor, you'd never guess that olive oil is the secret ingredient, giving the cake moistness and character. Because it's so moist, the cake keeps at room temperature for up to four days.

1¼ ounces (½ cup) unsweet-ened Dutch-processed cocoa powder, preferably Droste

1 teaspoon pure vanilla extract

½ teaspoon pure almond extract

4½ ounces (1 cup) unbleached all-purpose flour; more for the pan

¼ teaspoon baking soda

¼ teaspoon table salt

3 large eggs plus 1 egg yolk, at room temperature

⅔ cup mild but fruity extra-virgin olive oil; more for the pan

1⅓ cups granulated sugar

¼ cup confectioners' sugar, for dusting

Position a rack in the center of the oven and heat the oven to 325°F. Generously oil an 8-inch round cake pan (or an 8½-inch springform pan) that's at least 2 inches high with olive oil and line the bottom of the pan with parchment or waxed paper. Oil the paper and dust it lightly with flour. (The batter will almost fill a 2-inch pan.)

In a small saucepan, boil about ½ cup of water. Meanwhile, sift the cocoa through a sieve over a small bowl. Stir 6 tablespoons of the boiling water into the cocoa until it's smooth and glossy (if the mixture is very thick, you can add as much as 2 tablespoons more boiling water; if you use Hershey's cocoa, for instance, you may need to do this). Stir in the vanilla and almond extracts. Set aside to cool slightly. In another small bowl, mix the flour, baking soda, and salt; set aside.

In the bowl of a stand mixer, combine the eggs and yolk, olive oil, and sugar. Using the whisk attachment, beat on medium-high speed until thick, lemon colored, and creamy, 2 to 3 minutes, scraping down the sides of the bowl.

Reduce the speed to low and gradually add the warm (not hot) cocoa mixture until it's well combined, scraping down the sides of the bowl once. Gradually mix in the dry ingredients until just combined, scraping down the sides of the bowl.

continued

Before dusting, lay a stencil on top of the cake (you'll find the flat side of the cake has a more level surface) to add a pretty touch.

Pour the batter into the prepared cake pan and bake until a toothpick comes out with a few moist crumbs clinging to it but with no wet batter, 55 to 60 minutes. Put the pan on a rack and carefully run a paring knife around the inside edge to release the cake. Let cool for 10 minutes. Using a second rack to sandwich the cake pan, flip the pan over. Carefully lift the pan from the cake, gently peel off and discard the parchment, and let the cake cool completely.

Before serving, dust the top of the cake with confectioners' sugar.

Coffee-cocoa snack cake

Coffee intensifies the chocolate flavor of this super-moist cake. Mixing
in the flour by hand helps to keep the cake's crumb tender. Serve plain
to eat out of hand, or top with a warm ganache and serve with a fork.

10 tablespoons very soft
    unsalted butter;
    more for the pan

1⅔ cups granulated sugar

2 large eggs, at room
    temperature

1 teaspoon pure vanilla
    extract

½ teaspoon table salt

1½ cups plus 2 tablespoons
    unbleached all-purpose
    flour; more for the pan

½ cup plus ⅓ cup unsweet-
    ened natural cocoa pow-
    der (not Dutch-processed)

1 teaspoon baking soda

1 teaspoon baking powder

1½ cups good-quality brewed
    coffee, cooled to warm

Position a rack in the center of the oven and heat the oven to
350°F. Generously butter a 9-inch-square baking pan. Line the
bottom of the pan with a square of parchment, butter the parchment, and then flour the bottom and sides of the pan. Tap out
any excess flour.

Cream the butter and sugar until smooth, using a wooden spoon
or the paddle attachment of a stand mixer. Add the eggs one at
a time, mixing until just incorporated (use a whisk if working by
hand). By hand, whisk in the vanilla and salt. Sift the flour, cocoa,
baking soda, and baking powder directly onto the batter. Pour in
the coffee. Gently whisk the ingredients by hand until the batter
is smooth and mostly free of lumps.

Pour the batter into the pan, spreading it evenly with a rubber
spatula. Bake until a skewer inserted in the center comes out with
only moist crumbs clinging to it, 40 to 43 minutes. Set the pan
on a rack to cool for 20 minutes. Carefully run a knife around the
edges of the pan, invert the cake onto the rack, and remove the
pan. Invert again onto another rack and let cool until just warm.
Serve immediately or wrap in plastic and store at room temperature for up to five days.

Fastest fudge cake with ganache drizzle

This cake is super easy to make, but it's delicious enough for company. Fabulous on its own, it's even better drizzled with warm ganache.

4½ ounces (1 cup) unbleached all-purpose flour

1 ounce (¼ cup plus 2 tablespoons) unsweetened natural cocoa powder (not Dutch-processed)

½ teaspoon baking soda

¼ teaspoon table salt

¼ pound (½ cup) unsalted butter, melted and warm

1¼ cups packed light brown sugar

2 large eggs

1 teaspoon pure vanilla extract

½ cup hot water

1 cup Ganache Drizzle (facing page) (optional)

Position a rack in the lower third of the oven and heat the oven to 350°F. Grease the bottom of an 8x2-inch or 9x2-inch round cake pan or line it with parchment.

In a small bowl, whisk the flour, cocoa, baking soda, and salt. Sift only if the cocoa remains lumpy after whisking. In a large bowl, combine the melted butter and brown sugar with a wooden spoon or rubber spatula. Add the eggs and vanilla, and stir until well blended. Add the flour mixture all at once and stir just until all the flour is moistened. Pour the hot water over the batter; stir just until it's incorporated and the batter is smooth. Scrape the batter into the prepared pan. Bake until a toothpick inserted in the center comes out clean, about 30 minutes for a 9-inch pan or 35 to 40 minutes for an 8-inch pan. Let cool in the pan on a rack for 10 minutes. Run a thin knife around the edge and invert the cake (peel off the parchment if necessary). Invert it again onto the rack and let cool completely.

Once cool, set the rack over a baking sheet or foil. Pour the warm ganache over the cake and use an icing spatula to spread it over the top of the cake and down the sides. Let set for about an hour before serving.

ganache drizzle

If you have a bit of this ganache left over after icing the fudge cake or snack cake, use it as a sauce for ice cream or another dessert. It keeps for a week in the refrigerator. Rewarm gently.

½ pound bittersweet or semisweet chocolate, finely chopped

1 cup heavy cream; more as needed

Granulated sugar (optional)

Put the chocolate in a medium heatproof bowl. In a small saucepan, bring the cream to a boil. Pour the hot cream over the chocolate and whisk gently until the chocolate is completely melted and smooth. (If using a 70% bittersweet chocolate, the ganache might be a bit thick; add more cream, a tablespoon at a time, to thin it. You might also want to add a couple of teaspoons of sugar when you add the hot cream.)

Most ganache or chocolate sauce recipes call for blending the chocolate with heavy or whipping cream, but you can substitute crème fraîche to add a subtle but lovely tang.

Mocha chip cupcakes with chocolate-sour cream frosting

Chocolate curls look adorable on these cupcakes, but you can just as easily decorate them with shiny dragées, a smattering of sprinkles, or nothing at all.

4½ ounces (1 cup) unbleached all-purpose flour

½ teaspoon baking soda

¼ teaspoon table salt

¼ pound (½ cup) unsalted butter, softened at room temperature

1 cup granulated sugar

2 large eggs

1½ teaspoons pure vanilla extract

3 ounces unsweetened chocolate, melted and cooled slightly

2 teaspoons instant espresso powder, dissolved in ½ cup cool water

¼ pound (⅔ cup) semisweet chocolate chips

1 recipe Chocolate-Sour Cream Frosting (page 130)

Position a rack in the lower third of the oven and heat the oven to 350°F. Line 12 standard-size muffin cups with paper liners.

Sift the flour, baking soda, and salt together into a small bowl. In a large bowl, beat the butter with a stand mixer fitted with the paddle attachment (or with a hand-held mixer) on medium speed until the butter is smooth, 30 to 60 seconds. With the mixer running, slowly pour in the sugar. Stop the mixer, scrape the bowl and beaters, and then beat on medium-high speed until the mixture is light and fluffy, 2 to 3 minutes. Beat in the eggs, one at a time, on medium speed, beating until the batter is smooth after each addition (about 30 seconds). Scrape the bowl after each addition. Add the vanilla and melted chocolate (which may be slightly warm) and beat until smooth and blended. Add the dry ingredients in three installments, alternating with the espresso in two additions, mixing on low speed after each addition only until the batter is smooth. Stir in the chocolate chips by hand.

Portion the batter evenly among the prepared muffin cups. (Use two rounded soupspoons: one to pick up the batter, one to push it off.) Don't smooth the batter. Bake until the cupcakes spring back when gently pressed in the center, 20 to 22 minutes. Let them cool in the muffin tin for 5 minutes on a rack. Carefully remove the cupcakes from the tin, set them on the rack, and let cool completely.

continued

Put a generous spoonful of the frosting on top of each cupcake and use the back of the spoon to spread and swirl it. Garnish as you like. Let the frosting set for about 30 minutes before serving.

chocolate-sour cream frosting

Yields about 1¼ cups

Sour cream gives this frosting a pleasantly subtle tang.

⅓ cup sour cream (not low-fat)

¾ teaspoon pure vanilla extract

Pinch table salt

6 ounces confectioners' sugar (1½ cups, spooned and leveled)

2 ounces unsweetened chocolate, melted and cooled slightly

Whole milk, if necessary

In a medium bowl, whisk the sour cream, vanilla, and salt to blend. Gradually whisk in the confectioners' sugar until smooth. Add the chocolate and beat it in with the whisk until the frosting is smooth and creamy. The frosting must be thick and spreadable. If it's too thick, thin it with droplets of milk. If it's too thin, chill it briefly, stirring occasionally, until adequately thickened.

Chocolate cupcakes
with dark chocolate frosting

Yields 16 cupcakes

Sour cream makes these flat-topped cupcakes even more
moist and fudgy the day after you bake them.

For the frosting

¾ cup evaporated milk

1 cup granulated sugar

Pinch table salt

¼ pound unsweetened
    chocolate, melted

For the cupcakes

6 ounces (1½ cups) unbleached
    all-purpose flour

¾ teaspoon baking soda

½ teaspoon table salt

2 cups granulated sugar

1 cup strong, hot brewed coffee

½ cup sour cream

½ cup vegetable oil

2 large eggs

¼ pound unsweetened
    chocolate, melted

Make the frosting: In a blender, blend the evaporated milk, sugar, and salt until the sugar is dissolved. Add the chocolate and blend until the mixture is thick and glossy, about 3 minutes. Store at room temperature, covered with plastic, until ready to use. It will keep for up to two days.

Make the cupcakes: Heat the oven to 350°F. Line 16 cups of two standard muffin tins with foil liners (or grease the cups).

Sift the flour, baking soda, salt, and sugar into a medium bowl. In a large bowl, whisk the coffee, sour cream, oil, and eggs; whisk in the chocolate. Add the dry ingredients, whisking until there are no lumps. Pour the batter into the prepared muffin tins, filling each cup about three-quarters full. Bake until a toothpick inserted into the middle of a cupcake comes out clean, 19 to 20 minutes. Let the cupcakes cool in the pan for 15 minutes, and then remove them from the pan and cool them further. Ice generously with the frosting.

pies & tarts

Chocolate-raspberry tart
with a gingersnap crust

It's easy to make this simple tart look stunning because the ganache
is chilled slightly so the raspberries don't sink into the chocolate layer
as you arrange them. An added bonus for entertaining—you can make
the tart up to a day ahead.

Vegetable oil for the pan

About 40 gingersnap wafers
(to yield 1½ cups finely
ground)

¼ cup melted unsalted butter

3½ cups fresh raspberries

½ pound semisweet or
bittersweet chocolate,
finely chopped

1¼ cups heavy cream

Small pinch table salt

Position a rack in the middle of the oven and heat the oven to
325°F. Oil the sides and bottom of a 9½-inch fluted tart pan with
a removable bottom. In a food processor, grind the gingersnaps
until they're the texture of sand. Transfer to a bowl, add the melted
butter, and work it in by squishing the mixture together with your
hands. Press into the sides and bottom of the oiled tart pan. Set
the pan on a baking sheet and refrigerate for 20 minutes to firm.
Bake the tart crust on the baking sheet until fragrant, about
15 minutes, checking and rotating if needed to make sure the
crust doesn't get too dark. Set on a rack to cool.

Meanwhile, pass 1 cup of the berries through a food mill fitted
with a fine disk or force them through a fine sieve, mashing with
a wooden spoon, into a medium bowl. You'll have about ½ cup
purée; set it aside and discard the contents of the sieve.

Put the chopped chocolate in a medium bowl. Heat the cream
just until boiling. Pour the hot cream over the chopped chocolate;
whisk to blend, creating a ganache. Stir in the raspberry purée and
the salt. Pour the ganache into the cooled tart shell. Refrigerate
until the ganache is fairly firm, about 1 hour. Arrange the remaining raspberries on top of the ganache; they should completely
cover the surface. Chill until the ganache is completely firm, about
30 minutes, and serve.

Chocolate-glazed peanut butter tart

Reese's® Peanut Butter Cup fans will think they've died and gone to heaven when presented with this dessert. Plan ahead: The easy cookie crust must be baked and cooled before filling, and the filling must be chilled before glazing.

For the filling and crust

1½ cups whole milk

¼ teaspoon table salt

3 large egg yolks

⅓ cup very firmly packed light
brown sugar

4 teaspoons unbleached
all-purpose flour

4½ ounces (½ cup) creamy
peanut butter (preferably
natural, made with only
peanuts and salt)

½ teaspoon pure vanilla
extract

1 Press-In Cookie Crust
(facing page), preferably
chocolate, baked and cooled

For the glaze

3 ounces bittersweet
chocolate, finely chopped

2 ounces (¼ cup) unsalted
butter, cut into 6 pieces

1 tablespoon light corn syrup

Make the filling: In a medium saucepan, bring the milk and salt to a simmer over medium heat, stirring occasionally. Meanwhile, in a small bowl, whisk the egg yolks, brown sugar, and flour until well blended. Slowly add the hot milk, whisking constantly. Pour the mixture back into the saucepan. Cook over medium heat, whisking constantly, until it thickens and comes to a full boil, about 3 minutes. Continue to cook, whisking constantly, for 1 minute. Remove the pan from the heat and add the peanut butter and vanilla; whisk until well blended.

Pour the hot peanut butter mixture into the crust and spread evenly with a rubber or offset spatula. Gently press a piece of plastic wrap directly onto the filling's surface to prevent a skin from forming. Refrigerate the tart until cold, about 2 hours, before proceeding with the recipe.

Make the glaze: Melt the chocolate with the butter and corn syrup in a medium metal bowl set over a pan of simmering water (don't let the bowl touch the water) and whisk until the butter is melted and the mixture is smooth, about 1 minute. Carefully remove the plastic wrap from the top of the chilled filling. Drizzle the glaze over the filling and spread it evenly to cover the tart completely. Refrigerate the tart in the pan until the glaze sets, about 30 minutes and up to 12 hours.

press-in cookie crust

Yields one crust for one 9 ½-inch tart

With only three ingredients, this crust mixes up quickly and effortlessly.

1 cup finely ground cookies (about 25 Nabisco® Famous Chocolate Wafers, 8 whole graham crackers, or 35 vanilla wafers)

2 tablespoons granulated sugar

1½ ounces (3 tablespoons) unsalted butter, melted

Position a rack in the center of the oven and heat the oven to 350°F. Have ready an ungreased 9½-inch fluted tart pan with a removable bottom.

In a medium bowl, mix the cookie crumbs and sugar with a fork until well blended. Drizzle the melted butter over the crumbs and mix with the fork or your fingers until the crumbs are evenly moistened. Put the crumbs in the tart pan and use your hands to spread the crumbs so that they coat the bottom of the pan and start to climb the sides. Use your fingers to pinch and press some of the crumbs around the inside edge of the pan to cover the sides evenly and create a wall about a scant ¼ inch thick. Redistribute the remaining crumbs evenly over the bottom of the pan and press firmly to make a compact layer. (A metal measuring cup with straight sides and a flat base works well for this task.)

Bake the crust until it smells nutty and fragrant (crusts made with lighter-colored cookies will brown slightly), about 10 minutes. Set the baked crust on a rack and let cool. The crust can be made up to one day ahead and stored at room temperature, wrapped well in plastic.

Chocolate truffle tart with whipped vanilla mascarpone

Serves 12 to 16

Though it's elegant to look at, this tart has a flavor that brings you right back to childhood—it tastes just a little bit like s'mores, and who doesn't love them? You'll need to allow at least 4 hours chilling time before topping the tart.

For the filling and crust

¾ pound bittersweet chocolate, finely chopped

1 cup whole milk

2 ounces (¼ cup) unsalted butter, cut into 4 pieces

1 teaspoon pure vanilla extract

¼ teaspoon table salt

1 Press-In Cookie Crust (page 137), preferably graham cracker, baked and cooled

For the topping

½ pound mascarpone cheese, at room temperature

¾ cup heavy cream

¼ cup granulated sugar

½ teaspoon pure vanilla extract

Make the filling: Melt the chocolate, milk, and butter together in a medium metal bowl set over a pan of simmering water (don't let the bowl touch the water). Add the vanilla and salt. Whisk the mixture until well blended and smooth. Set aside, whisking occasionally, until room temperature and slightly thickened, about 1 hour. (For faster cooling, refrigerate the filling until thickened to a pudding consistency, about 30 minutes, whisking and scraping the sides of the bowl with a rubber spatula every 5 minutes.)

With a rubber spatula, scrape the mixture into the crust and spread evenly, taking care not to disturb the edge of the crust. Let cool completely, cover, and refrigerate until the filling is set, at least 4 hours and up to 8 hours, before proceeding.

Make the topping: In a medium bowl, combine the mascarpone, cream, sugar, and vanilla. Using an electric mixer, beat on low speed until almost smooth, 30 to 60 seconds. Increase the speed to medium high and beat until the mixture is thick and holds firm peaks, another 30 to 60 seconds. Don't overbeat.

With a rubber or metal spatula, spread the topping over the chocolate filling, leaving lots of swirls and peaks. Serve the tart right away or cover loosely and refrigerate, in the pan, for up to 4 hours.

138   PIES & TARTS

TRUE TART PANS MAKE UNMOLDING EASY

A removable-bottom tart pan is a must for any baker. They give your tarts a professional look, and they allow you to slip off the outer ring without marring the beautiful crust. Tart pans come in many sizes, so be sure to use what's specified in your recipe, otherwise you'll have too much or too little dough and filling.

To remove a baked tart from the pan, set the pan on a wide can and let the outside ring fall away. If it's stubborn, grip the ring with your fingers to coax it off.

Slide a long, thin metal spatula between the pan base and the crust and ease the tart onto a flat serving plate.

A COOKIE CRUST COMBINES CRUNCH WITH BUTTERY FLAVOR

Cookie crusts are easy to make and bring a wonderful textural contrast to smooth tart fillings. Gingersnaps, chocolate wafers (such as Nabisco Famous Chocolate Wafers), and plain or chocolate graham crackers are good choices. It's easiest to pulse the cookies to fine crumbs in a food processor, but you can also put them in a zip-top bag and pulverize with a rolling pin or heavy pan. To firmly pat down both the sides and bottom of a cookie crust, use a flat-bottomed, straight-sided metal measuring cup or a similarly shaped glass.

Chocolate caramel tart with macadamia nuts and crème fraîche whipped cream

Serves 12 to 16

This luxurious tart is a fantastic grand finale for a birthday celebration. Who needs cake when you can have caramel, chocolate, macadamia nuts, and whipped crème fraîche? Macadamia nuts aren't obligatory, either; you could substitute lightly toasted pecans or walnuts.

For the crust

6 ounces (1⅓ cups) unbleached all-purpose flour, plus a little more for rolling

3 tablespoons granulated sugar

¼ teaspoon kosher salt

4 ounces (½ cup) cold unsalted butter, cut into small cubes

2 tablespoons heavy cream

1 large egg yolk

continued

Make the crust: In a stand mixer fitted with the paddle attachment, combine the flour, sugar, salt, and butter and mix on medium speed until the butter blends into the flour and the mixture resembles a coarse meal. Mix the cream and yolk together in a small bowl. With the mixer on low speed, gradually add the cream mixture and mix until just combined. Do not overwork the dough.

Transfer the dough to a work surface and bring it together with your hands. Shape the dough into a 1-inch-thick disk. If the dough seems too soft to roll out, put it in the refrigerator for 5 to 10 minutes to firm it up a little. Set the dough on a lightly floured work surface, sprinkle a little flour over it, and roll it out into a ⅛-inch-thick circle 14 to 15 inches in diameter, reflouring the dough and work surface as necessary.

Starting at one side, roll and wrap the dough around the rolling pin to pick it up. Unroll the dough over an 11-inch fluted tart pan with a removable bottom and gently fit it loosely in the pan, lifting the edges and pressing the dough into the corners with your fingers. To remove the excess dough, roll the rolling pin lightly over the top of the tart pan, cutting a nice, clean edge. Cover loosely with plastic and chill for 1 hour.

continued

For the filling

1¼ cups macadamia nuts

2 cups heavy cream

1½ ounces (3 tablespoons) unsalted butter, cut into chunks

1 cup plus 1½ tablespoons granulated sugar

¼ cup light corn syrup

½ vanilla bean, split and scraped

6 ounces 70% bittersweet chocolate, chopped (about 1¼ cups)

½ cup whole milk

¼ cup crème fraîche

Make the tart: Position a rack in the center of the oven and heat the oven to 375°F. Prick the bottom of the crust with a fork and line it with a piece of parchment paper or several opened-out basket-style coffee filters. Fill the lined tart shell with dried beans or pie weights and bake until set around the edges, about 15 minutes. Take the tart out of the oven, and carefully lift out the paper and pie weights (if using coffee filters, spoon out most of the weights first). Return the tart to the oven and bake until the crust is golden brown all over, another 10 to 15 minutes. Cool completely on a rack.

While the crust is baking, spread the nuts on a baking sheet and toast (in the same oven) until they are golden brown and smell nutty, 10 to 12 minutes. Let them cool, and then chop coarsely.

In a small pot, bring ¾ cup of the cream and the butter to a simmer. Set aside. Combine 1 cup of the sugar with the corn syrup, vanilla bean seeds and pod, and ¼ cup water in a 3- or 4-quart heavy-based pot. Boil over high heat, stirring frequently with a wooden spoon, until the mixture becomes caramel-colored. Remove from the heat and immediately (but slowly and carefully—you don't want the hot sugar to overflow or splatter) whisk in the hot cream mixture.

Pour the caramel into the baked tart shell and pick out the vanilla bean halves with a fork or tongs. Sprinkle about two-thirds of the macadamia nuts on top of the caramel. Let cool completely in the refrigerator.

When the tart is cool, put the chocolate in a large bowl. In a small pot, bring ½ cup of the cream, the milk, and the remaining 1½ tablespoons sugar to a boil over medium-high heat. As soon as it boils, pour it over the chocolate. Let stand for 2 minutes and then stir very gently with a whisk until smooth and thoroughly combined. Let cool at room temperature for 5 minutes and then pour the chocolate filling over the completely chilled tart, covering the nuts and caramel.

Chill in the refrigerator for at least 4 hours or until completely set. Unmold the tart, using a long thin metal spatula to release it from the pan bottom. Place it on a cutting board or a serving plate, depending on how you intend to serve it.

Just before serving, whip the remaining ¾ cup cream and the crème fraîche to soft peaks. Slice and plate the tart in the kitchen or at the table. Top each serving with a dollop of the whipped cream and scatter the remaining macadamia nuts over and around.

MAKE AHEAD & FREEZE You can roll out and freeze the tart dough up to a week in advance. Defrost in the refrigerator overnight before baking.

Triple chocolate cheesecake

The luscious texture of cheesecake plus the seductive flavor of chocolate—
what more could you want in a dessert? The texture is best the next day,
and one cheesecake serves a crowd, so this is a perfect choice for a big
dinner party or holiday gathering.

For the crust

1½ cups very finely crushed
   chocolate cookie crumbs
   (from about 30 Nabisco
   Famous Chocolate Wafers)

3 tablespoons granulated
   sugar

⅛ teaspoon ground cinnamon
   (optional)

2 ounces (¼ cup) unsalted
   butter, melted

For the filling

8 ounces bittersweet
   chocolate

½ cup sour cream

2 teaspoons pure vanilla
   extract

continued

Many cheesecake recipes call for all-purpose
flour to stabilize the cream cheese, but cocoa
powder offers a similar binding effect without the
gluey mouth-feel. The instant coffee granules or
espresso powder in the filling adds a final note of
smoky richness that puts this cake over the top.

Make the crust: Heat the oven to 400°F. In a medium bowl, stir
the cookie crumbs, sugar, and cinnamon (if using) until blended.
Drizzle with the melted butter and mix until well blended and the
crumbs are evenly moist. Dump the mixture into a 9-inch springform pan and press evenly onto the bottom and about 1 inch up
the sides of the pan (to press, use plastic wrap, a straight-sided,
flat-based coffee mug, or a tart tamper). Bake for 10 minutes and
set on a rack to cool. Reduce the oven temperature to 300°F.

Make the filling and bake: Melt the chocolate in a metal bowl set
over a pan of simmering water (don't let the bowl touch the water);
let cool slightly. Mix the sour cream, vanilla, and coffee granules in a
small bowl. Set aside and stir occasionally until the coffee dissolves.

With a stand mixer fitted with the paddle attachment, beat the
cream cheese, cocoa, and salt until very smooth and fluffy, scraping down the sides of the bowl and paddle frequently (and with
each subsequent addition). Add the sugar and continue beating
until well blended and smooth. Scrape the cooled chocolate into
the bowl; beat until blended. Beat in the sour
cream mixture until well blended. Add the
eggs, one at a time, and beat until just blended.
(Don't overbeat the filling once the eggs have
been added or the cheesecake will puff too
much.) Pour the filling over the cooled crust,
spread evenly, and smooth the top.

continued

1 teaspoon instant coffee
granules or espresso powder

24 ounces (three 8-ounce
packages) cream cheese,
at room temperature

3 tablespoons unsweetened
natural cocoa powder,
sifted if lumpy

¼ teaspoon table salt

1¼ cups granulated sugar

3 large eggs, at room
temperature

Bake at 300°F until the center barely jiggles when the pan is nudged, 50 to 60 minutes. The cake will be slightly puffed, with a few little cracks around the edge. Let cool to room temperature on a rack and then refrigerate until well chilled, at least a few hours and overnight for the best texture and flavor.

To serve: Unclasp the pan's ring, remove it, and run a long, thin metal spatula under the bottom crust. Carefully slide the cake onto a flat serving plate. Run a thin knife under hot water, wipe it dry, and cut the cake into slices, heating and wiping the knife as needed.

MAKE AHEAD & FREEZE This cheesecake freezes beautifully, making it easy to get ahead in your party planning. Put the completely cooled, unmolded cake in the freezer, uncovered, until the top is cold and firm—this will prevent the surface from getting marked. When firm, wrap the cake in two layers of plastic and one layer of foil. The cake will keep for up to two months. Thaw for several hours or overnight in the refrigerator.

for the smoothest cheesecake, don't overwhip the batter

IT'S IMPORTANT TO AVOID OVERWHIPPING THE filling for cheesecake so you don't end up with a puffed, cracked cake.

Start with the cream cheese at room temperature (about 70°F).

Use the paddle attachment of a stand mixer to cream the cheese without aerating it.

Don't add the eggs until you're sure that the cream cheese is super smooth and that the sugar, cocoa, and chocolate are well combined. Add the eggs one at a time and beat on low speed until just blended.

Chocolate-espresso pecan pie

This updated classic transcends the sugary sweetness of a typical pecan pie with the addition of chocolate and coffee (with espresso powder and coffee liqueur). The flavor is best if you let the pie cool completely and then refrigerate it for several hours or overnight—which means it's a great choice for entertaining because you can make it ahead.

For the crust

6 ounces (1⅓ cups) unbleached all-purpose flour; more for rolling out the crust

1 teaspoon granulated sugar

¼ teaspoon plus ⅛ teaspoon kosher salt

2 ounces (¼ cup) chilled unsalted butter, cut into ½-inch pieces

2 ounces (¼ cup) vegetable shortening, chilled and cut into ½-inch pieces (put it in the freezer for 15 minutes before cutting)

continued

Make the crust: Pulse the flour, sugar, and salt in a food processor just to blend. Add the butter and shortening and pulse several times until the mixture resembles coarse cornmeal, 8 to 10 pulses. Transfer the mixture to a medium bowl. Tossing and stirring quickly with a fork, gradually add enough cold water (2 to 4 tablespoons) that the dough just begins to come together. It should clump together easily if lightly squeezed but not feel wet or sticky. With your hands, gather the dough and form it into a ball. Flatten the ball into a disk and wrap it in plastic. Chill the dough for 2 hours or up to 2 days before rolling. The dough can also be frozen for up to two months; thaw it overnight in the refrigerator before using.

Remove the dough from the refrigerator and let it sit at room temperature until pliable, 10 to 15 minutes. On a lightly floured surface with a lightly floured rolling pin, roll the dough into a ⅛-inch-thick, 13-inch-diameter round. Be sure to pick up the dough several times and rotate it, reflouring the surface lightly to prevent sticking—a giant spatula or the bottom of a removable-bottom tart pan works well to help move the dough around. Transfer the dough to a 9-inch Pyrex pie pan and trim the edges so there's a ½-inch overhang. Fold the overhang underneath itself to create a raised edge and then decoratively crimp or flute the edge. (Save the scraps for patching the shell later, if necessary.) Chill until the dough firms up, at least 45 minutes in the refrigerator or 20 minutes in the freezer.

continued

For the filling

3 ounces unsweetened chocolate, coarsely chopped

2 ounces (4 tablespoons) unsalted butter

4 large eggs

1 cup light corn syrup

1 cup granulated sugar

¼ teaspoon kosher salt

2 tablespoons instant espresso powder (or instant coffee)

2 tablespoons coffee liqueur (Kahlúa or Caffé Lolita®)

2 cups lightly toasted, coarsely chopped pecans

About ½ cup perfect pecan halves

Position a rack in the center of the oven and heat the oven to 350°F. Line the pie shell with parchment and fill with dried beans or pie weights. Bake until the edges of the crust are light golden brown, 25 to 30 minutes. Carefully remove the parchment and beans or weights. If necessary, gently repair any cracks with a smear of the excess dough. Transfer the shell to a rack to cool.

Make the filling: Melt the chocolate and butter in the microwave or in a small metal bowl set over a pan of simmering water (don't let the bowl touch the water), stirring with a rubber spatula until smooth.

In a medium mixing bowl, whisk the eggs, corn syrup, sugar, and salt. Dissolve the instant espresso in 1 tablespoon hot water and add to the egg mixture, along with the coffee liqueur and the melted chocolate and butter. Whisk to blend.

Evenly spread the toasted pecan pieces in the pie shell. To form a decorative border, arrange the pecan halves around the perimeter of the pie shell, on top of the pecan pieces, keeping the points of the pecans facing in and the backs just touching the crust. Carefully pour the filling over the pecans until the shell is three-quarters full. Pour the remaining filling into a liquid measuring cup or small pitcher. Transfer the pie to the oven and pour in the remaining filling. (The pecans will rise to the top as the pie bakes.)

Bake the pie until the filling puffs up, just starts to crack, and appears fairly set, 45 to 55 minutes. Transfer it to a rack and allow it to cool completely (at least 4 hours) before serving.

TWO GOOD METHODS FOR MELTING CHOCOLATE

Most directions for melting chocolate suggest using a double boiler (in lieu of melting it in a pan directly on the heat, which could easily scorch the chocolate). But chocolate expert Alice Medrich has refined an even safer method. Instead of suspending the bowl of chopped chocolate over a pot of water, she puts the bowl right into a wide skillet of very hot but not simmering water.

Here's why she likes this method: In a double-boiler setup, the water can easily start boiling without you realizing it, since it's covered by the bowl of chocolate. Steam is hotter than boiling water, and it can scorch the chocolate if you're not careful. With a bowl of chocolate heating in a few inches of water in a wide skillet, you can see the water and control the temperature as needed. With either method, the idea is to keep the temperature moderate and to avoid any water or steam touching the chocolate.

A microwave works well, too. Though you might find it fussier than using a water bath, the microwave is a good tool for melting. Heat the chocolate on 50% (medium) power for 1 minute and then stir. Continue heating in 15-second bursts, stirring between each round, until fully melted.

For any melting method, chop the chocolate first. White and milk chocolates scorch easily, so it's best to chop them finely to melt them with minimal heat. Dark chocolate is more forgiving, so chop it into almond-size pieces, which will take longer to melt but means less knife work up front.

Occasionally stir the chocolate, as well as any other ingredients you're melting with it, such as butter, until melted and smooth. Take the bowl from the pan, wipe the bottom dry, and let the melted chocolate cool slightly, unless otherwise directed by your recipe.

Watch the water: Just a few drops can make the chocolate seize into an unworkable mass, so be sure all tools are bone dry, and don't cover melting chocolate with a lid because condensation drips.

Chocolate silk pie

You can probably find this old-fashioned pie in your mother's recipe box, but with its intense filling, this version feels as sophisticated as any trendy ganache-based tart, especially when you use a good-quality chocolate. Here we've added a touch of almond extract and a hint more salt than is traditional, to give the filling an extra flavor boost. The longer you beat the mixture after each egg is added, the fluffier the filling will be, so make it dense and rich or light and moussey as you like. Top it with Cacao-Nib Whipped Cream (page 286) to add another layer of chocolate nuance. The filling contains raw eggs, so if you're concerned, use pasteurized eggs or ¾ cup of egg substitute.

3 ounces unsweetened chocolate, finely chopped

8 ounces (1 cup) unsalted butter, slightly softened

1 cup superfine sugar

½ teaspoon pure vanilla extract

½ teaspoon almond extract

⅛ teaspoon table salt

3 large eggs

1 baked 9-inch pie crust (see Chocolate Espresso Pecan Pie on page 147 for a crust recipe)

1 recipe Cacao-Nib Whipped Cream (page 286)

Semisweet or bittersweet chocolate shavings, for garnish

Melt the chocolate in a medium metal bowl set over a pan of simmering water (don't let the bowl touch the water); let cool slightly.

Put the butter and sugar in a mixing bowl and beat with an electric mixer until light and fluffy and the sugar doesn't feel grainy anymore, about 2 minutes. Slowly beat in the cooled melted chocolate, the vanilla and almond extracts, and the salt. Beat in the eggs one at a time, adding the next egg only once the mixture is smooth again.

Scrape the filling into the prepared pie crust and chill until firm, at least 2 hours or overnight.

To serve, dollop some Cacao-Nib Whipped Cream on each slice and sprinkle with some chocolate shavings.

Chocolate chunk tart with toasted almonds and coconut

Like an Almond Joy® for grown-ups, this tart features a moist coconut filling studded with toasty almonds and bittersweet chocolate nuggets. You can use mini chocolate chips if you like, but good-quality chocolate will give the tart the sophistication it deserves. Be sure to bake and cool your chocolate cookie crust before making the filling.

1 cup sweetened shredded
   coconut

½ cup sliced almonds

1 cup canned coconut milk

1 large egg, beaten well

3 tablespoons granulated sugar

1 teaspoon pure vanilla extract

⅛ teaspoon table salt

2 ounces bittersweet chocolate,
   chopped into pieces the size
   of small peas, or ⅓ cup mini
   chocolate chips

1 Press-In Cookie Crust, made
   with chocolate wafers
   (page 137), baked and cooled

Heat the oven to 350°F and place a rack in the middle of the oven.

Spread the coconut flakes on a baking sheet in an even layer; do the same with the almonds. Toast until light brown and very fragrant, 6 to 8 minutes, stirring both the coconut and the almonds once or twice. Check at about 5 minutes; the coconut in particular can go from toasted to burned quite fast. Transfer to a plate to cool.

In a medium bowl, stir together the coconut, almonds, coconut milk, egg, sugar, vanilla, and salt and mix until combined. Fold in the chocolate pieces. Scrape into the prepared cookie crust and bake until the filling is just set and the top gently browned, 20 to 25 minutes. Cool on a rack before serving.

puddings,

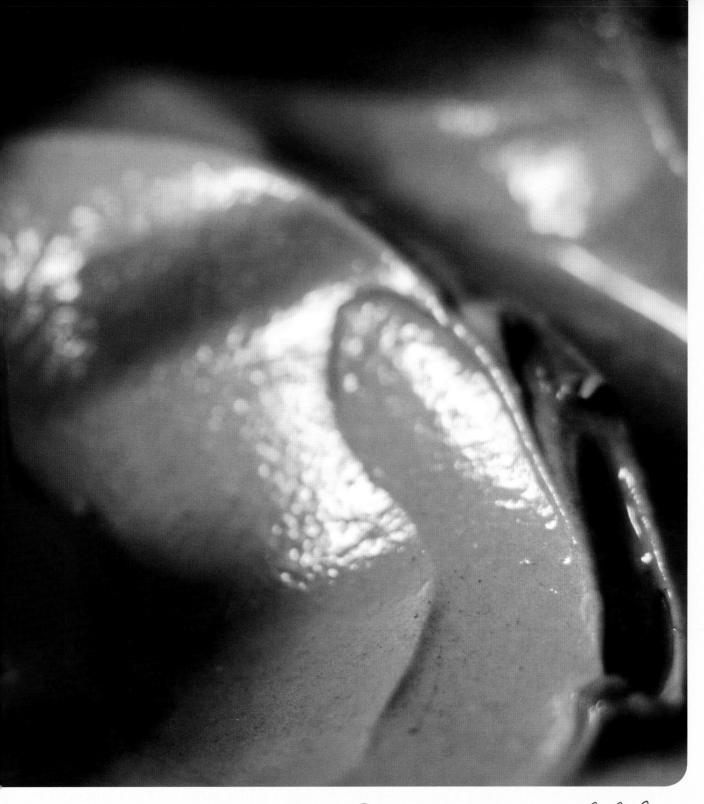

mousses & soufflés

Chocolate pots de crème

Serves 8

Pots de crème are all about creamy texture, intense flavor, and contented silence. Even a table of chatty diners suddenly goes quiet while spooning bites of this heavenly dessert. Pots de crème are also convenient, since you can (and should) make them the day before you plan to serve them. If you're doing a lot of baking, save the leftover egg whites for another recipe calling for just whites, such as the Chocolate Soufflé Cookies on page 26 or the Chocolate Pavlova with Tangerine Whipped Cream on page 182.

1 quart heavy cream

⅔ cup granulated sugar

½ vanilla bean, seeds scraped
   and pod reserved
   (or 2 teaspoons pure
   vanilla extract)

2 ounces bittersweet
   chocolate, finely chopped
   (to yield a generous ⅓ cup)

1 ounce (¼ cup) unsweetened
   natural or Dutch-processed
   cocoa powder, sifted

10 large egg yolks

Put a large pot of water on to boil for the water bath. Position a rack in the middle of the oven and heat the oven to 325°F. Put eight 6-ounce ramekins in a large roasting pan or baking dish with high sides.

Make the chocolate cream: In a medium saucepan over medium-high heat, heat the cream, ⅓ cup of the sugar, and the vanilla seeds and pod (if you're using vanilla extract, don't add it yet) until just below boiling. In a bowl, mix the chocolate and cocoa. Slowly add the hot cream, stirring constantly, until the chocolate is melted and the mixture is smooth. Return the mixture to the saucepan.

In a clean bowl, combine the egg yolks with the remaining ⅓ cup sugar; beat until smooth. Gently whisk a ladleful of the hot chocolate cream into the yolks and then whisk the yolk mixture into the saucepan with the rest of the chocolate cream. Cook slowly, stirring constantly, until the mixture reaches 170°F on an instant-read thermometer, 3 to 4 minutes. Strain immediately through cheesecloth or a fine sieve. If you're using vanilla extract, stir it in now.

Bake the pots de crème: Portion the mixture evenly among the ramekins in the roasting pan. Pull out the oven shelf, put the roasting pan on it (be sure it's stable), and pour enough boiling

continued

water into the pan so that it comes halfway up the sides of the ramekins. Cover the ramekins with a sheet of foil (simply lay the sheet on top, don't crimp the edges) and bake for 25 to 45 minutes—start checking early as how fast they cook will depend in large part on the ramekins. The custards are best when set about ¼ inch in from the sides, the centers respond with a firm jiggle (not a wavelike motion) when you nudge the ramekins, and the centers of the custards register 150°F to 155°F on an instant-read thermometer (the hole left by the thermometer will close up as the custards firm). Let the custards cool to room temperature in their water bath.

Remove the custards from the bath, cover them with plastic, and refrigerate for at least 8 hours and up to 2 days before serving.

four tips for perfect pots de crème

THIS DESSERT IS ALL ABOUT LUSCIOUS TEXTURE. If the pot de crème is undercooked, it will be tasty but runny, but overcooking can make it grainy, so a double doneness test is key.

Whisk thoroughly but gently. Vigorous whisking can aerate the custard and result in a foamy, perforated-looking surface instead of a smooth one.

Cook the custard slowly to 170°F on the stovetop. Some recipes cook the custards only in the oven, but this method calls for a few minutes of gentle cooking on the stove. The temperature rises quickly, so as the thermometer approaches 170°F, pull the pot off the heat.

Use very hot water for the water bath. This keeps the custard at a consistent but gentle heat as it goes from the stove to the oven.

To test for doneness, jiggle—and use a thermometer as a backup. When you nudge the ramekin, the custard will be firm about ¼ inch of the way in from the sides but the center will respond with a jiggle. If you see a wavelike motion, that means it's still too liquid. To confirm, use an instant-read thermometer, which should register 150°F to 155°F (the hole left by the thermometer will close as the custard firms). If in doubt, take the custards out of the oven on the early side, since they firm as they chill.

No-cook chocolate pudding

Here's a dessert that will please adults and kids alike. If you heat the cream in the microwave, use an 8-cup Pyrex measuring cup as your mixing bowl—the pour spout is extremely useful.

1¾ cups heavy cream

2 tablespoons unsweetened cocoa powder, preferably Dutch-processed

½ pound bittersweet chocolate, finely chopped (1½ cups)

2 ounces (¼ cup) unsalted butter, cut into 4 pieces

2 tablespoons granulated sugar

1 teaspoon pure vanilla extract

Pinch table salt

Sweetened whipped cream and chocolate shavings for garnish (optional)

Have ready six 4- to 6-ounce ramekins or teacups. Heat the heavy cream in a small saucepan or microwave until just boiling. Remove from the heat and whisk in the cocoa until smooth. Add the chocolate, butter, sugar, vanilla, and salt, and whisk until the chocolate and butter are melted and the mixture is smooth. Pour the mixture into the ramekins or cups. Depending on the size of your ramekins, they'll be filled about two-thirds to three-quarters of the way. Cover with plastic (not touching the surface of the puddings) and refrigerate until chilled and thickened, at least 6 hours and up to 3 days. Serve with a dollop of sweetened whipped cream and a few chocolate shavings, if you like.

Silky, sumptuous chocolate pudding

This pudding isn't much harder to make than the chocolate pudding from a box you had growing up, but it's leagues beyond that in terms of deliciousness. The pudding is baked in individual ramekins, but you can also use coffee cups or any other container that can withstand temperatures of 300°F. Serve with whipped cream and chocolate shavings, if you like.

8 ounces semisweet chocolate

½ cup granulated sugar

6 large egg yolks

4 cups heavy cream

1 teaspoon pure vanilla extract

¼ teaspoon table salt

Coarsely chop the chocolate and reserve it in a large mixing bowl. In a medium bowl, whisk ¼ cup of the sugar into the egg yolks. In a medium saucepan, mix the remaining ¼ cup sugar with the cream and the vanilla extract. Heat the cream to just below the boiling point. Add a little of the cream to the egg yolks and stir vigorously for smoother mixing; set aside. Pour the rest of the hot cream over the chopped chocolate. Gently stir the chocolate with a spatula until it has melted. Add the egg-cream mixture and the salt to the chocolate and stir to mix. Through a fine sieve, strain the pudding into a large measuring cup or pitcher (so it's easy to pour) or a bowl.

Heat the oven to 300°F. Fill six 8-ounce ramekins or eight 6-ounce ramekins with the pudding, leaving at least ¼ inch of space at the top. Put the ramekins in a baking pan no more than 1 inch deeper than your molds. Fill the pan with warm water about halfway up the sides of the molds. Cover the pan with foil and bake until the pudding is no longer runny, about 1 hour. When cooked, a lighter-colored spot about the size of a quarter appears on the surface of the puddings. Remove the ramekins from the water bath, cover, and refrigerate for at least 3 hours before serving.

Classic chocolate mousse

Here's a dessert from the classic French repertoire that fits beautifully into the most contemporary menu. Rich, intense, and a perfect showcase for today's high-quality chocolates, this mousse is a delicious way to end a special dinner party or to turn a simple meal into a celebration. This recipe makes a large amount, but any leftovers keep well in the refrigerator for a few days, or you could cut the recipe in half (use just 3 egg whites).

2 cups heavy cream

¾ ounce (¼ cup) unsweetened natural cocoa powder

13 ounces bittersweet chocolate, chopped

¼ pound (½ cup) unsalted butter, softened at room temperature and cut into small pieces

2 teaspoons pure vanilla extract or 1 to 2 tablespoons brandy or Cointreau®

Pinch table salt

7 large egg whites, at room temperature

½ cup granulated sugar

Whipped cream, for serving

Set up an ice bath by partially filling a large bowl with cold water and some ice.

Combine the cream and cocoa in a large saucepan set over medium heat. Bring to a full boil, whisking occasionally to blend in the cocoa. Slide the pan off the heat and immediately add the chopped chocolate and the butter; whisk slowly until melted and smooth.

Scrape the chocolate mixture into a large bowl. Add the vanilla (or liqueur) and salt. Set the bowl over the ice bath and stir constantly with a rubber spatula, scraping the sides very frequently, until the chocolate cools to room temperature (don't stop stirring or lumps will form). Remove the bowl from the ice bath.

Put the egg whites in a large clean bowl. Whip with an electric mixer on medium-low speed until very foamy. Increase the speed to medium high and beat until the whites form very loose, soft peaks. Slowly add the sugar. Continue beating until the whites are shiny and form floppy peaks.

continued

If you're concerned about eating uncooked egg whites, you can substitute a pasteurized egg white product.

Working quickly, scoop about a third of the whites into the cooled chocolate mixture and fold together with a rubber spatula or a whisk until blended. Scrape the remaining whites into the chocolate and fold together gently but thoroughly. Cover and chill at least 1 hour so the mousse can set up. Serve scoops in small dishes, with a dollop of whipped cream, if you like.

THE KEYS TO LUSCIOUS MOUSSE

The way to make a mousse that's both fluffy and creamy is to control the texture of the components all along the way.

When cooling the chocolate over the ice bath, stir constantly for a smooth consistency. Scrape the sides frequently with a rubber spatula, as the chocolate is quick to set and can develop lumps.

Before beating the whites, be sure your beater and bowl are super clean; the slightest hint of grease can ruin beaten egg whites. The whites are perfectly beaten when the tips of the peaks flop over loosely onto themselves. For this mousse, slightly underwhipped whites are better than slightly overwhipped ones.

Lighten the chocolate with some of the whites to make folding easier. Then fold in the remaining whites, aiming to incorporate them into the chocolate without deflating too much of the foam. Work gently but quickly—as the whites sit, they lose their softness and become lumpy.

Bourbon-chocolate mousse

This silky mousse—with a slight boozy kick—is delicious topped with a dollop of whipped crème fraîche and sprinkled with cocoa powder.

½ cup heavy cream

3 tablespoons confectioners' sugar

2 tablespoons bourbon

1 teaspoon pure vanilla extract

4 ounces bittersweet chocolate, finely chopped (¾ cup)

4 large egg whites, preferably at room temperature

Pinch table salt

Put 4 small (at least 6 ounce) individual serving bowls in the refrigerator.

Bring the heavy cream and sugar to a boil in a small saucepan and remove the pan from the heat (don't just turn off the burner). Stir in the bourbon and vanilla. Add the chocolate and let it sit for 5 minutes without stirring. Whisk the chocolate and cream until smooth and then transfer the ganache to a large bowl. Don't refrigerate.

In a medium bowl, beat the egg whites and the salt with a hand mixer on high speed just until they form stiff peaks when you lift the beaters.

With a rubber spatula, fold about one-quarter of the beaten whites into the ganache to lighten it. Then gently fold in the remaining whites, taking care not to deflate them. Divide the mousse among the chilled bowls and refrigerate for at least 30 minutes but preferably for 1 hour and up to 24 hours.

The egg whites in this recipe are not cooked, but we don't recommend using pasteurized egg whites because they tend to separate after they're folded into the ganache.

Gianduia mousse

Hazelnut and chocolate, called gianduia, is a much-loved flavor combo in Europe, and we're beginning to appreciate it in the U.S. also—just think Nutella®. The hazelnut butter in this quick-to-make, creamy mousse adds a bit of texture that's a real palate pleaser. Try the mousse as a pie filling in your favorite graham cracker crust or tart crust; serve well chilled. This mousse is best when served within 6 hours of the time it's made.

For the mousse

6 ounces bittersweet or semisweet chocolate, finely chopped

1½ cups heavy cream

⅔ cup Hazelnut Butter, at room temperature (facing page)

2 teaspoons pure vanilla extract

For the garnish

½ cup heavy cream

½ teaspoon pure vanilla extract

2 tablespoons finely ground toasted hazelnuts (see Hazelnut Butter, facing page, for toasting directions; grind the toasted nuts in a food processor)

To make the mousse: In a 2-quart metal bowl set over a saucepan of simmering water, melt the chocolate, stirring with a rubber spatula until the chocolate is completely smooth. In a separate small saucepan, heat ½ cup of the cream over medium heat to just below the boiling point. Remove the bowl of chocolate from the pan of water and wipe the bottom and sides dry. Pour the hot cream into the melted chocolate and stir together with the spatula until well blended. Add the hazelnut butter and stir until well combined. Stir in the 2 teaspoons vanilla.

In a chilled mixing bowl, using chilled beaters, beat the remaining 1 cup of cream until it holds soft peaks. With a rubber spatula, fold the whipped cream into the chocolate mixture in four batches, blending thoroughly after each addition. Pour the mousse into a 1½-quart soufflé dish or serving bowl, or into individual serving bowls or glasses. Cover with plastic wrap and refrigerate until set, at least 2 hours (or 1 hour if using it to fill profiteroles).

To make the garnish: In a chilled mixing bowl with chilled beaters, beat the ½ cup cream until frothy. Add the ½ teaspoon vanilla and continue beating until the cream holds soft peaks. Pipe or spoon the whipped cream on top of the mousse. Sprinkle the chopped hazelnuts over the whipped cream and serve.

hazelnut butter

If you can find hazelnuts (also called filberts) that are already skinned, by all means save yourself some work by using them. But when skinning them yourself, don't worry about getting every last bit of skin from the nut; the flavor and texture of the butter will be fine as long as you remove about half the skins.

8 ounces (1⅔ cups) hazelnuts

¼ cup vegetable oil, such as canola or sunflower

Pinch of table salt

Heat the oven to 350°F. Spread the hazelnuts in a single layer on a baking sheet and toast in the heated oven until the skins are mostly split and the nuts are light golden brown and quite fragrant, 15 to 18 minutes. Don't overcook the nuts or they'll become bitter.

Put the warm hazelnuts in a clean dishtowel. Fold the towel around the hazelnuts and let them steam for at least 5 minutes. Then rub the nuts in the towel to remove most of the skins (try to get at least 50 percent of the skins off). Let the hazelnuts sit for another 10 to 15 minutes to cool completely. Toasted, peeled hazelnuts can be cooled and frozen in a sealed plastic container for up to three months.

Put the nuts in a food processor; add the oil and salt, and pulse a few times. Then process, checking the consistency every few seconds, until the texture resembles that of natural, unhomogenized peanut butter or wet sand, 1 to 2 minutes.

MAKE & FREEZE This butter can be refrigerated in a sealed container for up to three months or frozen for up to six months. If frozen, thaw it slowly in the refrigerator overnight. Always bring the hazelnut butter to room temperature before use.

White chocolate mousse parfaits

The delicate flavor of white chocolate marries easily with many fruits, so don't limit yourself to this mango version of the parfait. Other delectable combinations include fresh raspberries or quartered strawberries with crushed chocolate cookies, reconstituted dried apricots with gingersnaps, and blueberries with vanilla wafers.

4 ounces good-quality white chocolate, chopped

1½ cups heavy cream

¼ teaspoon pure vanilla extract

Pinch table salt

1 ripe mango, cut into small chunks

20 gingersnaps or chocolate wafers, crushed

Melt the white chocolate in a small, heatproof bowl over simmering water or in a microwave. Stir until smooth. Set the chocolate aside and proceed immediately; the chocolate needs to be very warm for this speedy recipe to succeed.

Pour the cream into a medium bowl and add the vanilla and salt. Beat with an electric mixer on medium-high speed until the cream forms firm but not stiff peaks, about 2 to 3 minutes. (Don't go too far or the cream will curdle when the chocolate is beaten in.) Scrape the very warm white chocolate into the cream. Continue beating on medium-high speed until well blended and firm, about 30 seconds. The mousse should form a dollop when dropped from a spoon.

To serve, spoon the mousse into tall glasses, alternating with layers of the mango chunks and crushed cookies.

treat the lighter chocolates with care

WHITE CHOCOLATE CONTAINS HIGH PERCENTAGES of both cocoa butter and milk solids, so it's the most temperature sensitive of the chocolates. Be careful when you melt it—it burns easily, so use very low heat. In addition, the milk solids can coagulate with too much heat, leaving tiny lumps in the chocolate, so be sure to use a water bath or very low power on the microwave.

Mocha pudding cakes

Elegant enough for guests, these are also really easy to make; as they bake, the custard settles to the bottom while the spongy cake layer sets on top.

Softened butter for the ramekins

2 ounces (¼ cup) unsalted butter, melted and cooled slightly

1 cup granulated sugar

3 large eggs, separated, at room temperature

⅓ cup unsweetened Dutch-processed cocoa powder

2 tablespoons unbleached all-purpose flour

¼ teaspoon plus ⅛ teaspoon table salt

1¼ cups strong brewed coffee, at room temperature

⅓ cup whole milk, at room temperature

1 teaspoon pure vanilla extract

Lightly sweetened whipped cream for serving (optional)

Position a rack in the center of the oven and heat the oven to 350°F. Butter eight 6-ounce ovenproof ceramic ramekins or Pyrex custard cups and arrange them in a baking dish or roasting pan (a 10x15-inch or two 8x8-inch Pyrex dishes work well).

In a large bowl, whisk the melted butter with ⅔ cup of the sugar and the egg yolks until smooth and light, about 1 minute. Add the cocoa, flour, and salt, and pour in just enough of the coffee to whisk the flour smoothly into the egg yolk mixture. Then whisk in the remaining coffee, along with the milk and vanilla, until smooth. The mixture will be very fluid.

Put the egg whites in a large bowl. Beat with an electric mixer (a hand-held or a stand mixer fitted with the whisk attachment) on medium speed until the whites begin to foam, 30 to 60 seconds. Increase the speed to high and beat just until the egg whites hold soft peaks when the beater is pulled away from the whites, another 1 to 2 minutes. Reduce the mixer speed to medium. With the mixer running, very slowly sprinkle in the remaining ⅓ cup sugar; this should take about a minute. Stop the mixer and scrape the bowl. Beat on high speed until the whites hold medium-firm peaks when the beater is pulled away, about another 30 seconds.

continued

Scrape one-third of the egg whites into the egg yolk mixture and whisk until combined. Gently incorporate the remaining egg whites evenly into the batter, using the whisk in a folding/stirring motion. The batter will still be thin.

Portion the mixture evenly among the ramekins; the cakes don't rise much, so you can fill the ramekins to within 1/8 inch of the top. Pull out the oven rack and put the baking dish full of ramekins on the rack. Pour warm water into the dish to reach halfway up the sides of the ramekins. Bake until the tops of the cakes are slightly puffed and, when touched with a finger, feel spongy and spring back a bit but hold a very shallow indentation, 25 to 30 minutes. Using tongs, carefully transfer the ramekins to a rack. Let cool to room temperature and then refrigerate for at least 2 hours and up to 24 hours before serving, with whipped cream if you like.

Dark chocolate soufflé cakes with espresso-chocolate sauce

These soufflé cakes are pure chocolate goodness made practically foolproof. There's no tricky unmolding, and the superb bittersweet chocolate-sauce center doesn't need perfect timing to achieve. Don't worry about huge height for these soufflés, either, as they are even more flavorful after they have cooled and deflated slightly.

Softened butter and granulated sugar for the ramekins

For the espresso-chocolate sauce

1 teaspoon instant espresso powder

8 ounces bittersweet or semisweet chocolate, coarsely chopped

3 ounces (6 tablespoons) unsalted butter, cut into 8 pieces

Table salt

For the soufflé cakes

2 tablespoons unsweetened natural cocoa powder

2 large eggs, separated

1 large egg white

⅛ teaspoon cream of tartar

3 tablespoons granulated sugar

Put a metal or Pyrex pie plate or cake pan in the freezer to chill. Lightly butter six 6-ounce ramekins or custard cups. Coat with sugar and tap out the excess.

Make the sauce: In a small bowl, combine the espresso powder with 2 tablespoons warm water and stir to dissolve.

Melt the chocolate and butter in a medium bowl, stirring frequently until smooth. Add two pinches of salt, stir, and remove from the heat. Transfer 5 tablespoons of the chocolate mixture to the espresso and stir to blend. (Set the remaining melted chocolate aside.) Use a spatula to scrape the espresso mixture into a puddle on the chilled pie plate or cake pan and return it to the freezer until firm, about 10 minutes. When the espresso-chocolate mixture is firm, use a teaspoon to scrape it into six rough balls. Keep the balls on the plate and refrigerate until ready to use.

Make the soufflé cakes: Reheat the remaining chocolate mixture by setting its bowl in or over a skillet of hot water. When it's warm, remove it from the heat and whisk in the cocoa and the 2 egg yolks.

In a clean, dry bowl, beat the 3 egg whites and cream of tartar on medium speed in a stand mixer (or on high speed with a hand-held mixer) until the whites mound gently. Gradually beat in the

continued

sugar and continue beating until the whites form medium-firm peaks when you lift the beaters; the tips should curl over but still look moist, glossy, and flexible.

With a rubber spatula, fold about one-quarter of the egg whites into the chocolate to lighten it. Scrape the remaining whites into the bowl and gently fold in until blended, taking care not to deflate the whites. Take the chocolate balls out of the refrigerator and put one ball in the center of each ramekin. Divide the batter evenly among the ramekins and level the tops gently with the back of a spoon. You can now heat the oven and bake right away or cover the ramekins with plastic wrap and refrigerate for up to 2 days.

Bake the soufflé cakes: Position a rack in the lower third of the oven and heat the oven to 400°F. Remove the plastic from the ramekins and put the ramekins on a baking sheet. Bake until the soufflé cakes are puffed and possibly a little cracked on top (a toothpick inserted in the center will meet no resistance and will emerge mostly clean—the tip will be wet from the sauce at the bottom), 11 to 14 minutes (a minute or two longer if they were chilled overnight). Let cool for a few minutes before serving.

MAKE AHEAD The assembled, unbaked soufflé cakes can be wrapped in plastic and refrigerated for up to two days. They do not need to come to room temperature before baking, but baking time will need to be one or two minutes longer.

**Dark chocolate soufflé cakes
with espresso-chocolate sauce**

Chocolate-espresso mini-soufflés

This is a great dessert for hassle-free holiday entertaining, as you can make it up to a month in advance and stow it in the freezer. In fact, you must make the soufflés ahead so that they're chilled before they go in the oven.

Granulated sugar for the ramekins

1½ teaspoons instant coffee granules

3 tablespoons dark rum, brandy, Grand Marnier Liqueur®, or water (if serving these on the same day as making them, use 1½ tablespoons rum plus 1½ tablespoons water or the alcohol will overpower)

6 ounces bittersweet chocolate, finely chopped

3 ounces (6 tablespoons) unsalted butter, cut into pieces; more for the ramekins

¼ teaspoon table salt

3 large eggs, separated and at room temperature

3 ounces (¾ cup) confectioners' sugar

Fresh raspberries or lightly sweetened whipped cream, for garnish (optional)

Lightly butter six 6-ounce ramekins and dust with granulated sugar, tapping out the excess. Set the ramekins on a small baking sheet.

Stir the instant coffee into the liquor or water (or a combination of both). Set aside and stir occasionally until the coffee is dissolved. Melt the chocolate and butter in a large metal bowl set over a pan of simmering water (don't let the bowl touch the water). Remove from the heat and whisk until glossy and smooth. Stir in the coffee mixture and the salt. Whisk in the egg yolks, one at a time. Add about one-third of the confectioners' sugar and whisk until well blended and smooth. Set aside.

In a medium bowl, beat the egg whites with an electric mixer on medium-high speed until they're very foamy and just beginning to hold soft peaks. Increase the speed to high and gradually sprinkle in the remaining confectioners' sugar. Continue beating until the peaks are firm and glossy. Spoon about one-quarter of the beaten whites into the chocolate mixture and whisk until blended. Add the remaining whites and gently fold them in with a rubber spatula until just blended. Pour evenly into the prepared ramekins (the mixture will almost completely fill the ramekins). If you want to bake the soufflés within 24 hours, refrigerate them. (To refrigerate: Chill for about 30 minutes, and then cover in plastic and return to the refrigerator for up to 24 hours.)

To bake straight from the refrigerator: Heat the oven to 400°F. Unwrap the ramekins, set them on a baking sheet, and bake until they have puffed and risen about 1 inch above the ramekin, 15 minutes. The top will still be slightly sunken in the center; consider it a place to pop in a few berries or a dollop of whipped cream. Remove the soufflés from the oven and serve immediately.

MAKE AHEAD & FREEZE Put the filled ramekins in the freezer, uncovered, for 20 minutes. Then wrap each ramekin well in plastic and freeze for up to two weeks. To bake straight from the freezer, unwrap the ramekins and set on a small baking sheet or jellyroll pan. Let them sit for 20 minutes while heating the oven to 400°F. Bake on the baking sheet until they have puffed and risen about 1 inch above the ramekin, 18 minutes. (If they're a little underdone, they'll be a bit runny in the center; if a little overdone, they'll be a bit cakey in the center. It's best to stick to 18 minutes, as you don't want to use a method to test doneness that might deflate the soufflés. After you've made this recipe once in your own kitchen, you can adjust the timing as you like.) Remove from the oven and serve immediately.

White chocolate soufflé cakes with raspberry-chocolate sauce

One dip into this delicate cake, and the happy diner discovers a warm, pudding-like chocolate sauce. The trick to the deliciously gooey center is a lump of chilled, solidified chocolate sauce buried in the batter.

Softened butter and granulated
sugar for the ramekins

For the raspberry-chocolate sauce

½ cup fresh raspberries,
rinsed, or ¾ cup thawed
frozen raspberries

3 ounces bittersweet or
semisweet chocolate,
chopped

1 ounce (2 tablespoons)
unsalted butter

1 tablespoon granulated sugar

For the soufflé cakes

3 large eggs, separated,
at room temperature

3 tablespoons unbleached
all-purpose flour

⅛ teaspoon table salt

continued

Put a metal or Pyrex pie plate or cake pan in the freezer to chill. Lightly butter six 6-ounce ramekins or custard cups. Coat with sugar and tap out the excess.

Make the sauce: Purée the raspberries in a food processor. Transfer the purée to a fine sieve set over a small bowl. Strain the purée by pressing and scraping with a rubber spatula. Discard the seeds.

In a medium heatproof bowl set in or over a skillet of barely simmering water, combine the chocolate, butter, sugar, and 2 tablespoons of the raspberry purée (save any extra for another use). Stir frequently with a rubber spatula until melted and smooth. Scrape into a puddle on the chilled pie plate and return to the freezer until firm, 20 to 30 minutes. When the raspberry-chocolate mixture is firm, use a teaspoon to scrape it into six rough balls. Keep the balls on the plate and refrigerate until ready to use.

Make the soufflé cakes: Put the 3 egg yolks in a medium bowl near the stove and have another large, clean bowl at hand. Combine the flour and salt in a small, heavy saucepan. Whisk in just enough of the milk to make a smooth paste. Whisk in the remaining milk. Set the pan over medium heat and cook, whisking constantly, until the mixture has the consistency of a thick cream sauce, 2 to 3 minutes. Whisk about 2 tablespoons of the hot sauce into the yolks to warm them up gently. Scrape the yolks back into the saucepan and cook for a minute or two, whisking constantly, until the mixture becomes a thick pastry cream; it should be about

172   PUDDINGS, MOUSSES & SOUFFLÉS

¾ cup whole milk

6 ounces good-quality white chocolate, finely chopped

¼ teaspoon pure vanilla extract

Scant ¼ teaspoon cream of tartar

2 tablespoons granulated sugar

as thick as store-bought mayonnaise. Use a rubber spatula to scrape the pastry cream into the clean bowl. Add the white chocolate and whisk until it's fully melted and incorporated into the warm pastry cream. Stir in the vanilla. Set aside for a few minutes until tepid.

In a clean, dry bowl, beat the egg whites and cream of tartar on medium speed in a stand mixer (or on high with a hand-held mixer) until the whites mound gently. Gradually beat in the sugar and continue beating until the whites form medium-firm peaks when you lift the beaters; the tips should curl over but still look moist, glossy, and flexible.

With a rubber spatula, fold about one-quarter of the whites into the white chocolate pastry cream to lighten it. Scrape the remaining whites into the bowl and gently fold in until blended, taking care not to deflate the whites. Take the chocolate balls out of the refrigerator and put one ball in the center of each ramekin. Divide the batter evenly among the ramekins and level the tops gently with the back of a spoon. You can now heat the oven and bake right away or cover the ramekins with plastic and refrigerate for up to 2 days.

Bake the soufflé cakes: Position a rack in the lower third of the oven and heat the oven to 375°F. Remove the plastic and put the ramekins on a baking sheet. Bake until the cakes are puffed and golden brown on top—they'll quiver when tapped and seem soft in the center, 16 to 18 minutes. Let cool for a few minutes before serving.

Black forest trifle

Digging through the layers of a trifle to spoon out a serving is about as much fun as dessert can get. This version riffs on Black Forest cake, that famous combination of cherries and chocolate. Serve in a glass bowl.

For the cake

2 ounces semisweet chocolate, chopped

1 ounce unsweetened chocolate, chopped

5 ounces (1 cup plus 2 tablespoons) unbleached all-purpose flour

½ ounce (2 tablespoons) unsweetened Dutch-processed cocoa powder

½ teaspoon baking powder

½ teaspoon baking soda

¼ teaspoon table salt

3 ounces (6 tablespoons) unsalted butter, softened at room temperature

1 cup granulated sugar

2 large eggs

1 teaspoon pure vanilla extract

½ cup sour cream

⅓ cup strong brewed coffee

continued

Position a rack in the middle of the oven and heat the oven to 350°F. Butter the bottom and sides of a 9x2-inch round cake pan. Line the bottom of the pan with parchment and butter the parchment.

Make the cake: Melt the semisweet and unsweetened chocolate together in a metal bowl set over a pan of simmering water (don't let the pan touch the water). Let cool slightly.

Sift together the flour, cocoa, baking powder, baking soda, and salt. With a stand mixer using the paddle attachment, beat the butter and sugar on medium speed until light and fluffy, 2 to 4 minutes. Mix in the slightly cooled melted chocolate on low speed just until incorporated. Increase the speed to medium and add the eggs one at a time, beating well after each addition. Scrape the bowl, add the vanilla, and beat on medium speed for another minute. On low speed, mix in the sour cream just until it's incorporated. Add the flour mixture (in three additions), alternating with the coffee (in two additions); scrape the bowl as needed. The batter will be very thick, like chocolate mousse or frosting.

Scrape the cake batter into the prepared pan and smooth the top. Bake until the top feels firm and a toothpick inserted in the center comes out clean, about 35 minutes. The cake may sink a bit in the center, but that's fine. Let the cake cool for 20 minutes in the baking pan on a rack. Using a thin, sharp knife, loosen the sides of the cake from the pan, invert the cake onto the rack, and discard the paper liner. Let cool completely. (You can bake the cake one day ahead; wrap it when cool, and store at room temperature.)

For the cherries and kirsch syrup

One 15- or 16-ounce can pitted sweet cherries in heavy or extra-heavy syrup

¼ cup kirsch (cherry brandy)

Granulated sugar, to taste

For the whipped cream

3 cups cold heavy cream

½ cup granulated sugar

1 tablespoon kirsch

For assembling the trifle

1 cup semisweet chocolate shavings (from a 3- to 4-ounce block of chocolate)

Be sure to spread each layer to the edge of the bowl; this way the layers and colors will be clearly visible.

Prepare the cherries and kirsch syrup: Drain the cherries in a colander set over a large bowl (to catch the syrup) for 30 minutes. Reserve ½ cup of the syrup. Transfer the cherries to a small bowl, drizzle with 1 tablespoon of the kirsch, and set aside. Taste the syrup; it should be slightly tart and not too sweet. If necessary, stir in 1 to 2 teaspoons of sugar. Put the syrup in a small saucepan and simmer over medium heat until reduced by about half, about 3 minutes. Remove the pan from the heat and stir in the remaining 3 tablespoons kirsch. Set aside to cool. You can do this a day ahead; cover and refrigerate.

Make the whipped cream just before assembly: Put the cream, sugar, and kirsch in the large bowl of an electric mixer and whip on high speed until it holds firm peaks.

Assemble the trifle up to 6 hours ahead: Pick out the 10 best-looking cherries and blot them dry with paper towels. With a long, serrated knife, cut the cooled cake vertically (all the way across the cake) into ½-inch slices. Lay about a third of the cake slices in the bottom of a 2½- to 3-quart glass bowl or trifle bowl to create an even layer. Don't worry if the pieces break as long as they fill in the spaces. Brush this layer of cake lightly with some of the kirsch syrup, top with a third of the whipped cream, and randomly nestle half of the remaining cherries into the cream. Sprinkle with a third of the chocolate shavings. Repeat with two more layers. On the top layer of cream, arrange the best-looking cherries in a ring near the rim of the bowl and scatter the chocolate shavings inside the cherry ring. Refrigerate for at least 30 minutes and up to 6 hours. Serve chilled.

Coffee & cream icebox cake

Coffee and hazelnuts give this cake—a variation on Nabisco's Famous Wafer Roll recipe—a more sophisticated flavor. To be safe, buy two boxes of cookies, as some may break. This cake slices best after two days in the refrigerator.

1¾ cups heavy cream

1 tablespoon instant
  espresso powder

1 tablespoon granulated
  sugar

44 Nabisco Famous
  Chocolate Wafer cookies

¼ cup finely chopped,
  toasted hazelnuts
  for garnish

¼ cup crushed chocolate
  wafer cookie crumbs

Lightly grease a 6-cup loaf pan, then line it with two pieces of overlapping plastic wrap, allowing the excess to hang over the edges.

In a bowl, combine the cream, espresso powder, and sugar. Whisk until the cream holds firm peaks. Spoon about two-thirds of the whipped cream into the prepared pan. Tap the pan firmly on the counter to even the cream and eliminate any air bubbles.

Starting at a short side of the pan, arrange 11 cookies in the cream, standing them on their edge in a row like dominoes. Gently squeeze the cookies together as you go. Do the same with a second row of cookies, slightly overlapping the cookies from the second row with the cookies in the first row. Continue with two more rows for a total of four rows.

Press down on the cookies gently. Cover them with the remaining cream. Smooth the cream with a spatula, gently pressing to make sure any gaps between the cookies are filled. Tap the pan on the counter several times to eliminate any air pockets.

Cover the cake with the excess plastic wrap and refrigerate for at least 24 hours, preferably 2 days. When ready to serve, peel the plastic wrap from the top and gently tug on the plastic to loosen the cake from the sides of the pan. Set a cutting board on top of the pan and invert the cake onto the board. Lift the pan off and gently peel away the plastic wrap. Mix the hazelnuts with the cookie crumbs and sprinkle over the top of the cake. Slice carefully with a warm knife.

Chocolate-raspberry cookies & cream

Serves 6

Using some crème fraîche along with the heavy cream adds
dimension and a tiny bit of tang to this luscious, pretty pink filling,
but you can use all cream if that's easier.

3 cups frozen raspberries
   (about 12 ounces), thawed

5 tablespoons granulated
   sugar, more if needed

Few drops fresh lemon juice

Kosher salt

⅔ cup heavy cream

⅓ cup crème fraîche

21 Nabisco Famous
   Chocolate Wafer cookies

6 mint sprigs

Put 1 cup of the raspberries in a small bowl, sprinkle with 2 tablespoons of the sugar, mash with a fork, and let sit for a few minutes.

Meanwhile, put the remaining 2 cups of berries and 2 tablespoons of sugar in a food processor (or blender) and process until the berries form a purée. Strain through a fine-mesh strainer into a small bowl, pressing with a rubber spatula to get the seeds out. Squeeze in a few drops of lemon juice and a tiny pinch of salt. Taste and add more sugar or lemon if needed. The sauce should be thin enough to drizzle. If it seems too thick, add a few drops of water. Cover and refrigerate.

In a medium bowl, combine the cream, the crème fraîche, and the remaining 1 tablespoon of sugar and whip with a hand mixer until the mixture forms firm, thick peaks. Stir the mashed berries and sugar and lightly fold into the cream mixture with a rubber spatula, leaving streaks.

Reserve 6 of the cookies for decoration and crunch up the rest into uneven pieces—not too small. Fold the cookies into the cream. Cover with plastic wrap, pressing the wrap onto the surface of the cream, and chill until the cookie pieces are thoroughly softened, at least 2 hours and preferably overnight.

To serve, use an ice cream scoop or large spoon to scoop out a mound of cookies and cream into a small bowl or onto a plate. Drizzle a ribbon of raspberry sauce around the plate, tuck a cookie into the cream, and decorate with a mint sprig.

fun

& fancy desserts

Chocolate pavlova with tangerine whipped cream

Serves 8 to 10

When you need a dessert with knockout crowd-appeal, a pavlova—basically a big meringue—delivers. The meringue shell looks light, but it has a rich, brownie-like interior. Filled with tangerine-flavored whipped cream and fresh fruit, this dessert tastes as lovely as it looks.

4 large egg whites, at room temperature

⅛ teaspoon cream of tartar

⅛ teaspoon table salt

1 cup plus 2 tablespoons granulated sugar

1½ teaspoons cornstarch

1 tablespoon red-wine vinegar

¾ ounces (¼ cup) unsweetened Dutch-processed cocoa powder, sifted

1 cup heavy cream

Finely grated zest of 1 tangerine (about 1¼ teaspoons)

1½ cups fresh fruit, such as raspberries, sliced strawberries, peeled and sliced mango, or a mix

3 kiwis, peeled and sliced into half moons

Position a rack in the center of the oven and heat the oven to 350°F. Cut a piece of parchment so that it fits flat on a baking sheet. With a pencil, draw a 9-inch circle in the center of the parchment (tracing a 9-inch cake pan works fine). Line the baking sheet with the parchment, pencil side facing down (you should still be able to see the circle).

With an electric hand mixer or stand mixer with the whisk attachment, whip the egg whites, cream of tartar, and salt in a large, dry bowl on medium speed until foamy, about 30 seconds. Gradually add 1 cup of the sugar and then the cornstarch and vinegar; whip on medium high until the whites hold stiff peaks and look glossy, another 3 to 5 minutes. Add the sifted cocoa and mix on low speed until mostly combined, 20 to 30 seconds, scraping the bowl as needed. Finish mixing the cocoa into the meringue by hand with a rubber spatula until well combined and no streaks of white remain.

Pile the meringue inside the circle on the parchment. Using the spatula, spread the meringue to even it out slightly—it doesn't need to align perfectly with the circle, and it shouldn't be perfectly smooth or overworked.

Bake for 10 minutes and then reduce the heat to 300°F and bake until the meringue has puffed and cracked around its edges, another 45 to 50 minutes. Turn off the oven, prop the oven door

continued

open, and leave the meringue in the oven to cool to room temperature, at least 30 minutes. The delicate meringue won't collapse as much if it cools gradually.

Just before serving, put the meringue on a serving platter. In a chilled medium stainless-steel bowl, beat the cream with the remaining 2 tablespoons sugar until it holds soft peaks. Whip in the tangerine zest, making sure it's evenly distributed. Pile the whipped cream on the meringue, spreading it almost out to the edge, and then top with the fruit. To serve, slice into wedges with a serrated knife.

TIPS FOR MAKING THE CHEWY-CRISP PAVLOVA SHELL

Meringues can sometimes be finicky, so follow these tricks to guarantee a good result.

1. Whip the egg whites until they are extremely glossy. Cream of tartar helps them achieve the stiff peaks needed for meringue.

2. Use a rubber spatula to spread the meringue out into a round. It need not be perfect; natural swirls and ridges give it character.

3. Every pavlova is unique. If your meringue collapses more or less than this photo, don't panic; a concave center makes a wonderful bowl for the cream and fruit.

Chocolate rice pudding parfait with gianduia whipped cream & caramelized rice krispies

This dish is just a lot of fun; how can it not be with a garnish made of Rice Krispies®? Serve in clear glasses—martini glasses work great—so you can see the dessert's pretty layers. The various components of the dessert can be made ahead (as far as a month ahead in the case of the garnish), which means you can easily spread out the work.

For the chocolate rice pudding

3 cups whole milk

2½ tablespoons granulated sugar

Pinch table salt

⅓ cup raw arborio rice

5 ounces good-quality bittersweet chocolate or gianduia chocolate, chopped

2 ounces (¼ cup) unsalted butter, cut into small pieces

½ cup golden raisins, simmered in water until plump and then drained (optional)

1 recipe Cream Cheese Mousse (page 187)

continued

Make the rice pudding: In a saucepan, combine the milk, sugar, salt, and rice. Bring to a boil over medium-high heat. Cook at a vigorous simmer, stirring occasionally, until the rice is tender but not breaking apart and the pudding is still a little soupy but thicker than cream, about 15 minutes. Stir in the chopped chocolate and butter until well combined; the mixture will thicken. Mix in the raisins, if desired. Divide among the eight glasses you're using and chill until needed.

Meanwhile, make the Cream Cheese Mousse. Spoon equal amounts of the mousse over the pudding in the glasses. Chill until needed, at least 30 minutes.

Make the caramelized Rice Krispies: In a 3-quart or larger pot, bring the superfine sugar and 2 tablespoons water to a boil over medium-high heat. Boil for 1 minute. Sprinkle the Rice Krispies over the syrup, stirring gently to coat (the mixture will clump). Keep stirring gently over medium high (the rice will separate) until the rice is golden brown (the pan may smoke a bit), 4 to 5 minutes. Remove from the heat and immediately dump the caramelized Rice Krispies onto a baking sheet to cool. When ready to

continued

For the caramelized Rice Krispies

¼ cup superfine sugar

2 cups Rice Krispies

For the gianduia whipped cream

1 cup heavy cream

3 ounces gianduia chocolate (or good-quality bittersweet chocolate), chopped

use, break up clumps with your hands. (The Rice Krispies will keep for up to a month in an airtight container.)

Make the gianduia whipped cream: In a saucepan, bring the cream to a boil. Add the chopped chocolate and whisk vigorously until melted. Transfer to a stainless-steel bowl. Refrigerate, covered, until the cream is well chilled, about 3 hours. Whisk the cream until it forms soft peaks. Chill until needed.

Assemble the parfaits: Remove the glasses with the pudding and mousse from the refrigerator. Sprinkle on a generous layer of caramelized Rice Krispies and then a spoonful of the gianduia whipped cream. Finish with another sprinkling of Rice Krispies. Serve right away.

GELATIN NEEDS A TWO-STEP METHOD

Working with gelatin isn't difficult, but few modern recipes use it, so many cooks are unfamiliar with it. The most common form is powdered gelatin, which comes in small packets. Before it is added to a recipe, the gelatin must first be softened (called "blooming") and then melted. Follow these tips when working with gelatin.

- For every 2 teaspoons powdered gelatin, use about ¼ cup liquid for blooming.

- One ¼-ounce packet of Knox® brand powdered gelatin contains about 2¼ teaspoons.

- Always add softened gelatin to warm or hot mixtures; adding the gelatin to a cold mixture will make it firm up immediately, creating a stringy or lumpy texture.

- Another form, called sheet gelatin, is preferred by some pros. Two sheets equal 1 teaspoon Knox brand powder (other powder brands may differ in their gelling power). Soften sheet gelatin by soaking it in cold water for about 10 minutes. Squeeze to drain excess liquid before melting in the liquid ingredients in the recipe.

cream cheese mousse

This mousse, which can also be deliciously layered with strawberry compote or orange marmalade, can be made up to two days ahead of serving the parfaits. Have your parfait glasses filled with the pudding before you begin.

1⅓ cups heavy cream

⅓ cup granulated sugar

3 large egg yolks

1½ teaspoons powdered gelatin

One 8-ounce package cream cheese

3 tablespoons confectioners' sugar

In a bowl, beat the cream until it forms soft peaks; cover with plastic wrap and refrigerate.

In a very small saucepan, combine the sugar and 2 tablespoons of cold water and boil to 248°F on a candy thermometer (you may need to tip the pan to get an accurate reading). Meanwhile, in a small bowl, beat the egg yolks with an electric mixer (a hand-held works best) until blended. (If you're concerned about uncooked egg yolks, you can use in-shell pasteurized eggs, found in the fresh egg section.) When the syrup reaches 248°F, turn the mixer on high speed and pour the sugar syrup into the mixing yolks, avoiding the beaters and the sides of the bowl. Beat on medium speed until the mixture cools and becomes pale and ribbony, about 4 minutes; set aside.

In a small bowl, sprinkle the gelatin over 2 tablespoons of cold water and let it soften and swell, about 2 minutes. Meanwhile, warm the cream cheese until soft in a bowl set over a pan of simmering water or in a skillet of hot water, being careful not to overheat it. Whisk until it's smooth. Add the confectioners' sugar and the softened gelatin, whisking until smooth and completely blended. Remove the bowl from the heat and let the mixture cool to room temperature, 10 to 15 minutes; it will thicken slightly. Fold the egg yolk mixture into the cream cheese, and then gently fold in the whipped cream.

Fried chocolate-hazelnut wontons with orange dipping sauce

These whimsical dumplings make use of ready-made ingredients, yet they feel restaurant-special. Nutella® spread gives a lusciousness to the filling, and the wonton wrappers make the pastries crisp and delicate. Look for wonton wrappers in the produce section of the supermarket.

24 wonton wrappers, preferably square

One 13-ounce jar Nutella (or other chocolate-hazelnut spread), chilled

¾ cup heavy cream

½ cup thawed orange juice concentrate

2 teaspoons Grand Marnier

¼ teaspoon pure vanilla extract

3 cups vegetable oil for frying

Confectioners' sugar, for serving

Set out a bowl of water and a pastry brush. If necessary, trim the wonton wrappers into squares. Lay the wrappers on a work surface, orienting them so they look diamond shaped instead of square. Working quickly, put 1 heaping teaspoon of chilled Nutella in the lower half of each diamond. Brush the edges of one wonton with a little water and fold the top point of the diamond down to meet the bottom, forming a triangle. Gently press around the filling to force out any air and pinch the edges to seal. Repeat with the remaining wontons. Set the wontons on a baking sheet, cover, and keep chilled.

In a small bowl, combine the heavy cream with the orange juice concentrate, Grand Marnier, and vanilla. Refrigerate the sauce until ready to serve.

Heat the oil to 365°F in a heavy-based 3-quart saucepan over medium heat. Set a baking sheet lined with a thick layer of paper towels next to the pot. Slip 6 to 8 wontons into the oil and fry, turning occasionally, until golden brown, 2 to 3 minutes. Scoop them out with a slotted spoon and drain on the paper towels while you fry the rest.

Arrange 4 wontons on individual serving plates and sprinkle with confectioners' sugar. Serve with small individual dishes of orange sauce for dipping.

Chocolate-filled beignets

Yields 50 to 60 beignets, with a bit of dough leftover

These golden pastries have a demure exterior, with a rich surprise inside. A marked contrast between the light, crisp dough and the rich, creamy chocolate is key to the appeal of these pastries. The better the chocolate, the better the beignet.

For the dough

⅔ cup whole milk

1 package (2¼ teaspoons) active dry yeast

18 ounces (4 cups) unbleached all-purpose flour

3 tablespoons granulated sugar

1½ teaspoons table salt

6 large eggs, lightly beaten

3 ounces (6 tablespoons) unsalted butter, melted and cooled slightly

Vegetable oil for frying

Confectioners' sugar, for dusting

For the ganache centers

14 ounces good-quality bittersweet chocolate, finely chopped

1 cup heavy cream

2 ounces (4 tablespoons) unsalted butter, very soft but not melted or greasy

Crème anglaise, for serving (optional)

Make the dough: Warm the milk in a small pan and add the yeast. Stir gently until dissolved. Put the flour, sugar, and salt in the bowl of a stand mixer fitted with the paddle attachment and blend the dry ingredients briefly.

Set the mixer on low speed and slowly pour in the milk mixture, mixing until the dry ingredients are moistened. Slowly dribble in the eggs, mixing for a few seconds between additions. Stop the mixer and scrape the sides and bottom to get any flour missed by the paddle. Start mixing again and slowly pour in the melted butter.

Increase the speed to medium and mix until the butter is incorporated and the dough becomes smooth and elastic and pulls away from the sides and bottom of the bowl, about 8 minutes. Test the dough by greasing your hands, picking up the dough, and stretching it gently—it should extend easily without tearing.

Put the finished dough in a buttered bowl, cover with plastic wrap, and refrigerate for at least 3 hours and up to 24 hours. Check the dough once in a while—if it's rising, gently push it down.

Make the ganache centers: Put the chopped chocolate in a large bowl. In a small saucepan, bring the cream to a boil. Pour the boiling cream over the chocolate, let it sit for 30 seconds to start melting, and then whisk until the chocolate is melted and smooth.

continued

You can shape and wrap the uncooked beignets and freeze them for up to 2 days on a baking sheet covered with plastic. (Don't let them touch one another or the dough wrapping may stick and rip later.) Take them from the freezer no more than 30 minutes before cooking; you want the dough to thaw but not get too soft or start rising. Fry them according to the directions in the recipe.

Let the ganache cool to room temperature, about 30 minutes, but be sure it stays liquid.

Make sure your butter is really soft and creamy (but not at all melted) and then whisk or beat it into the room-temperature ganache, a little at a time, until completely blended.

The ganache should be shiny, showing that it's emulsified. If it's grainy, mix with a hand blender or whisk to re-emulsify. Chill, stirring often, until set up but not hard, about 40 minutes. It should have the consistency of buttercream frosting.

Line a baking sheet with parchment or waxed paper. Fit a pastry bag with a large plain tip and fill the bag with the ganache. Pipe out 50 to 60 blobs about the size of malted milk balls. Smooth off any points. Freeze the centers until they're quite firm, at least an hour (up to 2 days if wrapped).

Make the beignets: Arrange your work station so you have the chilled beignet dough, the tray of ganache centers, a little flour for dipping your hands, and a lightly floured baking sheet to hold the wrapped beignets. Fill a large pot about one-third full with fresh oil and let it heat up as you shape the beignets. Have a deep-frying thermometer ready.

Dip your hands in the flour and pull off a small piece of dough about the size of a prune. Flatten the dough slightly between your fingers and then wrap it around the chocolate center. Try to make the wrapping as thin as possible, but avoid patches that are so thin you can see the center through them.

Pinch off the excess dough and massage the beignet with your fingertips to be sure all holes are closed and the seams are tight. Roll the beignet between your hands to smooth. Set the beignet on the floured baking sheet. Continue until all the centers are wrapped. If the dough starts to soften or rise too much while you're working, put everything in the freezer for a few minutes to chill.

When the oil registers 350°F on the thermometer, start frying, adding just a few beignets at a time. The beignets will float, so gently press them down with a spoon or a wire skimmer so they brown evenly.

Fry until deep golden brown, about 4 minutes, and drain on paper towels. Serve hot, dusted with confectioners' sugar, with a pitcher of Cocoa Crème Anglaise (page 285) on the side, if you like.

SHAPING BEIGNETS

Carefully shaping your beignets is key to achieving the ideal—a center of rich melted chocolate encased in a light and tender, evenly fried dough.

1. Flatten a small chunk of dough with your fingers, then wrap a chilled chocolate center, without stretching the dough too much.

2. Pinch off the excess dough, leaving an even layer; pinch and press a bit more to seal all the seams and holes.

3. Give your beignet a prettier shape by rolling it between your palms to create a smooth, even ball.

Chocolate terrine with whipped cream & almond brittle

Serves 12, with about 1¼ pounds of almond brittle

This luxurious dessert is like a big slice of satiny truffle filling, topped with crunchy brittle for contrast. It's easy to make but needs thorough chilling, so plan ahead.

For the terrine

8 ounces good-quality semisweet chocolate, coarsely chopped

6 ounces (12 tablespoons) unsalted butter, cut into 12 pieces; more for the pan

¾ cup granulated sugar

½ cup brewed coffee (fresh or leftover)

4 large eggs, beaten

For the almond brittle

2½ cups granulated sugar

2 tablespoons unsalted butter

5 ounces (1 cup) whole almonds, toasted, cooled, and coarsely chopped

1 cup heavy cream

Position an oven rack in the lower middle of the oven and heat the oven to 350°F. Grease an 8x5-inch loaf pan and line with heavy-duty foil, making sure not to puncture it.

Make the terrine: Fill a medium saucepan halfway with water and bring the water to a simmer. Put the chocolate and butter in a stainless-steel bowl large enough to fit over the pan without dipping into the water. Set the bowl over the simmering water, stirring the chocolate and butter with a whisk until melted and blended. Add the sugar and coffee, stirring slowly to dissolve the sugar. Continue cooking until the mixture is hot to the touch and the sugar is dissolved. Remove the bowl from the heat and whisk in the beaten eggs. Pour the chocolate mixture into the lined loaf pan.

Set a large baking dish on the oven rack. Set the loaf pan in the center of the baking dish and surround it with 1 inch of very hot water. Bake until the chocolate has begun to lose its shine, doesn't shimmy when jostled, and just begins to puff slightly around the edges, 40 to 50 minutes. Remove the terrine from the oven and set it on a wire rack to cool to room temperature. Cover with plastic wrap and chill in the refrigerator for at least 4 hours or overnight.

Meanwhile, make the almond brittle: Grease a rimmed baking sheet with oil or cover with a nonstick liner (not parchment). Put the sugar in a medium saucepan without catching any crystals on the sides of the pan. Add ³/₄ cup water, pouring it around the

continued

sides to rinse down any sugar that might be there. Let the mixture sit for 1 minute (don't stir) so that the water infiltrates the sugar. Over high heat, boil the mixture without stirring until it turns very light amber, about 10 minutes. (Test the color of the caramel by dripping a bit from a spoon onto a white plate.) Remove from the heat and stir in the butter with a wooden spoon just until melted and evenly blended. Stir in the nuts and then immediately pour the mixture across the prepared baking sheet. Let cool. Break the brittle into manageable pieces and then chop half of it for the terrine (save the rest for snacking). The brittle can be stored in an airtight container for up to a week.

Assemble the dessert: Lift the terrine out of the loaf pan, using the foil as a sling. Turn it over onto a platter or cutting board and peel off the foil. Using a knife that has been dipped in hot water and wiped dry, cut the terrine into $\frac{1}{2}$-inch slices. (For perfectly neat slices, trim off the ends of the loaf first.)

In a chilled, medium stainless-steel bowl, beat the heavy cream with a whisk or an electric mixer at medium-high speed until it holds soft peaks when the beaters are lifted. Serve each slice of the terrine with a dollop of the whipped cream and a tablespoon-size sprinkling of the chopped almond brittle.

Hazelnut & chocolate baklava
with espresso-frangelico syrup

Yields about
30 pieces

If you've only ever tasted baklava from a Greek diner, you owe it to yourself to make this buttery, fragrant, and thoroughly divine pastry at home. One batch makes a lot, so it's great for entertaining a crowd.

1 pound "twin pack" phyllo dough (two 8-ounce packs, each containing about twenty 9x14-inch sheets)

10 ounces (1¼ cups) unsalted butter

For the filling

1 pound raw shelled hazelnuts

6 ounces coarsely chopped semisweet or bittersweet chocolate

¼ cup granulated sugar

2 teaspoons ground cinnamon

For the syrup

1½ cups granulated sugar

2 teaspoons instant espresso powder

2 tablespoons Frangelico®

Thaw the phyllo overnight in the refrigerator. Put the phyllo box on the counter to come to room temperature, 1½ to 2 hours.

Make the filling and bake the baklava: Melt the butter and let cool slightly. Put the hazelnuts, chocolate, sugar, and cinnamon in a food processor. Process until the nuts and chocolate are finely chopped (the largest should be the size of small dried lentils), 15 to 30 seconds. Set aside.

Unfold one pack of the phyllo sheets and stack them so that they lie flat on your work surface. Cover the top with plastic wrap, letting some excess plastic fall over all four edges. Dampen and wring out a kitchen towel and drape it on top of the plastic wrap; this will hold the plastic in place and prevent the phyllo from drying out.

Melt the butter in a small saucepan. Brush the bottom of a 9x13-inch metal pan (preferably with straight sides and a light-color interior to prevent overbrowning on the edges) with some of the butter. Remove a sheet of phyllo from the stack, re-cover the rest (be sure to cover the remaining sheets each time you remove a new one), and put the sheet in the bottom of the pan. Brush the sheet with some of the melted butter but don't soak the phyllo (remember, you'll have about 40 layers of buttered phyllo by the time you're done). Repeat until you have layered and buttered about half the sheets from the first pack—about 10 sheets in all. If your pan has slightly angled sides, arrange the sheets so the excess

continued

falls on the same side of the pan and cut off the extra every few layers with a paring knife. Sprinkle about one-third of the filling evenly over the phyllo.

Repeat layering and buttering the remaining sheets from the first pack and sprinkle on another third of the filling. Open, unfold, and cover the second pack of phyllo. Layer and butter it as described previously, sprinkling the remaining filling after layering about half the phyllo, and ending with a final layer of phyllo (you may not need all of the butter). Cover loosely and put the pan of baklava in the freezer for 30 minutes (this makes it much easier to cut the pastry).

Position an oven rack in the center of the oven and heat the oven to 350°F. Use a thin, sharp knife (serrated works well) and a gentle sawing motion to cut the baklava on the diagonal at $1\frac{1}{2}$-inch intervals in a diamond pattern. Try not to compress the pastry by pressing down on it with one hand while cutting with the other. Not only are you cutting serving portions, you are also cutting pathways for the flavored syrup to permeate the pastry, so be sure to cut the pastry all the way to the bottom of the pan. Bake the baklava until golden, 40 to 45 minutes. Transfer to a rack and let cool completely. Run a knife along the cut lines to help the syrup absorb evenly.

Make the syrup: Put the sugar, espresso powder, and $\frac{2}{3}$ cup of water in a small saucepan and bring to a simmer over medium heat, stirring occasionally, until the sugar is dissolved, about 5 minutes. Remove the pan from the heat and stir in the Frangelico. Pour the syrup evenly over the entire surface of the baklava, allowing it to run down into the cut marks and along the sides of the pan. Allow the baklava to cool to room temperature before serving.

MAKE AHEAD The baklava is at its best about 24 hours after the syrup is added. It will keep at room temperature for up to 5 days, though the texture changes from flaky and crisp to more solid and crystallized as time goes by. Both textures are delicious and have their fans.

MAKING PERFECTLY FLAKY BAKLAVA LAYERS

Working with phyllo dough isn't difficult—it just takes a little patience.

1. Brush each layer of phyllo evenly with melted butter, but no drenching—you'll have plenty of butter by the time all 40 layers are brushed. And avoid the watery part of the butter at the bottom of your pan; use just the golden fat.

2. Cut through all the layers of phyllo, creating as even a pattern as you can; a serrated knife works well. This step creates your portion sizes and also pathways for the syrup to soak into the pastry.

3. Bake the pastry until it's thoroughly browned and crisp, then let it cool. Now it's ready to soak up the syrup and still keep its texture without getting too soggy.

Bittersweet chocolate-glazed éclairs

Yields about
12 éclairs

What a fun and delicious surprise for dinner guests—a delicate, cream-filled éclair, topped with shiny dark chocolate glaze. You rarely get this kind of treat outside of a pastry shop, which is why it's a brilliant finale to a special party. Most of the components of this French classic—the shells, vanilla pastry cream filling, and chocolate glaze—can be made well in advance. For the final assembly, all you need to do is lighten the pastry cream with whipped cream, spoon the mixture into the pastry shells, and glaze with chocolate.

1 cup heavy cream, well chilled

1 tablespoon confectioners' sugar

1 teaspoon pure vanilla extract

1 recipe Vanilla Pastry Cream (page 200)

1 recipe Éclair Pastry Shells (page 201)

1 recipe Bittersweet Ganache Glaze (page 203)

Combine the cream, confectioners' sugar, and vanilla in a chilled mixing bowl and whisk by hand or with an electric mixer fitted with the whisk attachment until the cream becomes fluffy and forms a soft peak that folds over when you lift the whisk. Be careful not to overwhip the cream or you risk it curdling when you fold it into the custard.

Whisk the Vanilla Pastry Cream until smooth, and then gently whisk in about one-third of the whipped cream to lighten the pastry cream. Scrape the rest of the whipped cream over the mixture and, using the whisk in a folding action, gently blend the two until the mixture is uniform and smooth.

Cut an éclair shell in half lengthwise with a serrated knife. Use your fingers to pinch out the doughy insides of both halves. Use two soupspoons—one to scoop and the other to push the cream off the spoon—to mound the filling into the entire length of the bottom half of the shell, about 2 to 3 tablespoons of filling per shell. Gently place the top half of the éclair shell on the custard and put the assembled éclair on a wire rack set over a rimmed baking sheet. Repeat with the remaining shells.

continued

When all the éclairs are assembled, warm the Bittersweet Ganache Glaze a little just until it's loose enough to flow off the side of a spoon in a wide, thick ribbon. (If the ganache is too hot, it will run off the éclairs and puddle below on the tray.) Spoon the ganache along the entire length of each éclair top. Put the sheet of glazed éclairs in the refrigerator and chill for at least 30 minutes or up to 3 hours before serving.

vanilla pastry cream

Yields about
3 cups

Vanilla pastry cream is the classic filling for chocolate éclairs. The cream needs to chill for at least 1 hour before use and may be made ahead and refrigerated for up to a day.

1 cup whole milk

3 large egg yolks

¼ cup granulated sugar

2 tablespoons cornstarch

⅛ teaspoon table salt

½ teaspoon pure
   vanilla extract

Warm the milk in a medium saucepan over medium heat until tiny bubbles appear. Meanwhile, in a medium heatproof bowl, whisk the egg yolks and sugar until pale yellow. Add the cornstarch and salt and whisk well. Pour the hot milk into the yolk mixture, ½ cup at a time, whisking constantly. Return the mixture to the saucepan and cook over medium heat, whisking constantly, until it thickens to the consistency of thick pudding, about 2 minutes. (It will look lumpy as it starts to thicken but will smooth out as you continue to whisk.)

Remove from the heat and scrape the pastry cream into a large, clean metal bowl. Whisk in the vanilla and then lay a sheet of plastic wrap directly on the surface. Refrigerate until thoroughly chilled, about 1 hour.

éclair pastry shells

Yields 12 to 13
éclair shells

If you have a bit of this ganache left over after icing the fudge cake
or snack cake, use it as a sauce for ice cream or another dessert.
It keeps for a week in the refrigerator. Rewarm gently.

2 ounces (¼ cup) unsalted
butter

½ teaspoon table salt

4½ ounces (1 cup)
unbleached all-purpose
flour

3 large eggs

Position a rack in the middle of the oven and heat the oven to
400°F. Cut a sheet of parchment to fit in a heavy-duty 13x18-inch
rimmed baking sheet. Using a pencil, draw three sets of two lines
spaced 3 inches apart, running the length of the parchment. These
will be guidelines for piping the éclair dough. Line the baking sheet
with the parchment, penciled side down—you should be able to
see the lines through the parchment. If not, draw them darker.

In a medium saucepan, bring the butter, salt, and 1 cup of water
to a boil over medium-high heat. Reduce the heat to medium and
add the flour. Using a wooden spoon, stir vigorously to combine.
Continue to stir, using a figure-eight motion and smearing the
dough against the sides of the pan to cook the flour and work out
any lumps, for 2 minutes. The mixture will be thick and look like
a firm ball, or balls, of sticky mashed potatoes that pull away from
the pan sides. During this process, it's normal for a thin layer of
dough to stick to the bottom of the pan and sizzle.

Remove the pan from the heat and scrape the dough into the
bowl of a stand mixer fitted with the paddle attachment. On
low speed, mix until the dough feels merely warm to the touch,
not hot, 3 to 5 minutes.

With the mixer still on low, beat in the eggs one at a time. After
each egg is added, the dough will separate into small "curds" and
then come back together. After the dough pulls back together,
briefly (about 20 seconds) increase the speed to medium low to

continued

mix the dough well. Reduce the speed to low before adding the next egg. After the addition of the last egg, scrape the bowl well and beat on medium low for a final 30 seconds.

Scrape the dough into a pastry bag fitted with a large star tip. Twist the top of the bag to push the dough toward the tip. Hold the bag at a 60-degree angle and set the tip of the pastry tube on the paper, right at the top of one of the 3-inch-wide stripes you

BAKING PASTRY-SHOP PERFECT ÉCLAIRS

Making the pastry dough itself is simple, but giving your éclairs that special finesse takes a bit of precision.

1. **Don't try to eyeball the size of the éclair shells as you pipe—drawing 3-inch bands will ensure consistency. Use a large star tip to create a pretty pattern on the surface; the ridges also help the shells rise evenly. Pipe in a tight, even zigzag.**

2. **Cut the cooled shells completely in half in order to fill them with a good dollop of cream; you don't want any empty spots in your éclair.**

3. **To decorate your éclairs with a wide stripe of glossy glaze, be sure the chocolate is the perfect temperature—warm enough to flow from a spoon, but not so warm that it's runny.**

drew earlier. Squeeze the pastry bag and, using the lines on the parchment as a guide, pipe out 3-inch lengths of dough in a tight zigzag pattern, spacing the éclairs about 1 inch apart.

Bake until the shells are puffed, crisp, and thoroughly golden brown, 45 to 50 minutes. If you find that they're baking unevenly, rotate the pan. Remove from the oven, transfer to a rack, and let cool completely, about 15 minutes, before filling or storing.

bittersweet ganache glaze

Yields about ¾ cup

This simple ganache makes a shiny glaze for chocolate éclairs. The corn syrup is optional for this recipe but it helps keep the chocolate glossy when refrigerated.

½ cup heavy cream

4 ounces bittersweet chocolate, chopped (preferably 55% to 63% bittersweet chocolate)

1 teaspoon light corn syrup

Stovetop instructions: In a small saucepan, warm the cream over medium heat until it begins to simmer around the edges of the pan. Remove from the heat and add the chopped chocolate pieces and the corn syrup. Let stand for 5 to 7 minutes and then stir until smooth.

Microwave instructions: In a Pyrex cup, combine the chocolate, cream, and corn syrup. Microwave at 50% power for 30 seconds. Stir to combine. If just a few unmelted chunks of chocolate remain, let the heat of the mixture melt the remaining few chunks. If more than a few chunks remain, microwave at 50% power for another 30 seconds.

Chocolate roulade
with raspberry filling

Yields 1 roulade;

serves 12

When you need a showstopper holiday dessert, few can top this stunning roulade. Though similar in spirit to a bûche de Noël, or yule log, it's more sleek, elegant, and delicious, with its bright fruit filling. To keep your holiday a little saner, make the cake a day ahead of serving, so all you need to do the day of your party is glaze the cake and whip the cream.

For the chocolate sponge cake

3 ounces bittersweet
    chocolate, chopped

Softened butter for the pan

Flour for the pan

9 large eggs, separated

1 cup granulated sugar

1⅛ ounces (6 tablespoons)
    Dutch-processed cocoa
    powder, sifted; more for
    dusting

⅛ teaspoon table salt

continued

Make the cake: Position a rack in the middle of the oven and heat the oven to 350°F. In a double boiler, melt the chocolate with 2 tablespoons warm water. Let cool to room temperature.

Grease the bottom of an 18x13-inch rimmed baking sheet (a standard half sheet pan) with the softened butter. Line the pan with parchment; butter and then flour the parchment.

With an electric mixer, whip the egg yolks in a large bowl on medium-high speed until light in color and beginning to thicken, 2 to 3 minutes in a stand mixer or 3 to 5 minutes with a hand mixer. Add ½ cup of the sugar and whip until very thick and pale yellow, about 2 minutes. Reduce the speed to low and mix in the melted chocolate. With a rubber spatula, stir in the cocoa and salt until blended.

In a clean, dry bowl with clean, dry beaters (any grease will keep the whites from whipping), whip the egg whites with an electric mixer at medium speed until they're frothy and begin to increase in volume, about 30 seconds. In a steady stream, add the remaining ½ cup sugar. Increase the speed to medium high and whip until soft peaks form, 2 to 3 minutes in a stand mixer or 4 to 6 minutes with a hand mixer.

continued

For the raspberry filling and sauce

12-ounce package frozen raspberries, thawed

2 large egg whites

½ cup plus 2 tablespoons granulated sugar; more to taste

Table salt

5 ounces (10 tablespoons) unsalted butter, completely softened at room temperature

2 teaspoons raspberry liqueur, such as Chambord®

½ teaspoon fresh lemon juice; more to taste

For the chocolate glaze

3 tablespoons heavy cream

¾ cup granulated sugar

1½ ounces (½ cup) Dutch-processed cocoa powder

1½ teaspoons unflavored powdered gelatin

For serving

¾ cup heavy cream

2 teaspoons granulated sugar

½ teaspoon pure vanilla extract

With a rubber spatula, fold the whites into the chocolate mixture in two equal additions. You can fold in the first half vigorously to lighten the yolks, but fold in the second half gently, mixing just until the batter is evenly colored with no streaks of white. Don't overmix. Scrape the batter into the baking pan, gently spreading and smoothing it to make sure it's level. Bake until the top springs back lightly when touched, 22 to 25 minutes.

Meanwhile, spread a clean dishtowel (at least as big as the cake pan) on the counter. Using a sieve, dust the towel with cocoa powder, completely covering it (this will keep the cake from sticking to the towel as it cools).

Immediately after taking the cake from the oven, run a small knife around the inside edge to loosen it from the pan. Invert the cake pan onto the towel in one quick motion. Remove the pan. Carefully peel off the parchment. Using both hands and starting from one of the short ends, roll up the cake and the towel together. Let cool to room temperature.

Make the filling and sauce: Put the thawed raspberries in a food processor and process until completely puréed. Pass the purée through a fine sieve to strain out the seeds. You should have about 1 cup of purée.

Fill a wide pot or straight-sided skillet with 1 to 2 inches of very hot water. In the bowl of an electric mixer, whisk the egg whites, ½ cup of the sugar, and a generous pinch of salt until blended. Set the bowl in the pot of hot water; make sure the water comes up to at least the level of the mixture in the bowl. Whisk until the mixture is almost hot (about 120°F), about 90 seconds. Take the bowl out of the water. With an electric mixer on medium-high speed, whip the whites until cool and thick, 2 to 3 minutes. Reduce to medium speed, add the butter, 1 tablespoon at a time, and mix until the butter is completely incorporated. The filling should be soft and loose; it will firm up as it chills. (If it seems very runny, refrigerate it for up to 20 minutes.) With the mixer on low speed, blend in 2 tablespoons of the raspberry purée and the liqueur. Set the filling aside.

Make the sauce by stirring together the remaining raspberry purée, the remaining 2 tablespoons sugar, the lemon juice, and a pinch of salt. Add more sugar or lemon juice to taste.

continued

PUTTING THE "ROLL" IN ROULADE

The cake for a roulade needs to be flat and flexible, which is why you take this extra step.

1. Invert the baked cake onto a cocoa-dusted clean dishtowel (no fabric softener, please!) and peel away the parchment. The paper may pull off a thin layer of cake, but that's okay.

2. Gently but firmly roll the towel and cake together into a spiral. Letting the cake cool like this will help it hold the spiral shape once you fill it. If you tried to roll the cake after cooling it flat, it would simply crack too much.

3. Carefully unroll the cake, remove the towel, and spread with filling, then roll the cake a final time. Try to roll evenly so that your cake slices look pretty. Don't worry if the ends are messy—you'll trim those off anyway.

Carefully unroll the cooled, towel-wrapped cake. Spread the filling over the cake, covering it evenly to within 2 inches of the edges. Reroll the cake, without the towel this time. The filling may squish out of the ends a bit; this is fine. Line a rimmed baking sheet with foil and set a wire rack on the foil. Slide two large metal spatulas (or a spatula and your hand) under the roulade and transfer it to the rack. (Or, if working ahead, transfer it to a large sheet of plastic, wrap it snugly, and refrigerate for up to a day.)

Make the glaze: In a large saucepan, combine the cream, sugar, $\frac{1}{2}$ cup of water, and the cocoa. Bring the mixture to a boil and then reduce the heat to a simmer, whisking often, until very thick, like hot fudge sauce, 8 to 10 minutes from when the mixture began simmering. Pay close attention: This mixture boils over easily. Remove the pan from the heat. While the mixture is cooling, sprinkle the gelatin over $1\frac{1}{2}$ tablespoons of water and let sit to soften. Melt the softened gelatin over very hot water or in the microwave. Whisk the gelatin into the chocolate mixture and strain the glaze through a medium sieve into a metal bowl. Let the glaze cool at room temperature until thick but still pourable, about 5 to 10 minutes; the glaze should be about 110°F to 120°F. (If you've made the cake ahead, unwrap it and put it on a rack set over a foil-lined baking sheet.)

Glaze and serve the roulade: Pour the glaze over the roulade, using an offset spatula to help the glaze cover the top and sides evenly. Don't worry about covering the ends; they'll be trimmed later. Refrigerate uncovered for at least 30 minutes or up to 4 hours.

With a whisk or hand mixer, whip together the cream, sugar, and vanilla until soft peaks form.

The glaze will have "glued" the roulade to the rack, so slide a metal spatula between it and the rack to release it. Transfer the roulade to a cutting board, using two large offset spatulas to get underneath and pressing the spatulas against the rack as you go. Trim the ends of the roulade. Fill a tall container with hot water and have a dishtowel handy so that you can clean and dry the knife after cutting each slice. Using a long, sharp knife, cut ¾-inch straight slices, or cut pieces on an angle, rinsing and drying the knife after each slice. Arrange each slice on a dessert plate, then garnish with a small pool of raspberry sauce and a dollop of whipped cream.

MAKE AHEAD You can make the cake and filling and assemble the roulade (without the glaze) a day ahead. Wrap the unglazed, filled roulade with plastic, refrigerate it, and glaze it the next day. You can prepare the garnishes ahead, too, but whip the cream close to serving time.

Walnut, chocolate & rum-raisin crêpes with whipped-cream chocolate sauce

Yields about 20 crêpes, with filling for 18, and 2 cups of sauce

These crêpes, known as *gundel paliscinta*, are deep, dark, and delicious, and the sauce is both unusual and outstanding—the whipped cream folded in at the end gives it an amazing texture. In many Hungarian restaurants, these crêpes are flamed with Grand Marnier when presented—a dramatic touch but not necessary.

For the crêpes

2 large eggs

½ cup cold whole milk

½ cup cold sparkling water; more as needed

½ teaspoon table salt

6¾ ounces (1½ cups) unbleached all-purpose flour

Melted butter for frying the crêpes

For the filling

½ cup dark rum

½ cup golden raisins

½ cup heavy cream

½ cup granulated sugar

1¼ cups walnut halves, coarsely chopped

2 tablespoons chopped candied orange peel or ½ teaspoon grated orange zest

¼ teaspoon ground cinnamon

continued

Make the crêpes: Whisk the eggs with the cold milk, sparkling water, and salt. Whisking steadily, sift the flour over the egg mixture in a gradual but steady "rain" to make a smooth batter. Let sit for 20 minutes and then add more sparkling water if necessary to get the consistency of heavy cream.

Heat a 6- to 8-inch crêpe or omelet pan (nonstick is fine but not necessary). Brush with melted butter. Tilting and turning the pan with one hand, pour in enough batter to cover the pan's surface, about 3 tablespoons. Cook until golden on the underside, 1 to 2 minutes (don't undercook); flip or turn the crêpe with a small spatula or your fingers to cook the other side until just set, about 30 seconds more.

Adjust the heat so you get a definite sizzle when adding the batter, and thin the batter if the crêpes are too thick and flabby. Stack the finished crêpes on a plate as you go. Cover with plastic and refrigerate until using, up to 3 days ahead. You can also wrap the crêpes tightly and freeze them (put a piece of waxed paper between each one for easier separation).

Make the filling: Heat the rum and soak the raisins in it while assembling the other ingredients. In a small saucepan, bring the cream and sugar to a boil, stirring, and add the walnuts, orange peel (or zest), cinnamon, cocoa powder, and salt. Bring to a boil, stirring, and cook until the liquid has reduced almost completely but the nuts are still well coated and glossy, about 3 minutes. Stir

1 tablespoon cocoa powder

Pinch table salt

3 ounces bittersweet chocolate, chopped into ⅛-inch pieces

For the chocolate sauce

¼ cup cocoa powder

⅓ cup granulated sugar

2 teaspoons unbleached all-purpose flour

Pinch table salt

1 cup whole milk

3 ounces semisweet chocolate, finely chopped

½ cup heavy cream

in the raisins and rum and cool, then stir in the chocolate. You can make this filling a day or two ahead; keep refrigerated.

Make the chocolate sauce: In a medium saucepan, combine the cocoa powder, sugar, flour, and salt. Slowly whisk in the milk to make a smooth paste. Bring to a boil and cook for 30 seconds to cook off the floury taste, and then remove from the heat and add the chopped chocolate. Stir until smooth, cover loosely with plastic, and cool to room temperature, stirring occasionally to help it cool and prevent a skin from forming. Just before serving, whip the cream until it just forms soft peaks. Stir about one-quarter of the whipped cream into the chocolate, and then carefully fold the rest of the whipped cream into the sauce until well blended.

Assemble the crêpes: Spread about 2 tablespoons of the filling on the underside of a crêpe (reheat the filling slightly if it's cold from the refrigerator). Fold the crêpe in half, and then in half again to make a quarter circle. Repeat with the remaining crêpes, dividing the filling evenly.

In a large frying pan, heat 2 tablespoons of butter over medium heat until sizzling. Add the filled crêpes to the pan without crowding them (do this in batches if you need to). Cook the crêpes until warmed through and browned on each side, about 1 minute per side. Add more butter if necessary to the pan during cooking.

Arrange 3 crêpes on each plate and drizzle a generous ribbon of chocolate sauce on top, passing more sauce at the table. Serve immediately.

MAKE AHEAD You can fill and fold the crêpes a few hours ahead of serving and just keep them covered at room temperature.

ice creams

& frozen desserts

Ice cream sandwiches

Yields 12 ice cream sandwiches, each 2¾ inches square

Why should kids have all the fun? Here's a recipe for ice cream sandwiches that are sophisticated enough for grown-ups but still a treat for the whole family. Part of the fun is designing your own sandwich combinations by choosing the ice cream (store-bought), adding flavor to the chocolate cookie, and picking your favorite garnish. The sandwiches are perfect for picnics. Wrapped individually and stowed in a portable cooler with some ice packs, they'll stay good and firm up until serving time, even on the hottest summer day.

For the soft chocolate cookie

5⅔ ounces (1¼ cups) unbleached all-purpose flour

1½ ounces (½ cup) unsweetened, natural cocoa powder

½ teaspoon baking soda

¼ teaspoon table salt

3 ounces (6 tablespoons) unsalted butter, softened at room temperature

¾ cup granulated sugar

1½ teaspoons pure vanilla extract

⅔ cup cold whole milk

For assembly

1 quart or 2 pints ice cream

1½ cups press-on garnish

Make the cookie: Position a rack on the center rung of the oven. Heat the oven to 350°F. Lightly grease the bottom of an 18x13-inch rimmed baking sheet. Line the pan with parchment to cover the bottom and the edges of the pan's longer sides. Combine the flour, cocoa, baking soda, and salt in a medium bowl; whisk to blend. In a large bowl, beat the butter and sugar with a hand-held electric mixer on medium high until well blended and lightened in color, about 3 minutes. Beat in the vanilla. Add about a third of the flour mixture and beat on medium low until just blended. Pour in half of the milk and beat until just blended. Add another third of the flour and blend. Pour in the remaining milk and blend, and then beat in the remaining flour.

Distribute the dough evenly over the prepared pan in small dollops. Using one hand to anchor the parchment, spread the dough with a spoon or spatula. Drag a rectangular offset spatula over the dough to smooth it into an even layer, rotating the pan as you work. Brush or spray a sheet of parchment the same size as the pan with oil, and lay it, oiled side down, on the dough. Roll a straight rolling pin or a straight-sided wine bottle over the paper (or swipe it with a dough scraper) to level the batter. Carefully peel away the parchment. Bake until a pick inserted in the center

continued

comes out clean, 10 to 12 minutes. Set the pan on a wire rack and let cool to room temperature.

Assemble the layers: Lay two long pieces of plastic wrap in a cross shape on a baking sheet. Slide a knife along the inside edge of the pan containing the cookie to loosen it. Invert the cookie onto a large cutting board. Peel off the parchment. Using a ruler as a guide, cut the cookie crosswise into two equal pieces. Place one layer, top side down, in the middle of the plastic wrap (a wide, sturdy spatula will help the transfer).

Remove the ice cream from the freezer and take off the lid. It's important to work quickly from this point on. (If the ice cream gets too soft, pop it onto a plate and back into the freezer to harden up.) Using scissors or a sharp knife, cut the container lengthwise in two places and tear away the container.

Set the ice cream on its side. Cut the ice cream into even slices, 1/2 to 3/4 inch thick, and arrange them on top of the cookie layer in the pan, pairing the smallest piece next to the largest. Using a rubber spatula, gently yet firmly smear the ice cream to spread it evenly. (It helps to put a piece of plastic wrap on the ice cream and smear with your hands; remove the plastic before proceeding.)

Position the remaining cookie layer, top side up, over the ice cream. Press gently to spread the ice cream to the edges. Put a clean piece of plastic on top and wrap the long ends of the bottom sheet of plastic up and over the cookie layers and ice cream. Put the baking sheet in the freezer and chill until the sandwich is hard, about 4 hours and up to 2 days.

Cut and garnish the sandwiches: Take the baking sheet out of the freezer. Lift the package from the pan, transfer it to a cutting board, and line the pan with a fresh piece of plastic. Peel the top layer of plastic off the sandwich (you can leave on the bottom layer).

Working quickly, use a ruler and a long, sharp chef's knife to score the cookie, dividing it into twelve: three across the short side and four across the long side. Cut the sandwiches, wiping the blade clean as needed. (If your kitchen is very warm, put the pieces back into the freezer to firm up, or work with one strip at a time, keeping the rest in the freezer.)

Fill a small, shallow bowl with your chosen garnish and set it next to your work surface. Press some of the garnish onto some or all of the sides of the sandwich. Set the sandwiches back on the baking sheet and return to the freezer immediately. (If your kitchen is warm, keep the sandwiches in the freezer and garnish one at a time.) Once the sandwiches are hard, wrap them individually in plastic and store in the freezer.

ORGANIZATION IS A GOOD COOK'S SECRET INGREDIENT

No matter how excited you are about a recipe, don't launch into it without doing your prep work, called *mise en place*. This is especially important with desserts, where fragile batters, tempered chocolate, or softening ice cream don't like to be kept waiting.

Start by reading the entire recipe, to avert any surprises. Next, heat your oven and gather your equipment and ingredi-ents. If the recipe calls for an ingredient at a certain temperature, allow time for that to happen, and always prepare your pans before you start mixing dough or batter.

Next go through the ingredients list and measure, chop, or toast as directed. Now you're ready to go and can focus on creating perfect textures and flavors without needing to fumble for the right-size measuring spoon.

customizing your ice cream sandwich

YOU CAN DESIGN YOUR OWN SANDWICH COMBINATIONS BY CHOOSING THE ICE CREAM, ADDING FLAVOR to the chocolate cookie, and picking your favorite garnish. The flavoring possibilities are endless, but here are some delicious places to start.

Cookie variations

Chocolate-mint cookie Add ½ teaspoon peppermint extract when you add the vanilla.

Chocolate-orange cookie Add ½ teaspoon natural orange flavor or orange extract when you add the vanilla.

Chocolate-espresso cookie Mix in 1 level tablespoon instant coffee granules when you add the vanilla.

Chocolate-ginger cookie Add ½ teaspoon ground ginger to the dry ingredients.

Ice cream options

- Vanilla
- Chocolate chip
- Coffee
- Mint chocolate chip
- Mocha swirl
- Raspberry sorbet
- Dulce de leche or caramel

Garnish ideas

- Finely crushed hard peppermint candies
- Finely chopped or grated bittersweet or semisweet chocolate
- Minced crystallized ginger
- Finely chopped and toasted pecans
- Toasted sweetened coconut flakes
- Crushed amaretti cookies

Winning combinations

- Basic chocolate cookie with coconut ice cream and toasted coconut flakes
- Chocolate-mint cookie with vanilla ice cream and crushed peppermints
- Chocolate-orange cookie with raspberry sorbet
- Chocolate-ginger cookie with vanilla ice cream and minced crystallized ginger
- Chocolate-espresso cookie with dulce de leche ice cream and chopped pecans
- Chocolate-espresso cookie with coffee ice cream and crushed amaretti cookies

Frozen mocha

Serves 4 to 6

This intensely chocolatey dessert needs no ice cream maker, just a food processor. You can serve it in tall glasses as a grown-up "slushy" or freeze and scoop it like sorbet.

½ cup Dutch-processed cocoa

¾ cup granulated sugar

4 teaspoons instant espresso powder

2 cups plus 2 table- spoons whole milk

In a medium saucepan, combine the cocoa, sugar, espresso powder, and just enough of ½ cup water to make a smooth paste. Add the rest of the water. Bring to a simmer over medium heat, whisking constantly to prevent scorching. Continue to whisk and simmer for 1 minute. Remove the pan from the heat and stir in 2 cups of the milk. Pour into a shallow cake pan or ice-cube trays and freeze until hard.

Break up the frozen mixture with a fork and put it in a food processor. Add the remaining 2 tablespoons milk. Process until no lumps remain and the mixture is thick, slushy, and lightened in color. Immediately pour into goblets and serve. Or, refreeze the slush overnight to harden and serve it in scoops.

WORKING WITH COCOA

Cocoa starts dry but often needs to be turned into a liquid; follow these tips for the best results.

Measure cocoa like flour by spooning the unsifted cocoa into a measuring cup and leveling it off without compacting it. Sift it after measuring to remove any lumps. If the recipe calls for measuring sifted cocoa, sift the cocoa over the measuring cup and then level it off without compacting it.

When dissolving cocoa in liquid, stir just enough of the liquid into the cocoa to make a stiff paste. Stir and mash the paste until it's smooth and then stir in the rest of the liquid gradually. If you'll be adding sugar to the cocoa, do it before the liquid goes in.

Triple chocolate ice cream pie

Serves 8 to 12

This pie features a chocolate crust, chocolate ice cream, and chocolate sauce, with a few scoops of coffee and vanilla added for contrast.

6 ounces (about 30) chocolate wafer cookies

5 tablespoons unsalted butter, melted; more for greasing the pan

2 pints chocolate ice cream, slightly softened

Old-Fashioned Hot Fudge Sauce (page 280), at room temperature

1 pint coffee ice cream, slightly softened

1 pint vanilla ice cream, slightly softened

Position a rack in the middle of the oven and heat the oven to 350°F. Butter a 9-inch Pyrex or metal pie plate.

Put the cookies in a zip-top bag and crush them with a rolling pin (or process in a food processor) until you have fine crumbs. Measure 1½ cups of crumbs (crush more cookies, if necessary) and put them in a bowl. Add the melted butter and stir until the crumbs are moistened. Transfer to the pie plate and using your fingers, press the mixture evenly into the bottom and sides (but not on the rim). Bake for 10 minutes. Let cool completely on a wire rack.

Scoop 1 pint of the chocolate ice cream into the cooled crust and spread it evenly with a rubber spatula. Place in the freezer to firm up, about 30 minutes. Remove the pie from the freezer and, working quickly, drizzle ½ cup of the fudge sauce over the ice cream. Using a small ice cream scoop, scoop round balls of the chocolate, coffee, and vanilla ice creams and arrange them over the fudge sauce layer (you may not need all of the ice cream). Drizzle with ¼ cup of the remaining fudge sauce. Freeze until firm, about 2 hours. If not serving right away, loosely cover the pie with waxed paper and then wrap with aluminum foil. Freeze for up to 2 weeks.

To serve, let the pie soften in the refrigerator for 15 to 30 minutes (premium ice cream brands need more time to soften). Meanwhile, gently reheat the remaining fudge sauce in a small saucepan over medium-low heat. Pry the pie out of the pan with a thin metal spatula. (Set the pan in a shallow amount of hot water for a minute to help the crust release.) Set the pie on a board, cut into wedges, and serve drizzled with more hot fudge sauce.

Coffee ice cream with sour cream ganache, toffee chips, and toasted almonds

Here's a dessert that's perfect for impromptu entertaining because you can toss it together using ingredients from the pantry. The sour cream in the chocolate sauce gives it a nice tang, which keeps the sweetness of this dish in check.

6 ounces semisweet chocolate, chopped (or use chocolate chips)

⅓ cup sour cream, at cool room temperature

¼ teaspoon pure vanilla extract

1 quart coffee ice cream, slightly softened

¼ cup toffee chips (such as Skor® English toffee bits)

3 tablespoons sliced almonds, toasted

Melt the chocolate in the top of a double boiler over barely simmering water, stirring frequently, until completely melted. (Or put the chocolate in a Pyrex bowl and heat in the microwave, uncovered, until melted and hot, about 1 minute on high.) Stir in the sour cream and vanilla. Continuing to stir, drizzle 3 to 4 tablespoons water into the sauce until it reaches a smooth, pourable consistency. Ladle the warm sauce on top of individual scoops of coffee ice cream and scatter with the toffee chips and almond slices.

If you can't find toffee chips at the store, make your own by putting a toffee candy bar, such as a Heath® bar, into a heavy zip-top bag and crushing with a rolling pin.

Luscious milk chocolate ice cream

This is an ice cream for those who love to luxuriate in the creaminess of milk chocolate, which is enhanced by the cream in the custard base. Serve with a drizzle of Bittersweet Chocolate-Rum Sauce (page 283) for some contrast, or keep things mellow by skipping a sauce and tucking a butter cookie next to your scoop.

1½ cups whole milk

1½ cups heavy cream

1 tablespoon natural cocoa powder

⅓ cup granulated sugar

7 ounces good-quality milk chocolate, finely chopped

8 large egg yolks

In a heavy-based saucepan, combine the milk and cream. Sift the cocoa powder over the mixture and whisk thoroughly to combine. Sprinkle about half the sugar into the saucepan and slowly bring the mixture to a simmer; don't let it boil.

Put the chopped chocolate in a medium bowl and fill a large bowl with ice water.

While waiting for the milk mixture to simmer, whisk the egg yolks with the remaining sugar. Whisk vigorously until the yolks thicken and become a paler shade of yellow, 3 to 4 minutes.

To combine the egg and milk mixtures, slowly pour half the simmering milk into the yolks while whisking constantly to temper it. Whisk that mixture back into the milk in the saucepan. Reduce the heat to low and stir constantly with a wooden spoon or rubber spatula in a figure-eight motion until the custard is thick enough to coat the back of a spoon (about 170°F), 10 to 15 minutes.

Pour the cooked custard over the chocolate. Whisk until all the chocolate is melted. Set the custard bowl over the bowl of ice water; stir until the custard is completely cool. Pour through a fine sieve if there are any lumps and then refrigerate for several hours or overnight.

Pour the custard into an ice cream machine with at least a 1-quart capacity and freeze following the manufacturer's directions.

Triple strawberry-chocolate ice cream sundaes

Serves 4 to 6

Strawberries and chocolate are a sublime pairing, especially when the berries are sweet and fragrant from the farmers' market and you choose a high-quality, fruity chocolate. Here, we get a triple dose of both ingredients: chocolate in the ice cream, the sauce, and the coating on the dipped berries, while strawberries take the form of a roasted compote, a whipped cream, and a stunning chocolate-cloaked garnish.

For the roasted strawberries

1 quart (about 1 pound) small ripe fresh strawberries, hulled

½ cup granulated sugar

For the strawberry whipped cream

10 small ripe fresh strawberries, hulled

¾ cup heavy cream

2 tablespoons confectioners' sugar

Pinch table salt

To assemble the sundaes

1 quart chocolate ice cream

Half-recipe Double Chocolate Sauce (page 282)

¼ cup toasted sliced almonds

4 to 6 Chocolate-Dipped Strawberries (page 275)

Roast the strawberries: Position a rack in the middle of the oven and heat the oven to 450°F. Toss the strawberries in a bowl with the sugar. Transfer to a rimmed baking sheet. When the oven is hot, roast the strawberries, giving them a stir every 5 minutes, until they're soft and fragrant, about 15 minutes total. Transfer the baking sheet to a rack to cool for 5 minutes, then scrape the berries with their sauce into a small bowl. Chill in the refrigerator until cold, about 2 hours or up to a day.

Make the whipped cream: Purée the strawberries in a food processor until smooth. Pour through a fine sieve set over a bowl, pressing hard on the solids. (You should have about ¼ cup purée.) Discard the solids. Refrigerate the purée until very cold, about 15 minutes.

In a deep bowl, beat the cream with an electric mixer on medium-high speed just until the cream begins to thicken. Add the sugar and beat just until soft peaks form when the beaters are lifted. Slowly beat in half of the strawberry purée and the salt. Beat just to stiff peaks. Drizzle the remaining purée over the cream and gently fold it in with a rubber spatula. Refrigerate, covered, until ready to assemble the sundaes.

continued

Assemble the sundaes: In tall glasses, layer scoops of the chocolate ice cream with the roasted strawberries. Drizzle with Double Chocolate Sauce, top with a dollop of strawberry whipped cream, a scattering of almonds, and a chocolate-dipped strawberry. Serve immediately.

HANDLING AND STORING STRAWBERRIES

Strawberries are delicate, so handle them as little as possible to prevent bruising. When you bring them home, carefully sort out any that are mushy, moldy, or discolored. One bad berry can spoil the whole bowl. Spread the berries in a single layer on a baking sheet or shallow baking dish lined with paper towels.

Stored in the refrigerator, they can keep for up to three days, but the sooner you eat them, the better. Don't wash them until ready to use them, and then be gentle and use as little water as possible. Don't hull berries until after you've washed and dried them.

Chocolate ice cream with cinnamon, dulce de leche, and toasted pecans

Yields about 1 quart

This chocolate ice cream has a distinctive, almost roasty flavor. You can substitute semisweet chocolate for the Mexican chocolate, increasing the sugar to ¾ cup and adding a scant ½ teaspoon ground cinnamon (preferably Ceylon) along with the chocolate. Some specialty shops or Hispanic markets carry dulce de leche in jars, but it's easy to make your own (see recipe on page 228).

½ cup granulated sugar

2½ teaspoons cornstarch

Pinch table salt

1¾ cups whole milk

7 ounces Mexican chocolate, coarsely chopped (such as Ibarra® brand)

¼ cup Dulce de Leche (page 228)

3 large egg yolks

½ cup chilled evaporated milk

¾ cup chilled whipping or heavy cream

½ cup coarsely chopped pecans

In a medium saucepan, combine the sugar, cornstarch, and salt. Gradually stir in the milk over medium heat and add the chocolate, whisking often until the chocolate has melted and the milk is hot and just about to simmer, about 5 minutes. Add the dulce de leche and whisk until it melts, 1 to 2 minutes. Remove the pan from the heat.

In a large bowl, beat the egg yolks until blended, about 30 seconds. Whisk about ½ cup of the hot milk-chocolate mixture into the yolks and then beat in another ½ cup. Slowly whisk in the remaining hot liquid and then pour the mixture back into the pan. Heat the mixture over medium to medium-high heat, stirring constantly, until it reaches 180°F and just begins to thicken. Remove from the heat and whisk in the evaporated milk and cream, whisking until the mixture begins to cool. Strain to remove any cooked pieces of egg and refrigerate until it's colder than about 60°F, at least 2 hours or as long as 24 hours, stirring occasionally.

Add the pecans and freeze the mixture in an ice cream machine (following the manufacturer's instructions) until the ice cream is very thick and cold. Transfer to a resealable plastic or stainless-steel container and freeze until it's firm enough to scoop, at least 3 hours.

continued

dulce de leche

This recipe makes more caramel than you'll need for the ice cream recipe, but that's a good thing. It keeps in the refrigerator for at least a week, at the ready for nibbling or drizzling on grilled fresh pineapple.

One 14- or 14½-ounce
   can sweetened
   condensed milk

¼ teaspoon pure
   vanilla extract

In a saucepan, combine the sweetened condensed milk with the vanilla extract. Simmer very gently, stirring frequently, until very thick and golden brown (it may get lumpy but will eventually smooth out), about 20 minutes.

Chocolate ice cream with cinnamon, dulce de leche, and toasted pecans

Tropical banana split with toasted-coconut ice cream and bittersweet chocolate rum sauce

Yields about 1¼ quarts
ice cream; serves 4,
with ice cream left over

Even when fully frozen, this very coconutty ice cream remains soft and looks almost sticky, which just adds to the gooey fun of this twist on the ice cream parlor favorite. Toast the coconut flakes in a 350°F oven for 6 to 8 minutes, stirring once or twice, but check at about 5 minutes—coconut flakes go from toasted to burnt quite fast, so keep an eye on them.

For the ice cream

1 cup granulated sugar

2½ teaspoons cornstarch

Pinch table salt

1 cup whole milk

¾ cup whipping or heavy cream

2 large egg yolks

½ cup chilled evaporated milk

1 cup chilled unsweetened
    canned coconut milk

¼ cup sweetened coconut
    flakes, toasted

continued

Make the ice cream: In a medium saucepan, combine the sugar, cornstarch, and salt. Gradually stir or whisk in the milk and cream, bring to a boil, and then reduce the heat to a simmer for 1 minute. Remove the pan from the heat.

In a large bowl, beat the egg yolks until blended, about 30 seconds. Whisk about ½ cup of the hot milk-cream mixture into the yolks and then beat in another ½ cup. Slowly whisk in the remaining hot liquid and then pour the mixture back into the pan. Heat the mixture over medium to medium-high heat until it reaches 180°F and begins to thicken, stirring constantly; it will look like it's about to boil. Remove the pan from the heat and whisk in the evaporated milk and coconut milk, whisking until the mixture begins to cool. Strain to remove any cooked pieces of egg and refrigerate until it's colder than about 60°F, at least 2 hours or as long as 24 hours, stirring occasionally.

Add ¼ cup of the toasted coconut flakes, and freeze the mixture in an ice cream machine (following the manufacturer's instructions) until the ice cream is very thick and cold. Transfer to a resealable plastic or stainless-steel container and freeze until it's firm enough to scoop, at least 3 hours.

For the banana splits

½ cup cold whipping cream

1 teaspoon confectioners' sugar

¼ teaspoon pure vanilla extract

2 tablespoons unsalted butter

1 tablespoon lightly packed dark
   brown sugar

4 small, ripe bananas, peeled
   and split lengthwise

Half-recipe Bittersweet
   Chocolate-Rum Sauce
   (page 283)

⅓ cup sweetened coconut
   flakes, toasted

Assemble the banana splits: Whip the cream until it forms soft peaks; add the confectioners' sugar and vanilla and continue whipping until dollopy. Keep in the fridge until ready to serve.

Arrange 4 shallow bowls or banana split dishes on the counter. Heat a large sauté pan over medium high. Add the butter and brown sugar and stir to combine. When bubbling, add the bananas, cut side down, and sauté until slightly softened and golden, but do not let them get mushy, 2 to 3 minutes. Transfer two banana halves to each dish, laying them parallel to each other, cut side up. Let cool slightly, then top each set of banana halves with two or three small scoops of coconut ice cream, drizzle with the chocolate sauce, add a dollop of whipped cream, and sprinkle with the ⅓ cup toasted coconut. Serve immediately.

breads

Individual orange & chocolate bread puddings

You can assemble the bread puddings and keep them in the refrigerator up to a day ahead. Remove from the refrigerator 30 minutes before baking, let them come to room temperature, and bake when ready to serve.

8 slices good-quality American-style white bread (about 8 ounces)

2 tablespoons unsalted butter, softened; more for the ramekins

⅓ cup orange marmalade

3 ounces (½ cup) chopped semisweet chocolate (or ½ cup semisweet chocolate chips)

2 large eggs

1 cup whole milk

½ cup heavy cream

⅓ cup granulated sugar

½ teaspoon pure vanilla extract

Heat the oven to 375°F. Lightly butter four 1¼-cup ramekins. Remove the crusts from the bread and spread one side with the butter and marmalade. Cut the bread into quarters and arrange four quarters in the base of each ramekin, overlapping to fit. Sprinkle with half of the chocolate and repeat with the remaining bread and chocolate to make two layers.

Whisk the eggs, milk, cream, sugar, and vanilla in a medium bowl or large glass measuring cup. Pour equal portions of the egg mixture over the bread. Set the ramekins on a baking sheet and bake until puffed and golden brown, 20 to 25 minutes. Let cool for 5 minutes before serving.

Chocolate-banana-ginger bread pudding

Yields one 9x13-inch bread pudding; serves 12

A bread pudding can sound like a humble dessert, but when you make it with generous amounts of bittersweet chocolate, ripe fragrant bananas, spicy ginger, and buttery croissants, "delectable" is probably a better descriptor.

7 large egg yolks

3 large eggs

1 cup granulated sugar

1 teaspoon table salt

6 cups half-and-half

3 cups chopped bittersweet or semisweet chocolate, divided

1 tablespoon pure vanilla extract

10 cups 1-inch cubes day-old croissant

3 ripe bananas, thinly sliced

½ cup chopped crystallized ginger

In a large heatproof bowl, whisk the yolks and eggs. Slowly whisk in the sugar and salt until thoroughly combined. Pour the half-and-half into a medium saucepan. Heat over medium-high heat until steaming but not bubbling. Add 2 cups of the chocolate to the half-and-half and whisk until the chocolate is completely melted. Slowly whisk the half-and-half mixture into the egg mixture until thoroughly combined. Strain the mixture through a fine sieve into a large Pyrex measuring cup or heatproof bowl. Add the vanilla extract.

Put the bread cubes in a 9x13-inch baking dish and pour the custard on top. Make sure the bread is as submerged in the custard as possible and let cool at room temperature for about an hour. Cover with plastic wrap and refrigerate for at least 5 hours and up to 24 hours.

Heat the oven to 325°F. Transfer the bread mixture to a large mixing bowl and gently fold in the bananas, the remaining 1 cup chopped chocolate, and the crystallized ginger. Return the mixture to the baking dish.

Cover the pudding loosely with foil and bake at 325°F for 70 minutes. Remove the foil and continue to bake until no liquid custard is visible when you poke a small hole in the center with a paring knife, 20 to 40 minutes more.

Toasted bread with chocolate

Bread and chocolate is a popular snack for kids in Spain. Add a drizzle of olive oil and a pinch of salt for a sophisticated touch that grown-ups will love, too.

Eight ½-inch-thick slices good bread, such as a rustic peasant bread or a real baguette

Best-quality extra-virgin olive oil for drizzling

4 ounces best-quality bittersweet chocolate, very coarsely chopped (scant 1 cup)

Sea salt, kosher salt, or any specialty salt

Position a rack 4 inches from the broiler element and heat to high. Put the bread on a baking sheet and toast until light golden on both sides, 1 to 2 minutes per side. Drizzle the bread with olive oil. Distribute the chocolate evenly on top of the bread. Turn off the broiler and return the bread to the oven until the residual heat melts the chocolate, about 1 minute. Smooth the chocolate with a table knife, if you want. Sprinkle a pinch of salt on each slice and serve.

Chocolate chunk scones

On their own or slathered with some sweet butter, these scones are the perfect partner for a cup of coffee or tea. Choose a good-quality bittersweet or semisweet chocolate because the better the chocolate, the better the scones will taste.

9 ounces (2 cups) unbleached all-purpose flour

⅓ cup granulated sugar

1 tablespoon baking powder

½ teaspoon table salt

5½ ounces bittersweet or semisweet chocolate, coarsely chopped (to yield 1 cup)

3 ounces (6 tablespoons) cold unsalted butter, cut into cubes

¾ cup heavy cream

2 large egg yolks, lightly beaten

For finishing

1 large egg, lightly beaten with 1 tablespoon milk for glazing

1 to 1½ teaspoons granulated sugar

Position an oven rack in the lower third of the oven and heat the oven to 400°F. Line a heavy baking sheet with parchment. In a large bowl, whisk the flour, sugar, baking powder, and salt. Add the chopped chocolate, tossing until the pieces are evenly distributed and coated with flour. Cut in the butter with a pastry blender or two table knives until the largest pieces of butter are about the size of peas.

In a small bowl, stir the cream and egg yolks just to blend. Add this all at once to the flour mixture. Stir with a fork to begin combining the wet and dry ingredients and then use your hands to gently knead the mixture together until all the dry ingredients are absorbed into the dough and it can be gathered into a moist, shaggy ball. Don't overknead—this dough is sticky but benefits from minimal handling. Set the rough ball in the center of the prepared baking sheet and pat it gently into a round about 1 inch thick and 7 inches in diameter. Don't be tempted to make the round any flatter.

With a sharp knife or a pastry scraper, cut the round into eight wedges; separate the wedges. Brush the scones with the egg-milk glaze (you won't need to use all of it) and sprinkle with the sugar. Bake until the scones are deep golden and a toothpick inserted into the center of a wedge comes out clean, 18 to 22 minutes. Slide the parchment onto a rack and let the scones cool for 10 to 15 minutes before serving.

MIXING AND SHAPING TIPS

1. Cut the butter into the flour until the largest chunks are the size of peas. Two table knives can stand in for a pastry cutter.

2. Knead just until you can gather the dough into a shaggy ball.

3. Pat the shaggy ball into a manageable round.

4. Section the round into eighths with a dough scraper or a knife.

Individual cinnamon coffee cakes with chocolate-cherry-almond swirl

When it comes to breakfast, a coffee cake made with yeast, well, takes the cake. The cakes freeze like a dream. Wrap unglazed cooled cakes in plastic wrap and freeze for up to a month. Defrost them overnight (or for a few hours) in the refrigerator and warm them in a low oven just before glazing and serving.

For the dough

½ cup warm whole milk (about 105°F)

1½ teaspoons active dry yeast

⅓ cup plus 2 teaspoons granulated sugar

9 ounces (2 cups) unbleached all-purpose flour

½ teaspoon table salt

1 teaspoon ground cinnamon

2 large eggs, lightly beaten

5 ounces (10 tablespoons) very soft unsalted butter

½ cup sliced almonds, toasted

continued

A day before baking, make the dough: In the bowl of a stand mixer, gently whisk the warm milk with the yeast to combine. Sprinkle with 2 teaspoons of the sugar. Let the yeast proof until air pockets float up, making the mixture look spongy, 5 to 10 minutes.

Add the remaining dough ingredients and mix with the paddle attachment on medium-low speed until the dough comes together, and then continue mixing for 6 minutes to knead the dough, scraping the sides of the bowl once or twice. The dough should be loose and seem more like a tacky batter.

Scrape the dough into a greased bowl that's at least twice the dough's size, cover tightly with plastic, and refrigerate overnight.

Make the filling: The next morning, put the chocolate in a food processor and pulse to chop coarsely. Add the dried cherries, almonds, sugar, and cinnamon and pulse until quite fine. Add the egg white and process just until the ingredients form a rough paste. (Cover the leftover yolk and refrigerate.)

Assemble the bread: Grease 8 cups of a 12-cup muffin pan. Scrape the chilled dough onto a liberally floured surface. Using a well-floured rolling pin, gently roll the dough into a 12x8-inch rectangle. Work quickly; the warmer the dough gets, the harder it is to handle. Spread the filling by hand over the dough, leaving a 1-inch border on all four sides. It's all right if it's a bit uneven.

For the filling

¼ pound semisweet chocolate

6 ounces (about 1 cup)
   dried cherries

1 cup sliced almonds, toasted

⅓ cup granulated sugar

½ teaspoon ground cinnamon

1 large egg, separated

½ teaspoon whole milk

For the glaze

1 cup confectioners' sugar

4 to 5 teaspoons strong
   brewed coffee

Starting with a long side, roll the dough into a log. If the dough sticks to the work surface, use a bench knife or a spatula to lift it.

Brush the excess flour from the top and sides of the dough roll. Using a sharp knife, trim the ends of the roll just enough to expose the spiral of filling. Discard the trimmings. Cut the roll into 8 equal slices (each about 1½ to 2 inches wide). Set each slice, spiral side up, in a greased muffin cup, brushing the flour from the bottom of each piece as you go. Press very gently to be sure each piece reaches the bottom of the cup. Pour a few tablespoons of water into the empty, ungreased cups.

Cover the dough with a clean, damp dishtowel or an oversize plastic storage container (to make a little "greenhouse") and let rise until light and billowy, 1½ to 2 hours. (Be patient. Remember your dough is cold and the rate of rising will depend on the temperature of the kitchen.)

Meanwhile, heat the oven to 350°F. Make an egg wash by mixing the reserved egg yolk with the ½ teaspoon milk. Just before baking, brush the dough with the egg wash. Bake until puffed and deep golden, 20 to 25 minutes. Let cool for 10 to 15 minutes. Carefully siphon or drain the water from the extra cups and wipe dry. Loosen under the edge of the cakes' caps with the tip of a paring knife. If the cakes grew together during baking, cut between them to separate. Turn onto a cooling rack set over paper towels or parchment.

Make and apply the glaze: In a cup, mix the confectioners' sugar and coffee to make a smooth paste. It should be thick but still pourable. Drizzle over the cakes after they have cooled slightly. Serve as soon as the glaze has set.

Chocolate french toast sandwiches

Need dessert quick? Check your pantry, because you're likely to have everything on the list for this delicious twist on French toast.

4 slices white sandwich bread (such as Pepperidge Farm® sandwich bread), fresh or slightly stale

1½ to 2 ounces good-quality semisweet chocolate (preferably from a thin bar)

2 large eggs

2 tablespoons granulated sugar

½ cup half-and-half

1 teaspoon pure vanilla extract

¼ teaspoon kosher salt

2 tablespoons unsalted butter

Confectioners' sugar

Cut each piece of bread into four triangles by slicing diagonally. Cut or break the chocolate into 8 pieces, roughly the same triangle shape as the bread pieces but slightly smaller by at least ¼ inch all the way around.

In a medium bowl, vigorously whisk together the eggs and sugar until well combined. Add the half-and-half, vanilla, and salt and whisk until combined. Put the bread pieces in the bowl and press down gently to make sure they're all soaked.

Heat 1 tablespoon of the butter in a medium nonstick skillet over medium heat. When the butter is melted and sizzling, add half of the bread pieces in one layer, leaving a little space between each. Cook until nicely browned, about 2 minutes. Turn each piece over with a spatula and cook until the other side is nicely browned, 1½ to 2 minutes.

Transfer the bread pieces to a plate lined with paper towels and take the skillet off the heat. Put a triangle of chocolate on half of the bread pieces, and top each with another piece of bread (save the best-looking pieces for the tops). Let them sit while you return the pan to the heat, melt the remaining 1 tablespoon butter, cook the remaining bread, and fill it with the remaining chocolate. When all the chocolate sandwiches are made, arrange two, overlapping slightly, on each of four plates. Sprinkle the confectioners' sugar generously over all and serve warm.

Chocolate chip muffins

These muffins are a perfect morning snack. Serve them plain or, for a sweeter treat, dress them up with an easy-to-make glaze. They'll keep for a day or two in an airtight container, but their first day is the best.

1 pound (3½ cups) unbleached all-purpose flour

4 teaspoons baking powder

½ teaspoon baking soda

½ teaspoon table salt

1⅓ cups granulated sugar

5 ounces (10 tablespoons) unsalted butter, melted and cooled slightly

1 cup whole milk, at room temperature

1 cup crème fraîche or sour cream, at room temperature

2 large eggs, at room temperature

1 large egg yolk, at room temperature

1 teaspoon pure vanilla extract

1½ cups chocolate chips

¾ cup coarsely chopped, toasted pecans or walnuts (optional)

continued

Make the muffins: Position a rack in the center of the oven and heat the oven to 350°F. Lightly oil (or spray with nonstick cooking spray) the top of a standard 12-cup muffin tin and then line with paper or foil baking cups. (Spraying the pan keeps the muffin tops from sticking to the pan's surface.)

In a large bowl, sift together the flour, baking powder, baking soda, and salt; mix well. In a medium bowl, whisk the sugar, butter, milk, crème fraîche or sour cream, eggs, egg yolk, and vanilla until well combined. Pour the wet ingredients into the dry, and fold gently with a rubber spatula just until the dry ingredients are mostly moistened; the batter will be lumpy, and there should still be quite a few streaks of dry flour. Fold in the chocolate chips, and the nuts, if using, until just combined. Don't overmix; the batter will still be lumpy.

If you have an ice cream scoop with a "sweeper," use it to fill the muffin cups. Otherwise, use two spoons to spoon in the batter, distributing all of the batter evenly. The batter should mound higher than the rim of the cups by about ¾ inch or more, especially if using nuts (overfilling gives you those great big bakery-style muffin tops).

Bake until the muffins are golden brown and spring back lightly when you press the middle, 30 to 35 minutes. (The muffin tops will probably meld together.) Let the muffin tin cool on a rack for 15 to 20 minutes. Use a table knife to separate the tops and

continued

For the glaze

12½ ounces (3 cups)
  confectioners' sugar

¼ teaspoon ground cinnamon
  (optional)

then invert the pan and pop out the muffins. Serve the muffins as is or glaze them.

Make the glaze: Combine the confectioners' sugar, 6 tablespoons water, and cinnamon, if using, and whisk until smooth. The glaze should be thin enough that it will drip off of a spoon; if it's more like a spreadable icing, thin it with more water, 1 tablespoon at a time. The glaze can be made up to 2 days in advance; store in an airtight container at room temperature.

When the muffins have cooled down but are still slightly warm, put them on a rack over foil to catch any glaze that drips off. Dab the glaze on the muffins with a pastry brush, or spoon the glaze on and let it drip over the sides. It should leave a smooth, somewhat translucent coating. You may not need all of the glaze. Wait 20 to 30 minutes for the glaze to set—it won't dry completely—before serving.

If you love great big muffin tops like the kind you get at the coffee shop, be sure to mound the batter higher than the rims of the cups, by ¾ inch at least. The tops might melt together into one big mass, but that's fine; once cooled, just cut them apart with a knife.

Rich chocolate muffins

**Yields about
20 medium muffins**

These deeply chocolate muffins benefit from a quality chocolate, such as Callebaut®. If 20 muffins are too much for you, know that the batter will keep, covered and refrigerated, for up to a week, which means you can spread out your muffin enjoyment.

10 ounces bittersweet chocolate, finely chopped

8 ounces unsweetened chocolate, finely chopped

1¼ pounds (2½ cups) unsalted butter

1 pound (3½ cups) unbleached all-purpose flour

4½ cups granulated sugar

12 large eggs, cracked into a bowl

In a saucepan, melt the two chocolates with the butter. Let cool slightly. In a large bowl, mix the flour and sugar. Whisk the eggs into the dry ingredients. Pour the chocolate into the egg mixture and stir until well blended; chill for at least 3 hours.

Heat the oven to 350°F. Line a muffin tin with muffin papers. Scoop about ½ cup batter into each tin so that the curve of the batter is even with the rim of the cup. (Refrigerate any extra batter in an airtight container for up to a week.) Bake the muffins until the tops puff and crackle and are slightly soft to the touch, and a toothpick stuck in the center has moist but not wet crumbs clinging to it, about 30 minutes.

get an edge on chopping chocolate

SERRATED KNIVES ARE GREAT FOR CHOPPING chocolate, especially when you want evenly sized chunks for cookies. The serrations bite down into the chocolate to keep the blade from slipping, and since you don't have to press down as hard, the chocolate won't break into as many tiny shards.

Another nifty way to chop large blocks is with a "chocolate chipper." Poke the chipper into the block and pull down with both hands. The prongs pierce the chocolate and reduce it to easy-to-use pieces.

Pains au chocolat

The pride of any French bakery, pains au chocolat (pronounced pan oh sho-co-LAH) are doable for the home baker as well. The key is to take your time rolling out the croissant dough, so that you get delicate, crisp layers surrounding the chocolate filling. You don't want to overload the croissants with too much chocolate—just enough to give these pastries a bittersweet edge that contrasts with their butteriness.

For the dough

1 pound 2 ounces (4 cups) unbleached all-purpose flour; more for rolling

5 ounces (½ cup plus 2 tablespoons) cold whole milk

¼ cup plus 2 tablespoons granulated sugar

2 ¼ teaspoons table salt

1 ½ ounces (3 tablespoons) unsalted soft butter

1 tablespoon plus scant ½ teaspoon instant (rapid or quick-rise) yeast

10 ounces (1 cup plus 4 tablespoons) cold unsalted butter

8 ounces semisweet chocolate, chopped

1 large egg

Make the dough: Combine all the dough ingredients plus ½ cup and 2 tablespoons cold water in the bowl of a stand mixer fitted with the dough hook. Mix on low speed for 3 minutes, scraping the sides of the mixing bowl once if necessary. Mix on medium speed for 3 minutes. Transfer the dough to a lightly floured 10-inch pie pan or a dinner plate. Lightly flour the top of the dough and wrap well with plastic so it doesn't dry out. Refrigerate overnight.

Make the butter layer: The next day, cut the butter lengthwise into ½-inch-thick slabs. Arrange the pieces on a piece of parchment or waxed paper to form a 5-inch to 6-inch square, cutting the butter crosswise as necessary to fit. Top with another piece of parchment or waxed paper. With a rolling pin, pound the butter with light, even strokes. As the pieces begin to adhere, use more force. Pound the butter until it's about 7½ inches square and then use a knife or bench scraper to trim the edges of the butter. Put the trimmings on top of the square and either pound them in lightly with the rolling pin or smear them in with the bench scraper. Refrigerate.

Laminate the dough: Unwrap and lay the dough on a lightly floured work surface. Roll into a 10½-inch square. Brush excess flour off the dough. Remove the butter from the refrigerator—it should be pliable but cold. If not, refrigerate a bit longer. Unwrap and place the butter on the dough so that the points of the butter

continued

square are centered along the sides of the dough (like a diamond). Fold one flap of dough over the butter toward you, stretching it slightly so that the point just reaches the center of the butter. Repeat with the other flaps and then press the edges together to completely seal the butter inside the dough. (A complete seal ensures butter won't escape.)

Lightly flour the top and bottom of the dough. With the rolling pin, firmly press the dough to elongate it slightly and then begin rolling instead of pressing, focusing on lengthening rather than widening the dough and keeping the edges straight. Roll the dough until it's an 8x24-inch rectangle. If the ends lose their square shape, gently reshape the corners with your hand. Using a pastry brush, brush any flour off of the dough. Pick up one short end of the dough and fold it back over the dough, leaving a third of the other end of dough exposed. Brush the flour off and then fold the exposed dough over the folded side. Put the dough on a baking sheet, cover with plastic wrap, and freeze for 20 minutes to relax and chill the dough.

Repeat the above step, positioning the dough with the seam on the left and rolling the dough until it's about 8x24 inches. Fold the dough in thirds as above, brushing off excess flour and turning under any rounded edges or short ends with exposed or smeared layers. Cover and freeze for 20 minutes more.

Give the dough a third rolling and folding as above. Put the dough on the baking sheet and cover with plastic wrap, tucking the plastic under all four sides. Refrigerate overnight.

Divide the dough: The next day, unwrap and lightly flour the top and bottom of the dough. With the rolling pin, "wake the dough up" by pressing firmly along its length—you don't want to widen the dough, but simply begin to lengthen it with these first strokes. Roll the dough into a long and narrow strip, about

8x44 inches. If the dough sticks as you roll, sprinkle with a bit of flour. Once the dough is about half to two-thirds of its final length, it may start to resist rolling and even shrink back. If this happens, fold the dough in thirds, cover, and refrigerate for about 10 minutes; then unfold the dough and finish rolling. Lift the dough an inch or so off the table at its midpoint and allow it to shrink from both sides—this helps prevent the dough from shrinking when it's cut. Check that there's enough excess dough on either end to allow you to trim the ends so they're straight and the strip of dough is 40 inches long. Trim the dough.

Lay a yardstick or tape measure lengthwise along the top of the dough. With a chef's knife, mark the top of the dough at 5-inch intervals along the length (there will be 7 marks in all).

Lay the yardstick along the bottom of the dough. Make a mark 2½ inches in from the end of the dough. Make marks at 5-inch intervals from this point all along the bottom of the dough. You'll have 8 marks that fall halfway between the marks at the top.

Make diagonal cuts by positioning the yardstick at the top corner and the first bottom mark. With a chef's knife or pizza wheel, cut the dough along this line. Move the yardstick to the next set of marks and cut. Repeat until you have cut the dough diagonally at the same angle along its entire length—you'll have made 8 cuts. Now change the angle of the yardstick to connect the other top corner and bottom mark and cut the dough along this line to make triangles. Repeat along the entire length of dough. You'll end up with 15 triangles and a small scrap of dough at each end.

Shape the croissants: Using a paring knife or a bench scraper, make a ½-inch- to ¾-inch-long notch in the center of the short side of each triangle.

continued

Hold a dough triangle so that the short notched side is on top and gently elongate to about 10 inches without squeezing or compressing the dough. Lay the croissant on the work surface with the notched side closest to you. Distribute the chocolate along the length of the notched side. With one hand on each side of the short end, begin to roll the dough away from you, toward the pointed end. Press down on the dough with enough force to make the layers stick together, but avoid excess compression, which could smear the layers. Roll the dough all the way down its length until the pointed end of the triangle is directly underneath the croissant. Now bend the two legs toward you to form a tight cres-

MAKING CROISSANTS STEP-BY-STEP

Follow these steps for folding, cutting, and shaping the croissants.

1. With the chilled dough rolled out and butter centered on top, fold one flap of dough toward you; repeat with the other flaps and press to seal the butter inside.

2. With the dough shaped to be about 8 inches by 24 inches, pick up one short end and fold it back over, leaving a third of the other end of dough exposed. Fold the exposed dough over the folded side.

3. Gently lengthen the dough to about 44 inches with a rolling pin and trim the ends.

cent shape and gently press the tips of the legs together (they'll come apart while proofing but keep their crescent shape).

Shape the remaining croissants in the same manner, arranging them on two large parchment-lined rimmed baking sheets (8 on one pan and 7 on the other). Keep as much space as possible between them, as they will rise during the final proofing and again when baked.

Proof the croissants: Make the egg wash by whisking the egg with 1 teaspoon water in a small bowl until very smooth. Lightly

continued

4. Make diagonal cuts along the length of the dough with a chef's knife or pizza wheel, creating triangles.

5. Pick up a triangle, holding it so that the short notched side is on top, and elongate to 10 inches, then lay the triangle on the work surface, add the chocolate, and roll the dough away from you.

6. The dough should be rolled all the way down its length, so that the pointed end of the triangle is underneath the croissant. Press the legs toward you to form a crescent shape. Continue to form all of the croissants.

7. Brush the croissants with the egg wash, then allow the croissants to proof. Brush on a bit more egg wash before baking.

brush it on each croissant. Refrigerate the remaining egg wash (you'll need it again).

Proof the croissants in a draft-free spot that's 75°F to 80°F. Wherever you proof them, be sure the temperature is not so warm that the butter melts out of the dough. They will take 1½ to 2 hours to fully proof. Signs of full proofing include: When viewed from the side, you should be able to see the layers of the dough. If you shake the sheets, the croissants should wiggle. And finally, the croissants will be distinctly larger (though not doubled) than they were when first shaped.

Bake the croissants: Shortly before the croissants are fully proofed, position racks in the top and lower thirds of the oven and heat it to 400°F convection or 425°F conventional.

Brush the croissants with egg wash a second time. Put the sheets in the oven. After 10 minutes, rotate and swap the sheets' positions. Continue baking until the bottoms are an even brown, the tops richly browned, and the edges show signs of coloring, 8 to 10 minutes more. If they appear to be darkening too quickly during baking, lower the oven temperature by 10°F. Cool on baking sheets on racks.

MAKE AHEAD The croissants are best served barely warm. However, they reheat very well, so any that are not eaten right away can be reheated within a day or two in a 350°F oven for about 10 minutes. They can also be wrapped in plastic or aluminum foil and frozen for a month or more. Frozen croissants can be thawed overnight prior to reheating or taken from the freezer directly to the oven, in which case they will need a couple of minutes more to reheat.

Russian chocolate braid

Yields 1 loaf

This is an old-fashioned sweet bread that's similar to a Jewish babka. The dough is super-tender as well as flavorful because of the addition of sour cream and potato—it can't get any more Russian than this.

1 recipe Sour Cream & Potato Sweet Dough (page 256)

1 cup Pastry Cream, chilled (page 257)

½ cup mini chocolate chips or chopped semisweet or bittersweet chocolate

1 large egg, beaten

Line a heavy baking sheet (or an insulated sheet or two sheets sandwiched together) with parchment or butter it. Roll the dough into a rectangle about 13x16 inches and about ⅛ inch thick. Stir the chilled pastry cream to soften it and then spread it over the dough in a thin layer. Scatter the chocolate chips evenly over the surface. Roll the rectangle into a cylinder from the wider side and pinch the long edge to seal. Put the cylinder on the baking sheet. Cut the cylinder in half lengthwise, splitting it into two thin half-cylindrical strips. Arrange the strips parallel to one another so that the filling is facing up, push them together, and wrap them around each other to form a twist, working from the center.

Position a rack in the middle of the oven and heat the oven to 350°F. Cover the shaped dough and proof until it's large, puffy, and remains indented when lightly pressed with your fingertip, about 45 minutes.

Brush the braid with the beaten egg, taking care not to smear the filling or dislodge the chocolate bits. Bake until golden brown, about 35 minutes, rotating the pan halfway through baking. Let cool on a rack for 1 hour before slicing.

continued

Much simpler to make than a true braided bread such as challah, chocolate-studded dough just gets twisted together so it bakes into a pretty pattern. Be careful to keep the cut side of the dough up as you work, so the chocolate filling doesn't spill out.

sour cream & potato sweet dough

Be sure to use a food processor that holds at least 7 cups.

8 ounces (1½ cups)
plus 3 tablespoons
unbleached all-purpose flour

1 teaspoon instant (Red Star®
QuickRise, SAF® Perfect Rise,
Fleischmann's® RapidRise, or
bread machine) yeast

1 very small potato, peeled,
boiled, and sieved (to yield
¼ cup)

2 large egg yolks

2 teaspoons pure vanilla
extract

¼ cup sour cream

3 tablespoons granulated sugar

½ teaspoon table salt

1½ ounces (3 tablespoons)
cold unsalted butter

In a large bowl, mix the 3 tablespoons of flour with the yeast and then whisk in 3 tablespoons water. Let the mixture sit covered until it has begun to puff, 10 to 15 minutes.

Fit a large-capacity food processor with the metal blade. Put the remaining flour in the bowl of the processor and then add the yeast mixture, potato, egg yolks, vanilla, and sour cream. Process the dough for about 1 minute. Remove it from the machine and knead it by hand on an unfloured countertop for 1 minute to redistribute the heat. The dough will be very stiff at this point. Continue this alternating kneading: Process for 30 seconds and then knead on the counter for about 30 seconds, until the dough is very smooth (this should take two to three rounds of processing).

Put the dough back in the food processor and add the sugar and salt, kneading again in the processor and then on the counter until the sugar has dissolved (the dough will soften considerably and become very sticky; this is fine).

Finally, return the dough to the processor, add the butter, and do another alternating kneading round until the butter is well incorporated and the dough is very soft and smooth, about 1 minute. The dough won't clean the bowl at this point. It's all right if it feels quite soft and warm after processing. Kneading the dough on the counter will help it to cool down and firm up.

Transfer the dough to a container at least four times its volume (no need to grease the container); seal well. (At this point, the dough can instead be rolled in flour and then sealed in a plastic bag and refrigerated for up to 4 days. If you do mix ahead and chill the dough, pull it out of the fridge 3 to 4 hours before baking.) Let the dough ferment at room temperature for about 3 hours or until it has expanded to three times its volume and an indent remains when you press it with a floured finger.

pastry cream

Yields 1 cup

This is a very stiff pastry cream that can hold up in the Russian Chocolate Braid without oozing out. Make the pastry cream just after you make the dough to allow it enough time to cool.

1 cup whole milk

2-inch piece vanilla bean, slashed lengthwise and seeds scraped out, or ½ teaspoon pure vanilla extract

¼ cup granulated sugar

3 tablespoons unbleached all-purpose flour

¼ teaspoon table salt

2 large egg yolks

In a medium saucepan, warm the milk over medium heat (if you're using a vanilla bean, add it now) just until a skin forms. Take the pan off the heat. In a medium mixing bowl, combine the sugar, flour, and salt. Add the yolks, beating with a wooden spoon. Whisk in the warm milk in a thin stream, whisking constantly. Return the milk mixture to the saucepan. Cook over medium heat, whisking constantly, until the mixture is extremely thick and gluey (you'll need to switch to a wooden spoon), about 5 minutes. If you're using vanilla extract, stir it in now. Immediately force the pastry cream through a sieve. Gently press a sheet of waxed paper or plastic onto the surface of the hot pastry cream to prevent a skin from forming. Let cool and then refrigerate until ready to use it.

candies & confections

Simple chocolate truffles

In this recipe, truffles are rolled in cocoa powder or ground nuts right after they're coated with melted chocolate. Dutch-processed cocoa powder is best for coating the truffles because it's brighter in color and less acidic than natural cocoa powder, but if you can find only natural cocoa, use it instead.

12 ounces semisweet chocolate (55% to 60% cacao), coarsely chopped or broken into pieces (2 slightly heaping cups)

1 cup heavy cream

2 tablespoons unsalted butter, softened

1 cup cocoa powder (preferably Dutch-processed); more as needed

8 ounces semisweet chocolate, chopped (about 1½ cups)

1 cup (6 ounces) finely chopped toasted nuts (such as almonds, hazelnuts, walnuts, pecans, peanuts, and pistachios), optional

Grind the chocolate in a food processor until it reaches the consistency of coarse meal, about 30 seconds. Bring the cream to a boil in a small saucepan over medium heat. Add the cream to the food processor and process until smooth, about 10 seconds.

Add the butter to the warm (but not hot) ganache while it's still in the food processor. Process until smooth, about 10 seconds. Transfer to a medium bowl, cover tightly with plastic wrap, and refrigerate until firm, at least 2 hours or overnight.

Put the cocoa powder in a large bowl. Using 2 teaspoons, shape rounded, heaping teaspoonfuls of truffle mixture and drop them onto a large, parchment-lined baking sheet.

When all of the truffles are scooped, dip them in the cocoa and use your palms to roll the truffles into smooth 1-inch balls (don't worry about making them perfect; slightly irregular truffles have an appealing homemade appearance). Transfer the truffles to the refrigerator.

Melt the chocolate in a medium heatproof bowl set in a small skillet of barely simmering water, stirring occasionally until smooth. Transfer the bowl to a work surface. Working in batches, use your fingers or a couple of forks to coat the truffles with the melted chocolate.

continued

Coat the truffles again with the remaining cocoa or chopped nuts (if using), and return them to the baking sheet. If using your hands, you'll have to stop and wash off the chocolate in between batches.

Let the truffles sit at room temperature for at least 15 minutes before serving.

MAKE AHEAD Truffles will keep for up to five days in an airtight container in the refrigerator. Bring them to room temperature before serving.

making a truffle "sampler"

ONCE YOU LEARN HOW TO MAKE TRUFFLES, THE flavor possibilities are endless. An assortment of three varieties wrapped in a cute box makes a fantastic gift.

Toffee & Fleur de Sel
Add ½ cup ground toffee bits (Heath bars ground coarsely in a food processor work well) and ¼ teaspoon fleur de sel to the ganache. Use 1¼ cups finely ground toffee bits mixed with 1 teaspoon fleur de sel for the coating. (You'll need a total of six 1.4-ounce Heath bars.)

Liqueur Filling
Add 3 tablespoons of a flavored liqueur of your choice to the ganache before refrigerating. Good choices include Frangelico, Baileys®, Godiva®, Kahlúa, and amaretto.

Mexican Chocolate
Add 2 tablespoons Kahlúa liqueur, 2 teaspoons instant espresso, and ½ teaspoon ground cinnamon to the ganache. Coat the truffles with 1 cup (6 ounces) ground toasted almonds.

PB&J
Add ⅔ cup strawberry jam to the ganache and process until smooth. Coat the truffles with 2 cups (10 ounces) ground salted peanuts. (Yields about 54 truffles because of the added jam.)

Mint
Add ½ teaspoon pure peppermint extract to the ganache.

Classic chocolate truffles

Yields about 80
1-inch truffles

Pure chocolate sophistication, these are truffles for the candy connoisseur.
The process is time-consuming, but the results are more delicious than what
you find in most chocolate shops—a satiny smooth filling with a whisper of a
crackly chocolate coating, lightly cloaked in a dusting of cocoa. Be sure to use
the best chocolate you can find.

2¾ pounds good-quality
   bittersweet or semisweet
   chocolate

1 cup heavy cream

4 ounces (8 tablespoons)
   unsalted butter,
   at room temperature

¼ cup good-quality liqueur
   (such as rum, Cognac,
   Armagnac, or Grand Marnier)

8 ounces Dutch-processed
   cocoa powder (optional)

Make the ganache: Using a serrated knife or the heel of a chef's
knife, chop 12 ounces of the chocolate by shaving shards from the
bar and then crosscutting to get chips no bigger than peanuts.
Transfer to a small stainless-steel bowl—you'll use this portion
for the ganache.

Chop the remaining 2 pounds of chocolate the same way, and set
aside to use for dipping.

Heat the cream in a small saucepan until it just comes to a boil and
pour it over the chopped 12 ounces of ganache chocolate. Using
a wooden spoon, stir quickly in small circles in the center of the
bowl. The chocolate center will become a viscous, shiny emulsion.

Gradually stir in larger circles, bringing in more chocolate from the
sides. Keep enlarging the shiny center until all the chocolate has
been incorporated. If the emulsion cools before all the chocolate has
melted, briefly flash the bowl over a pan of hot (not simmering)
water for a few seconds, being careful not to overheat the ganache and
lose the emulsion. When there are no more lumps, continue stirring
for 1 minute more; don't overmix. Set the ganache aside to cool.

Meanwhile, in another bowl, beat the butter with a wooden
spoon until it's very soft, smooth, and creamy. When the ganache
has cooled to room temperature and thickened noticeably, add the

continued

butter in small pieces, a few at a time. The butter should blend without melting. Stir until no butter bits remain. Gradually pour in the liqueur, stirring constantly to maintain the smooth emulsion.

Shape the truffles: If you want to pipe the truffles immediately, chill the ganache in the refrigerator until it's cool but not firm, 10 to 15 minutes. Otherwise, cover the bowl with plastic wrap and let it sit at room temperature until ready, up to a day. When you're ready to pipe, the ganache should be as smooth and as soft as peanut butter (but not as sticky).

Fill a pastry bag fitted with a ½-inch tip one-third of the way with the ganache. Holding the bag vertically, pipe the ganache onto parchment-lined baking sheets, aiming for 1-inch drops. Refrigerate the truffle centers until quite firm, about 1 hour.

Shape each truffle center into a smooth ball by rolling it between your palms. (Your palms will be covered in chocolate after rolling a few truffles, so get in a messy mood!) If you sense that the truffles are melting too much as you roll, dip your hands in ice

choosing chocolate for ganache

PEOPLE SAY THAT FOR COOKING YOU SHOULD USE only a wine you would drink, and the same holds true for chocolate. Chocolate is one of only two ingredients in ganache, so use only a chocolate that's good enough to eat straight from the package.

A chocolate that's between 55% and 60% is generally a good choice for ganache: Rich and moderately sweet without a strong bitter edge, it will produce consistent results. Ganache made with higher-percentage chocolate may be less stable and prone to curdling.

Don't ever cut corners by using chocolate chips. They usually contain added ingredients that help them hold their shape when baked but can translate into an overly thick, viscous ganache.

water, dry them well, and then continue rolling. (To smooth the truffles even more, refrigerate them for 30 minutes and then roll them a second time.) Refrigerate the shaped truffles on the baking sheet for 1 hour, or until ready to dip.

Get set up for dipping: Set two parchment-lined baking sheets on a long work surface, leaving enough space to one side for the melted chocolate and the truffle centers, in that order. If you're rolling the truffles in cocoa powder, sift it into a shallow dish and set it to one side of the work area.

Temper your chocolate, following the method on page 269. Set the bowl of tempered chocolate on the work surface and begin dipping the truffles. (Remember to pay attention to the temperature of the chocolate as you dip, heating it up gently as directed in order to keep in temper.)

Dip the truffles: Remove about one-quarter of the truffle centers from the fridge; set them on the work surface. Immerse one in the melted chocolate and spin it around with a fork to cover completely. Lift it out on the fork tines. Tap the fork on the sides of the bowl several times so the excess chocolate drips off and a thin chocolate shell forms around the truffle. You may have to tap 20 times or more.

Gently set the dipped truffles on the lined baking sheets, using a knife to nudge the truffle off the fork without scraping off any coating. When the utensils are sticky with chocolate, switch to clean ones to avoid scarring the shell. Continue with all the truffle centers.

If you're rolling in cocoa, instead of setting the freshly dipped truffles on parchment, tip them into the dish of sifted cocoa.

continued

a satiny ganache is at the center of a perfect truffle

Be sure your chocolate is chopped finely and evenly so that it melts easily from the heat of the cream.

To create a good emulsion, use a wooden spoon and stir in small circles, starting in the middle of the bowl. Expand your circle as the chocolate becomes glossy and smooth.

For a ganache with butter, make sure your butter is very soft and the ganache is no longer warm, so it incorporates the butter but doesn't cause it to melt.

When the dish is full of truffles, snap it back and forth to coat the truffles, and then gently transfer the truffles to a plate.

Store tempered truffles at a cool room temperature, preferably in a dry place with low humidity, for up to 3 days. In the refrigerator, they'll last for about a week or in the freezer for up to a month. Untempered truffles must be stored in the refrigerator or freezer. Store all refrigerated and frozen truffles in airtight containers to prevent condensation. Remove them an hour or two before serving, keeping them covered until they reach room temperature.

A DIP IN CHOCOLATE CREATES A DELICATE SHELL

To get a delicately thin coating on your truffles, encourage the excess chocolate to drip off by gently tapping your dipping fork several times on the edge of the bowl.

Scoot the dipped truffles to a parchment-covered baking sheet with the edge of a knife.

If you want a cocoa coating, tip the chocolate-coated truffle directly into a plate of cocoa powder. Shake the plate so the truffles roll around evenly, then transfer them to another plate to set.

Chocolate-raspberry truffles

Yields about 60
1-inch truffles

Raspberry loves chocolate, and these easy and luscious little treats perfectly express that affinity. When warmed, the chocolate mixture for the truffles doubles as a delicious sauce for ice cream.

1 cup fresh raspberries

1 pound semisweet or bittersweet chocolate, finely chopped

1½ cups heavy cream

Small pinch table salt

1 cup unsweetened Dutch-processed cocoa powder

Pass the berries through a food mill fitted with a fine disk or force them through a fine sieve, mashing with a wooden spoon, into a medium bowl. You'll have about ½ cup purée; set it aside and discard the contents of the sieve.

Put the chopped chocolate in a medium bowl. In a small saucepan, heat the cream just until boiling. Pour the hot cream over the chopped chocolate; whisk to blend. Stir in the raspberry purée and the salt. Refrigerate the mixture until completely chilled, about 1 hour. Pour the cocoa onto a plate. With a melon baller or spoon, scoop the chocolate and shape it into 1-inch balls. If the truffles are very soft, put them on a baking sheet and refrigerate briefly to firm. Roll the shaped truffles in the cocoa, coating them thoroughly. Sealed and refrigerated, they'll keep for about a week.

Macadamia trios

These macadamia-nut clusters are a simple but delicious candy made from tempered chocolate. Don't skip the tempering step or your chocolate may remain soft and won't be shiny. When made with good chocolate and fresh macadamias, these pretty candies are worlds better than those souvenir sweets from Hawaii.

1 pound good quality semi-sweet or bittersweet chocolate, chopped

120 (about 12 ounces) whole roasted macadamia nuts

Line two baking sheets with parchment. Temper the chocolate following the method in "Temper Your Chocolate for Shine and Snap" (facing page), melting 1¼ pounds of the chocolate and chopping the remaining ¼ pound even finer to use to "seed" the melted portion.

Fill a small resealable plastic bag with about 8 ounces of the chocolate and cut a small hole in one corner of the bag. Squeeze out 40 teaspoon-size drops of chocolate onto one of the baking sheets. Arrange three nuts in a triangle on top of each chocolate drop and allow to set. Drop the nut triplets, one at a time, into the tempered chocolate. With a dry fork, gently submerge the nuts until completely coated. Lift out of the chocolate, tapping gently on the edge of the bowl to shake off any excess chocolate. Set on a parchment-lined baking sheet to dry and set.

While working with the chocolate, you want to keep it between 88°F and 91°F. Placing the bowl on a heating pad set at the lowest temperature is a good way to do this. As you work, stir the chocolate occasionally, and if it cools too much, simply increase the temperature by adjusting the heat setting.

TEMPER YOUR CHOCOLATE FOR SHINE AND SNAP

Tempered chocolate has a professional- looking sheen, snaps cleanly, and is less likely than untempered chocolate to wilt at room temperature because it has a higher melting point. If those are important qualities for your candies, you'll want to temper the chocolate you use for dipping. You'll need only an accurate chocolate thermometer and a calm disposition.

Store-bought chocolate has been tempered during manufacturing. When you melt it, as you must do to dip the truffles, cookies, or other sweets, the chocolate loses its temper. To regain it, the chocolate must be heated, cooled, and then very gently warmed again, which encourages the cocoa butter crystals to harden into a specific pattern.

To temper 2 pounds of chopped chocolate for dipping truffles, chop about one-quarter of it into even finer pieces. Set these pieces aside in a bowl separate from the rest of the dipping chocolate. In a medium saucepan, simmer about an inch of water. Transfer the 1½ pounds of chopped chocolate to a stainless-steel bowl that is large enough to rest over—not in—the water.

Remove the pan of simmering water from the heat and set the bowl of chopped chocolate over it. Stir with a wooden spoon until the chocolate is completely melted; continue heating it over the pan of hot water until a chocolate thermometer registers between 120°F and 125°F. Remove the bowl from the saucepan, dry the bottom, and cool the chocolate to 86°F by adding the reserved finely chopped chocolate, 2 tablespoons at a time, stirring after each addition until the pieces melt. (This is known as the "seeding" method.)

When the temperature reaches 86°F and the pieces no longer melt (you might not use all the finely chopped chocolate), very gently raise the temperature to between 88°F and 91°F by flashing the bowl over the pan of hot water for 10 seconds at a time, drying the bottom of the bowl every time.

To test if the chocolate is in temper, spread a bit on a swatch of parchment or waxed paper and let it cool for a few minutes. The chocolate is in temper if it sets quickly. If the chocolate has white streaks and is tacky to the touch, it is not in temper; start the process again by heating the chocolate to 120°F.

Keep the chocolate in temper while dipping by holding it between 88°F and 91°F. To monitor the temperature, tape the thermometer to the bowl (the bulb shouldn't touch the bowl). If the temperature in the center of the bowl drops to 89°F, flash the bowl over the hot water in 10-second increments until the temperature hits 90°F.

Toffee-chocolate candy

Variations on this addictive candy show up in older American cookbooks. This version has been adapted a bit by the addition of vanilla, bittersweet chocolate, and toasted pecans. You could use all semisweet chocolate, or even milk chocolate, if you like. Put some of this candy in a festive holiday tin for gift giving.

6 ounces semisweet chocolate, chopped

6 ounces bittersweet chocolate, chopped

½ pound (1 cup) unsalted butter

1 cup granulated sugar

1 teaspoon light corn syrup

½ teaspoon kosher salt

1 teaspoon pure vanilla extract

½ cup finely chopped toasted pecans

Combine the two chocolates and set aside.

Set a small bowl of water and a pastry brush next to the stove.

In a heavy-based saucepan fitted with a candy thermometer, cook the butter, sugar, ¼ cup water, corn syrup, and salt over medium heat. Stir frequently with a wooden spoon until the butter melts and the sugar dissolves; then stir gently and only occasionally as the mixture approaches 300°F and begins to darken. Brush the sides of the pan down with a little water every once in a while to keep the sugar from crystallizing. When the mixture reaches 300°F (this will take about 18 to 20 minutes), remove the pan from the heat, carefully add the vanilla, and stir it in. With a heatproof rubber spatula, scrape the mixture into a metal 9x11-inch baking pan set on a cooling rack. Tilt the pan until the toffee covers the bottom of the pan evenly. Let cool for 2 minutes.

Sprinkle the toffee with the chopped chocolate and cover the pan with another baking pan (to keep things warm and help the chocolate melt) for a few minutes. Smooth the melted chocolate with a spatula (use a narrow offset spatula if you have one) and sprinkle on the pecans. Let cool completely (3 to 4 hours) and then break or chop into pieces; use a metal spatula or a blunt knife to pry the toffee out of the pan. To help the chocolate set faster on a warm day, refrigerate the candy.

Fast and easy nibby fudge

Cacao nibs are roasted and lightly crushed cacao beans—in other words, pure chocolate! Their bittersweet, toasty flavor and irresistible crunch is a wonderful contrast to this super-creamy fudge. You won't need a thermometer to make this fudge because marshmallow cream ensures a smooth texture.

⅔ cup evaporated milk

One 7-ounce jar marshmallow creme

2 ounces (¼ cup) unsalted butter; more for the pan

1½ cups granulated sugar

¼ teaspoon table salt

12 ounces semisweet chocolate, finely chopped

1 teaspoon pure vanilla extract

⅓ cup cacao nibs, divided

Line an 8x8-inch pan with foil, folding the excess over the sides to form handles. Grease the foil and set the pan aside.

Put the evaporated milk, marshmallow creme, butter, sugar, and salt in a large, heavy-bottomed saucepan. Bring to a boil over medium heat, stirring constantly with a heatproof spatula. Scrape the bottom and sides of the pan often, as this mixture is apt to burn.

Once the mixture comes to a boil, cook for 5 minutes, stirring constantly; it will caramelize a bit, which is fine. Remove from the heat, add the chocolate and the vanilla, and stir until the chocolate is melted and the mixture is smooth. Add half of the nibs, stir to combine, and pour into the prepared pan. Top with the remaining nibs and allow to set.

Once the fudge is firm, lift it out of the pan using the foil handles and cut it into small squares with a long, sharp knife on a cutting board.

Old-fashioned fudge
with crunchy cacao nibs

Yields 64
1-inch squares

Old-fashioned fudge isn't difficult, but it may give your forearms a workout during the beating stage. A successful batch of fudge is all about controlling the crystals that form at different stages; all it takes is one misstep to find yourself with a pan full of grainy candy. Follow the steps carefully and you'll be in the clear. Adding the cacao nibs gives this classic candy a crunchy new twist.

2 cups granulated sugar

¾ cup whole milk

Pinch table salt

1 tablespoon light corn syrup

4 ounces unsweetened chocolate, coarsely chopped

2 tablespoons unsalted butter; more for the pan

1 teaspoon pure vanilla extract

⅓ cup cacao nibs

Line an 8x8-inch pan with foil, folding the excess over the sides to form handles. Grease the foil and set the pan aside.

Butter the inside of a heavy 2-quart saucepan. Put the sugar, milk, salt, corn syrup, and chocolate in the saucepan and place over medium heat, stirring until the sugar dissolves and the mixture boils. Clip on a candy thermometer and cook until the mixture reaches 234°F (soft ball stage).

Immediately remove the pan from heat. Add the butter and, without stirring or swirling, cool the mixture until the thermometer reads 110°F (you may either allow this to happen naturally or plunge the base of the saucepan into an ice bath). Add the vanilla and beat vigorously with a wooden spoon until the fudge becomes quite stiff and loses its gloss (this may take up to 5 minutes). Quickly add the nibs and turn the fudge into the prepared pan, being careful not to scrape the insides of the saucepan too much, so you don't incorporate dried-out bits of fudge. Smooth the fudge so that the top is relatively even and allow to set before cutting.

Chocolate-dipped strawberries

Yields about
1 dozen

The secrets to perfection: Use the best strawberries and chocolate you can, and be sure your strawberries are bone-dry before you dip them into the melted chocolate or the chocolate will seize into a mass.

3 ounces bittersweet chocolate, chopped into almond-size pieces

2 teaspoons neutral vegetable oil, such as grapeseed or canola

1 pint medium-size ripe fresh strawberries (preferably with stems), rinsed and dried

Melt the chocolate with the oil in a small, deep heatproof bowl set in a skillet holding about 1 inch of barely simmering water, whisking occasionally until smooth. Remove the bowl from the heat.

Line a small rimmed baking sheet with waxed paper. Tilt the bowl to pool the chocolate on one side. Dip each strawberry into the chocolate to cover about two-thirds of the berry, or until the chocolate reaches the strawberry's shoulders. Turn the berry to coat it evenly, lift it out of the chocolate, and gently shake off any excess. Carefully lay it on the waxed paper. If the dipping chocolate begins to cool and thicken, return the bowl to the water bath to heat it briefly.

Let the berries stand at room temperature for 15 minutes and then refrigerate until the chocolate is set, 20 to 30 minutes. Carefully remove the berries from the waxed paper. Serve immediately or refrigerate, uncovered, for up to 8 hours before serving.

everything's special when dipped in chocolate

JUST ABOUT ANYTHING CAN BE DIPPED IN chocolate. Besides strawberries, good things to dip include biscotti, candied citrus zest, candied ginger, cocktail pretzels, coffee beans, dates, dried apricots, figs, grapes, nuts, and shortbread. Whatever you choose, dip only halfway to allow the item's original color and texture to contrast with the chocolate. For best results, use tweezers, forks, or specialized dipping tools.

Chocolate-nut bark

Toasting brings out the flavor in nuts, as well as makes them appealingly crunchy, but be sure to cool them completely before you add them to the chocolate or you'll destroy the temper.

1 pound good-quality
   chocolate

¾ pound toasted nuts,
   such as hazelnuts or almonds

Line a baking sheet with kitchen parchment. Temper the chocolate following the directions on page 269. Fold the cooled nuts into the tempered chocolate and spread the mixture in an even layer about ¼ inch thick on the prepared pan. Let set completely. Cut into squares with a sharp knife or break into bite-size pieces.

understanding why chocolate seizes

TO SOME PEOPLE, CHOCOLATE IS THE PERFECT food, but it does have one annoying habit: It can "seize" while you're melting it if a small amount of moisture gets into the chocolate. There's no question whether your chocolate has seized—it will transform from a smooth state to a grainy, matte, clumpy mess. Why does that happen and, more importantly, how can you fix it?

Chocolate is composed of fine, dry particles (cocoa and sugar) in rich fat (cocoa butter). If a few drops of water (or even a bit of steam) get stirred into melted chocolate, the dry cocoa and sugar particles will clump together and form a dull, dry, grainy mass.

You can usually fix seized chocolate by whisking in more water, which will provide enough liquid to wet all the seized particles and smooth the chocolate (but may change the proportions in your recipe).

To prevent seized chocolate, you need to melt the chocolate with a sufficient amount of liquid from the recipe. The magic amount necessary is 1 tablespoon of water (or a water-type liquid) for every 2 ounces of chocolate, meaning your liquid must be at least 25% the weight of your chocolate (water's weight and volume are the same, so this is easy to calculate, e.g. 1 tablespoon is ½ fluid ounce and also ½ ounce by weight).

The liquid can be pure water or milk, or you can use cream or butter, but you'll need to calculate the amount of water they contribute (cream is 60% water, butter is only 20% water). Specialty chocolates with high percentages of cocoa may need a bit more liquid.

If your recipe doesn't call for adding any liquid to the melted chocolate, just be careful not to let water or steam get in the bowl, and be sure to use dry utensils.

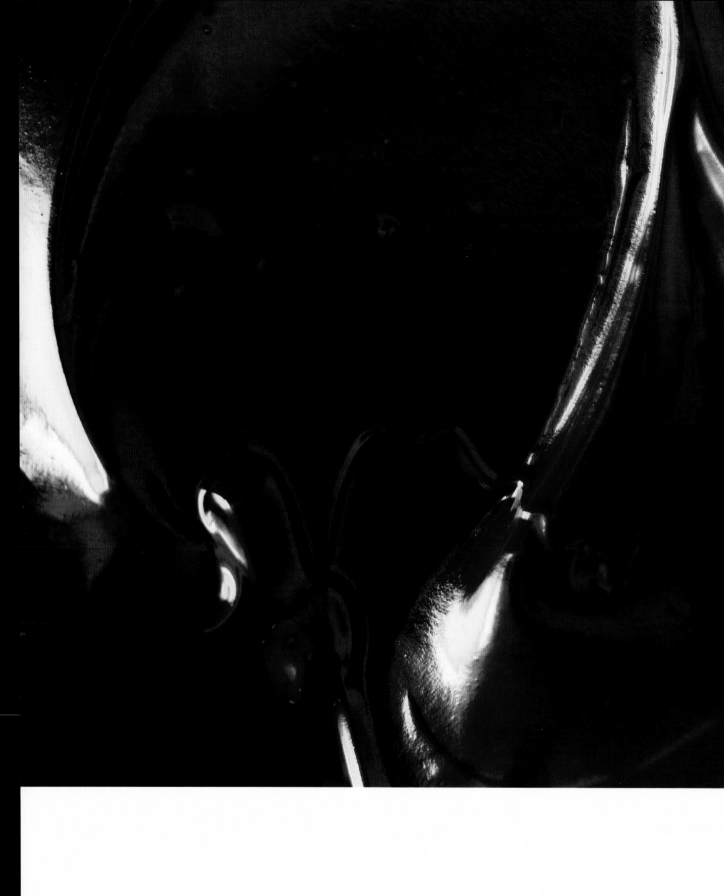

sauces & drinks

Old-fashioned hot fudge sauce

Cocoa powder, not bar chocolate, is featured in this fudgy sauce.
Like most chocolate sauces, it may be stored in the refrigerator
and reheated gently in a microwave or in a pan of simmering water.

6 tablespoons unsweet-
ened natural or Dutch-
processed cocoa
powder

1½ ounces (3 table-
spoons) unsalted
butter

1 cup granulated sugar

2 tablespoons light corn
syrup

1 teaspoon pure vanilla
extract

Put the cocoa in a small saucepan and pour in just enough of
$\frac{1}{3}$ cup boiling water to make a smooth paste. Add the rest of the
boiling water; stir to dissolve. Add the butter and cook over low
heat until the butter has melted. Gently stir in the sugar and corn
syrup with a wooden spoon just until combined. With a wet paper
towel or pastry brush, clean the sugar crystals from the sides of
the pot. Bring the mixture to a simmer. As soon as you see tiny
bubbles around the entire perimeter of the pot, set a timer for
8 minutes. Cook without stirring until the time is up, adjusting
the heat so that the sauce boils actively but not furiously.

Meanwhile, wash your wooden spoon to remove undissolved
sugar crystals and set it aside. Take the pan off the heat and use
the clean wooden spoon to gently stir the vanilla into the sauce.

Double chocolate sauce

Store-bought desserts, such as ice cream, pound cake, or cream puffs, get a homemade feel when topped with some of this quick-to-make but luscious chocolate sauce.

3 ounces bittersweet
   chocolate, finely chopped

1 ounce milk chocolate,
   finely chopped

½ cup heavy cream

Melt the two chocolates together in a medium metal bowl set over a pan of simmering water (don't let the bowl touch the water). In a small saucepan, heat the cream to just below boiling. Take the pan off of the heat, pour all of the hot cream onto the melted chocolate, and stir with a rubber spatula until the sauce is blended and cool, about 4 minutes. The sauce can be made up to 2 weeks ahead and stored in the refrigerator; before serving, warm the sauce in a metal bowl set over a pan of simmering water.

Bittersweet chocolate-rum sauce

This simple yet divine chocolate sauce may be made with bittersweet or semisweet chocolate. Taste the sauce on ice cream before adding more sugar; chocolate sauce that tastes too strong on its own is usually perfect with ice cream.

10 ounces bittersweet or semisweet chocolate, coarsely chopped

3 tablespoons dark rum

½ to 1 cup half-and-half; more as needed

Granulated sugar to taste (optional)

Combine the chocolate and rum in a heatproof bowl set over a pan of simmering water (don't let the bowl touch the water). If using a standard bittersweet or semisweet chocolate (without a percentage on the label), add ½ cup of the half-and-half; if using a chocolate labeled 66% to 70% chocolate liquor, add 1 cup of the half-and-half.

Melt the chocolate mixture, stirring frequently until the chocolate is melted and smooth. Note: A high-percentage of chocolate may cause the sauce to look curdled. If this happens, whisk in a little more half-and-half or some sugar or both.

To adjust the consistency and sweetness, spoon a little sauce over some ice cream and wait a minute for the sauce to cool before tasting. If the sauce tastes too bitter, stir in some sugar, a little at a time. If the sauce thickens with cooling more than you'd like, stir in more half-and-half by the tablespoon as needed.

Serve the sauce warm over ice cream, or let it cool, cover, and store for up to a week in the refrigerator. Reheat the sauce by setting the bowl in a skillet of barely simmering water.

Mexican chocolate sauce

Yields about

1½ cups

Don't worry about the cayenne in this recipe—the sauce won't taste
"hot," just lively with spice and fragrant with a touch of both vanilla
and almond extracts.

1 cup heavy cream

4 ounces semisweet
chocolate, chopped

1 teaspoon ground
cinnamon

1 teaspoon pure vanilla
extract

¼ teaspoon pure almond
extract

⅛ teaspoon cayenne
pepper

Heat the cream in a small saucepan until it just begins to simmer.
Remove it from the heat and add the chocolate, cinnamon, vanilla
extract, almond extract, and cayenne, and let sit undisturbed
for about 2 minutes to allow the chocolate to melt. Whisk until
everything is combined and the sauce is smooth. When you're
ready to serve, if the sauce seems a little thick, whisk in a few
spoonfuls of very hot water to loosen.

Cocoa crème anglaise

Yields 1¾ to 2 cups

Crème anglaise is a classic French vanilla custard sauce, so making it with cocoa powder is an unexpected, and delicious, twist. Recipes for the sauce vary quite a bit in their proportions of milk, cream, eggs, and sugar (some use no cream at all). This one is neither too rich nor too milky, with just enough yolk so it's thickened without tasting eggy. Making a paste with the cocoa powder before adding all the liquid helps prevent clumping.

2 tablespoons unsweetened Dutch-processed cocoa powder

1¼ cups whole milk

¾ cup heavy cream

⅛ teaspoon table salt

⅓ cup granulated sugar

4 large egg yolks

½ teaspoon pure vanilla extract

Put the cocoa powder in a heavy-based saucepan that holds at least 2 quarts and pour in enough of the milk to moisten the cocoa. Stir with a spoon or rubber spatula to make a paste, adding more milk if needed. Add the remaining milk, the cream, salt, and about half of the sugar and stir or whisk to blend. Bring just to a simmer over medium-high heat.

Fill a large bowl with a few inches of water and ice. Have ready a smaller metal bowl that will fit into the ice bath and a fine sieve. In a medium heatproof bowl, whisk the yolks with the remaining sugar. When the milk mixture is hot, whisk about ½ cup of it into the yolks, and then whisk the yolk mixture back into the milk. Cook, stirring constantly with a wooden spoon, until the sauce thickens ever so slightly and passes the spoon test; the temperature should be about 175°F. Immediately strain the sauce into the waiting metal bowl and set the bowl in the ice bath. Add the vanilla extract, and then stir occasionally until the sauce is cool. Press a piece of plastic wrap directly onto the surface of the sauce (to prevent a skin from forming), and refrigerate for up to 3 days.

Chocolate whipped cream

Yields almost
2 cups

Whipped cream can be much more than an ivory dollop; here it's flavored with chocolate to become a perfect topping for chocolate pudding or a slice of chocolate cake. For something different, substitute white chocolate for the semisweet to create a subtle and ultra-creamy topping.

2 ounces good-quality
   semisweet chocolate

¾ cup heavy or
   whipping cream

½ teaspoon pure vanilla extract

Small pinch table salt

Melt the chocolate in a medium metal bowl set over a pan of simmering water (don't let the bowl touch the water). Stir until smooth and leave to cool slightly. Using a balloon whisk or an electric mixer, whip the cream with the vanilla and salt until it forms very soft peaks. By hand, whisk in the melted chocolate until blended and the cream forms soft peaks that hold a shape.

Cacao-nib whipped cream

Yields about
2 cups

Heating the cacao nibs in the cream will encourage them to release a little cocoa butter, which further enriches the cream. The resulting nib cream is adorably speckled, with a flavor vaguely reminiscent of cocoa, but brighter. Use this to top your favorite chocolate pudding or even as a topping for berry-laden fruit desserts.

1 cup heavy cream

2 tablespoons cacao nibs,
   roughly chopped if large

2 teaspoons granulated sugar

Bring the cacao nibs and the cream to a boil in a small saucepan. Remove from the heat, cover, and let steep for 20 minutes. Strain the cream, pressing on the nibs to extract any additional liquid, and chill until very cold, at least 4 hours in the refrigerator (alternately, you may use an ice bath).

In a large bowl, whip the cream to soft peaks; sprinkle in the sugar and whip for another few seconds to blend. Use right away.

Double-chocolate malted milk shake

For the thickest shakes, use a dense, premium brand of ice cream, such as Ben & Jerry's®. And if you'd rather have just a chocolate milk shake, skip the malt powder at the end.

⅓ to ½ cup very cold whole milk; more as needed

3 scoops chocolate ice cream (about 2 ounces each), slightly softened; more as needed

1 tablespoon chocolate syrup, such as Hershey's® Special Dark

1 tablespoon plain malted milk powder; more to taste

Pour the milk into the mixing cup of a milk shake mixer or hand blender or into the jar of a regular blender. Add the ice cream and chocolate syrup. Blend on high speed until smooth. The blending time depends on the machine and the temperature of the ingredients. If necessary, add more milk or ice cream to adjust to your preferred consistency. When the shake is just about smooth, briefly blend in the malted milk powder. Serve immediately in a chilled glass.

Bittersweet hot chocolate

Yields 2 cups

Most hot chocolate drinks tend to be too sweet, so for a more grown-up version, don't add sugar to the hot chocolate itself but rather pass a sugar bowl so that guests can add their own. Choose your favorite high-quality bittersweet or semisweet chocolate for this recipe, because this drink allows the chocolate's distinct flavor nuances to shine.

5 ounces bittersweet or
    semisweet chocolate,
    coarsely chopped
    (a 70% is wonderful,
    but milder chocolates
    also work well)

Pinch table salt

1 cup whole milk

Lightly sweetened
    whipped cream

Granulated sugar, for serving

In a medium saucepan, combine the chocolate, salt, and about ⅓ cup of the boiling water. Stir until the chocolate is completely melted and smooth. Add another ⅔ cup boiling water and heat, whisking constantly, until the mixture begins to simmer at the edges. Whisk in the milk and continue to cook until steaming hot, but keep the temperature well under a boil (ideally no more than 180°F) for the best flavor and texture. Just before serving, whisk to a froth. Serve in small cups. Pass a sugar bowl and a small bowl of the whipped cream for people to add as they wish.

Frothy irish coffee hot chocolate

Yields about 2½ cups

You'll hope for cold weather so you have an excuse to make this spirited hot chocolate. Mix up a batch for your next cross-country ski outing.

2 cups whole milk

½ cup strong brewed coffee

3 ounces bittersweet or semisweet chocolate, chopped into small bits (¼-inch pieces are fine)

2 tablespoons whiskey

Bring the milk and coffee just to a boil in a small saucepan. Put the chocolate and whiskey in a blender and pour in the hot milk-coffee mixture. Let sit for 10 to 15 seconds so the chocolate begins to melt and then cover securely, place a folded towel over the lid, and blend until completely mixed and frothy, about 30 seconds.

If you don't want the hot chocolate to be frothy, heat the milk and coffee in a saucepan until it just begins to simmer. Remove the pan from the heat, add the chocolate and whiskey, let sit for a few seconds so the chocolate can begin to melt, and stir or whisk until well blended.

Cinnamon-ginger hot chocolate

Yields 2 cups

Spices make this warming drink fragrant and just a touch exotic.

¾ teaspoon ground cinnamon

½ teaspoon ground ginger

2 cups whole milk

3 ounces bittersweet or semisweet chocolate, chopped into small bits (¼-inch pieces are fine)

Put the milk in a small saucepan, whisk in the cinnamon and ginger, and bring just to a simmer. Remove the pan from the heat, add the chocolate, let sit for a few seconds so the chocolate can begin to melt, and then stir or whisk until well blended.

Equivalency charts

Liquid/dry measures

U.S.	METRIC
¼ teaspoon	1.25 milliliters
½ teaspoon	2.5 milliliters
1 teaspoon	5 milliliters
1 tablespoon (3 teaspoons)	15 milliliters
1 fluid ounce (2 tablespoons)	30 milliliters
¼ cup	60 milliliters
⅓ cup	80 milliliters
½ cup	120 milliliters
1 cup	240 milliliters
1 pint (2 cups)	480 milliliters
1 quart (4 cups; 32 ounces)	960 milliliters
1 gallon (4 quarts)	3.84 liters
1 ounce (by weight)	28 grams
1 pound	454 grams
2.2 pounds	1 kilogram

Oven temperatures

°F	Gas Mark	°C
250	½	120
275	1	140
300	2	150
325	3	165
350	4	180
375	5	190
400	6	200
425	7	220
450	8	230
475	9	240
500	10	260
550	Broil	290

Contributors

Jennifer Armentrout Chocolate Cherry Coconut Macaroons; Cocoa Crème Anglaise

Nancy Baggett Chocolate-Glazed Chocolate Hazelnut Cookies

Karen Barker Chocolate Espresso Pecan Pie

Karen and Ben Barker Bourbon Chocolate Cake

Sara Bir Fast and Easy Nibby Fudge; Old-Fashioned Fudge with Crunchy Cacao Nibs; Cacao-Nib Whipped Cream; Chocolate Chunk Tart with Toasted Almonds and Coconut

Carole Bloom Gianduia Mousse; Double Chocolate Sauce

Flo Braker Frangipane-Ripple Chocolate Pound Cake

Kay Cabrera Sour Cream Chocolate Cake with Coconut Buttercream Frosting

Greg Case Double Chocolate-Glazed Peppermint Brownies; Vanilla Layer Cake with Whipped Rum-Ganache Icing

Greg Case and Keri Fisher Chocolate-Espresso Mousse Torte; Simple Chocolate Truffles

Joanne Chang Chocolate-Nut Wafers; Double Chocolate Cookies; Chocolate-Banana-Ginger Bread Pudding; Chocolate Chip Muffins

Martin Courtman Chocolate Pots de Crème

Regan Daley Chocolate Chunk Scones

Paula Disbrowe and David Norman Mexican-Style Pecan-Chocolate Squares

Abigail Johnson Dodge Chocolate-Espresso Mini-Soufflés; Chocolate-Glazed Peanut Butter Tart; Chocolate-Mint Cut-Outs; Chocolate Nut Upside-Down Cake; Chocolate Truffle Tart with Whipped Vanilla Mascarpone; Classic Chocolate Mousse; Dark Chocolate Crackles; Double Chocolate Chunk Fudge Brownies; Flourless Chocolate Cake with Chocolate Glaze; Flourless Chocolate & Vanilla Marble Cake; Hazelnut Toffee Squares; Ice Cream Sandwiches; Kahlúa Fudge Bites; Kahlúa Truffle Triangles; Luscious Chocolate Mousse Layer Cake; Macadamia Double-Decker Brownie Bars; No-Cook Chocolate Pudding; Nutty Butterscotch & Chocolate Bars; Pistachio-Chocolate Shortbread Wedges; Press-In Cookie Crust; Triple Chocolate Cheesecake; White Chocolate Mousse Parfaits

Richard Donnelly Frothy Irish Coffee Hot Chocolate; Cinnamon-Ginger Hot Chocolate

Stephen Durfee Luscious Milk Chocolate Ice Cream

***Fine Cooking* staff** Chocolate Whipped Cream

Gale Gand Chocolate Pavlova with Tangerine Whipped Cream; Fried Chocolate-Hazelnut Wontons with Orange Dipping Sauce; Chocolate

Terrine with Whipped Cream & Almond Brittle

Annie Giammattei Mocha Cinnamon Chocolate Chip Cookies

Maggie Glezer Russian Chocolate Braid; Sour Cream & Potato Sweet Dough; Pastry Cream

Suzanne Goin Chocolate Caramel Tart with Macadamia Nuts and Crème Fraîche Whipped Cream

Bonnie Jean Gorder-Hinchey Chewy Chocolate Chip Cookies, Crisp Chocolate Chip Cookies

Mark Gray Macadamia Trios; Chocolate-Nut Bark

Lauren Groveman Coffee Ice Cream with Sour Cream Ganache, Toffee Chips, and Toasted Almonds

Jeffrey Hamelman Pains au Chocolat (adaptation)

Pierre Hermé Chocolate Rice Pudding Parfait with Gianduia Whipped Cream & Caramelized Rice Krispies

Heather Ho Coffee & Cream Icebox Cake

Martha Holmberg Chocolate-Raspberry Cookies & Cream; Chocolate Silk Pie; Mexican Chocolate Sauce

Sarah Jay Toasted Bread with Chocolate

Eva Katz Individual Orange & Chocolate Bread Puddings

Elaine Khosrova Apricot, Pistachio & Chocolate Chip Bars

Elinor Klivans Almond Crunch and Chocolate Confetti Chiffon Cake; Black Forest Trifle; Milk Chocolate Pecan Lace Cookie Sandwiches

Allison Ehri Kreitler Bourbon-Chocolate Mousse; Double-Chocolate Malted Milk Shake

Camilla Leonard Brownie Cream-Cheese Bites

Lori Longbotham Triple Chocolate Ice Cream Pie; Triple Strawberry-Chocolate Ice Cream Sundaes (adaptation); Chocolate-Dipped Strawberries

Emily Luchetti Chocolate Roulade with Raspberry Filling

Rocco Lugrine Chocolate-Filled Beignets

Alice Medrich Bittersweet Mocha Cookies; Chocolate Chunk Cookies with Dried Cherries & Pecans; Chocolate Soufflé Cookies; Cocoa Cookie Dough; Crunchy Cocoa Wafers; Dark Chocolate Soufflé Cakes with Espresso-Chocolate Sauce; Fastest Fudge Cake with Ganache Drizzle; Frozen Mocha; Old-Fashioned Chocolate Layer Cake with Mocha Milk Chocolate Frosting; Rich Cocoa Brownies; White Chocolate Soufflé Cakes with Raspberry-Chocolate Sauce; Old-Fashioned Hot Fudge Sauce; Bittersweet Chocolate-Rum Sauce; Bittersweet Hot Chocolate

Susie Middleton Chocolate French Toast Sandwiches; Toffee-Chocolate Candy

Cindy Mitchell Cakey Brownies; Chewy Brownies; Chocolate Brownie Cookies; Fudgy Brownies

Cindy Mushet Hazelnut & Chocolate Baklava with Espresso-Frangelico Syrup

David Page and Barbara Shinn Chocolate Cupcakes with Dark Chocolate Frosting; Silky, Sumptuous Chocolate Pudding

Greg Patent Mocha Chip Cupcakes with Chocolate-Sour Cream Frosting

James Peyton Chocolate Ice Cream with Cinnamon, Dulce de Leche, and Toasted Pecans; Tropical Banana Split with Toasted-Coconut Ice Cream and Bittersweet Chocolate Rum Sauce (adaptation)

Michelle Polzine Chocolate-Raspberry Tart with a Gingersnap Crust; Chocolate-Raspberry Truffles

Randall Price Walnut, Chocolate & Rum-Raisin Crêpes with Whipped-Cream Chocolate Sauce

Nicole Rees Brown-Butter Banana Cake with Chocolate Chips; Caramel Turtle Bars; Chocolate Chip Butter Pound Cake; Coffee-Cocoa Snack Cake; Deep, Dark Chocolate Stout Cake; Mocha Pudding Cakes; Port Ganache-Glazed Brownies with Dried Cherries

Paige Retus Individual Cinnamon Coffee Cakes with Chocolate-Cherry-Almond Swirl

Leslie Revsin Rich Chocolate Olive-Oil Cake

Tony Rosenfeld Flourless Chocolate-Almond Cake with Almond-Cherry-Caramel Glaze

Katherine Seeley Chocolate Strawberry Shortcakes

Kathleen Stewart Rich Chocolate Muffins

Carole Walter Chocolate-Vanilla Pinwheel Cookies

Kathleen Weber Chocolate-Orange Biscotti

Linda Weber Peanut Butter-Chocolate Chip Sandwich Cookies

Carolyn Weil Chocolate-Dipped Espresso Shortbread Cookies; Bittersweet Chocolate-Glazed Éclairs; Vanilla Pastry Cream; Éclair Pastry Shells; Bittersweet Ganache Glaze

Bill Yosses Classic Chocolate Truffles

Recipe index by chapter

Index